Liturgy of Change

MOVEMENT RHETORIC/RHETORIC'S MOVEMENTS

Victoria J. Gallagher

Also of Interest

The Democratic Ethos: Authenticity and Instrumentalism in US Movement Rhetoric after Occupy, A. Freya Thimsen
Activist Literacies: Transnational Feminisms and Social Media Rhetorics, Jennifer Nish

LITURGY

OF

CHANGE

Rhetorics of the Civil Rights
Mass Meeting

ELIZABETH ELLIS MILLER

THE UNIVERSITY OF
SOUTH CAROLINA PRESS

Published by the University of South Carolina Press
Columbia, South Carolina 29208

www.uscpress.com

Manufactured in the United States of America

32 31 30 29 28 27 26 25 24 23
10 9 8 7 6 5 4 3 2 1

Library of Congress Cataloging-in-Publication Data
can be found at http://catalog.loc.gov/.

ISBN: 978-1-64336-388-2 (hardcover)
ISBN: 978-1-64336-389-9 (paperback)
ISBN: 978-1-64336-390-5 (ebook)

CONTENTS

ILLUSTRATIONS

The University of South Carolina series "Movement Rhetoric/Rhetoric's Movements" builds on the Press's longstanding reputation in the field of rhetoric and communication and its cross-disciplinary commitment to studies of civil rights and civil justice. Books in the series address two central questions: In historical and contemporary eras characterized by political, social, and economic movements enacted through rhetorical means, how—and with what consequences—are individuals, collectives, and institutions changed and transformed? How and to what extent can analyses of rhetoric's movements in relation to circulation and uptake help point the way to a more equal and equitable world?

In keeping with the social movement scholarly tradition that serves as an inspiration for this series, Elizabeth Ellis Miller provides a unique and worthwhile contribution to the literature on the rhetoric of the US civil rights movement of the 1950s and '60s. Although rhetorical scholars have analyzed individual speeches delivered at mass meetings by figures like Fannie Lou Hamer and Ralph Abernathy, the mass meeting remains a significant but underexamined site both in rhetorical studies and historiography of the movement for Black freedom more generally. *Liturgy of Change* brings attention to the pattern of religious genres—song, prayer, and testimony—that structured the events and illuminates the ways these genres created rhetorical opportunities for ordinary people to speak up and develop their activism. This text is valuable for anyone interested in how individuals, collectives, and institutions are transformed through rhetorical action.

ACKNOWLEDGMENTS

This book emerged from a premise: the civil rights mass meeting is best understood through attention to the collective working together. This insight also reflects my work on this book, a project that only came to fruition because of many wonderful people working alongside me. Jessica Enoch helped me envision this book, and my career, and realize both. Her generosity to early career scholars is astounding. I'm very thankful to count her as my mentor and friend. Shirley Logan and Jane Donawerth's insights shaped this study, especially related to religious music and prayer.

I am thankful for supportive colleagues in the English Department at Mississippi State University (MSU), especially Bonnie O'Neill, Shalyn Claggett, and Dan Punday, who helped me problem solve and find time to write. Katherine Flowers read drafts and offered thoughtful suggestions and generally brought wisdom and humor to starting out as an assistant professor. Along with Katherine, Megan Smith, Eric Vivier, and Dhanashree Thorat shared advice and support over bagels and coffee: may the Assistant Professor Breakfast tradition continue after we move into the next phase of our careers. I am also grateful for the MSU English Department's generous financial support of this project.

I benefited too from kind friends who offered advice and feedback. Melanie Loehwing spearheaded opportunities for sharing work in rhetorical studies at Mississippi State and offered astute guidance on all things publishing. Ruth Osorio and Anne-Marie Womack, members of my writing group, responded to many drafts and cheered me on to the finish line. Participants in the Rhetoric Society of America Workshop on Sensory Rhetorics helped me sort through the book's organization. I'm grateful also to Scott Wible, Melanie Kill, Chanon Adsanatham, Scott Eklund, Heather Lindenman, Justin Lohr, Cameron Mozafari, Martin Camper, Danielle Griffin, Nathan Tillman, and Katie Bramlett.

The folks at the University of South Carolina Press are very good at their jobs. I am grateful to editors Aurora Bell and Victoria Gallagher who saw the manuscript through with care and expertise. Anonymous reviewers offered feedback that significantly improved the project.

My parents, Rusty and Mary Frances, deserve more gratitude than I can express. I am so thankful for their enduring support. My brothers, Jason and

David, and their wives, Robin and Sarah Ann, are great friends and gave me good reasons to move back to Mississippi. My sister, Jenni, defies categories: friend, mentor, colleague. She gives advice, cares for my children, and shares syllabi and lesson plans. I am lucky to have her in my corner. David W., Josie, and Olive have been on my team for a long time. The Millers—Steve, Marlene, Katie, Mikey, Lesley, Jonathan, Sarah, and Michael—celebrate my achievements and always ask good questions.

My participation in churches in Mississippi, Alabama, and Washington, DC kept the questions alive and inspired me to pursue this project. I am grateful to have had wise pastors and faithful friends encourage my writing and teaching wherever I have lived. Thanks especially to DC friends, Erin, Justin, Paul, Liz, Harris, Heather, and Katie T., and in Mississippi, Ashleigh, Josiah, Scott, Karin, Sara, Anje, Jamey, and David.

Finally, my daughters, Jane and Lila, were born in the final stages of this project. They did not do much to help me finish the book, but they sure make my days more fun. My husband, Matt, ensures we eat well and laugh often. He cheers me up when the going is tough and reminds me daily what is important. I am grateful to spend my life with him.

A version of chapter 5 was published as "Between Enclave and Counterpublic: Doubled Rhetorical Space and the Civil Rights Mass Meeting" in *Rhetoric & Public Affairs* 23, no. 2 (Summer 2020): 225–54.

Introduction

Recovering the Civil Rights Mass Meeting

The [mass] meeting moves with an inevitability . . . a sense of inner
form to it, high moments, low ones, expressions of joy, of sorrow, of
mirth, of courage and determination, and expressions again and again
of that larger view of life which, spontaneously, out of the hearts of the
people, out of their culture, their religion, gave them the grace to
have genuine compassion, forbearance, love for their enemies,
condemning the sin, not the sinners.

—PAT WATTERS, *DOWN TO NOW*

Civil rights activist Jo Ann Robinson recalls a "new spirit" among
Black people in Montgomery, Alabama, after their first day boycotting segregated buses. Remembering this December 1955 moment,
Robinson explains: "The one day of protest against the white man's
traditional policy of white supremacy had created a new person in
the Negro. The new spirit, the new feeling did something to Blacks individually and collectively . . . There was no turning back!" (*The Montgomery Bus
Boycott and the Women Who Started It*, 76). Robinson recognized that the
boycott sparked a change in Black identity, one she equates to becoming
"a new person." In her book, she goes on to recount how after this first day
of protest, people kept this new spirit and new feeling in the weekly mass
meetings over the course of the next year. Meetings served, Robinson writes,
as both "a communication center and [site] for keeping up morale" (76).

Explaining the first Montgomery mass meeting, for instance, civil rights
activist Fred Gray remembers: "There was electricity in the air. Such a feeling
of unity, success, and enthusiasm had never been in the city before . . . The
people were together. They were singing. They were praying" (*Bus Ride to
Justice*, 57). Activist and leader Ralph Abernathy recalls: "The fear left, the
fear that had shackled us across the years all left suddenly when we were in
that church together" (Abernathy, Interview, 5). As many as three or four

thousand people were in attendance that evening, with groups listening in on the meeting through loudspeakers in the basement and outdoor areas of the church. The program included hymns such as "Onward Christian Soldiers," prayers and Scripture reading, an address by Martin Luther King Jr. and the reading of resolutions.

The overall effect of this meeting, as activists explain above, was an energized unity. Black people in Montgomery experienced the excitement of gathering, they articulated their unique vision for democratic change, and they enacted these feelings and vision as a group. This experience of the meeting served to constitute, to bring into existence, a collective poised for protest in their town. The creation of this group and their new sense of themselves was just as important as any sociopolitical change they would go on to accomplish through direct action. As King would later reflect in *Stride Toward Freedom*, Montgomery was *already* changed by this meeting of Black people standing together, showcasing a new understanding of their "dignity and destiny" (53).

The significant experience and achievement of the mass meeting was not isolated to Montgomery, Alabama. Mass meetings working toward the objective of uniting African Americans occurred across the South for more than a decade. Although these events varied considerably according to place and organization, the meeting's purpose was largely the same: to bring local people together and to energize and equip them to make change in their towns and cities. As activist Bob Moses claimed in 1964: "Local people have really begun to find a way they can use a meeting as a tool for running their own lives. For having something to say about it. That's very slow, but it's happening" (quoted in Polletta, *Freedom Is an Endless Meeting*, 55). Historian Charles Payne likewise zeroes in on the meeting as a space in which to change one's sense of self: "Mixtures of the sacred and the profane, the mass meeting could be a very powerful social ritual. . . . By ritually acting out new definitions of their individual and collective selves, people helped make those selves become real" (*I've Got the Light of Freedom*, 263). As Payne and Moses observe, the mass meeting was a transformative experience for individuals and for collectives. By gathering regularly to sing, to pray, and to tell their stories, Black people across the United States reimagined the sociopolitical possibilities for themselves and their communities; in so doing, they transformed the South and the nation.

Liturgy of Change: Rhetorics of the Civil Rights Mass Meeting provides a rhetorical history of the transformative space so important to Robinson, Gray, Abernathy, and many others working to remake the Southern United States in the 1950s and 1960s. In this book, I reconstruct mass-meeting scenes; recovering the religious and rhetorical patterns of events; the genres that comprised them; and the ways that these genres shaped individuals and groups, enabling them to craft identities for civic and political action. This process of identity making was animated by a liturgy of change and its faithful genres, rooted in Black church traditions yet specific to the civil rights movement. As I use the term, "liturgy" refers to an embodied spirituality and set of genres that structure collective religious participation (Vondey, "The Making of a Black Liturgy," 150). In the case of the mass meeting, the liturgy invited participation in events designed to facilitate individuals' and groups' first steps into activism and then to provide a scaffold for ongoing rhetorical and democratic learning and action.

As a rhetorical history of a key event in the civil rights movement, a central objective of this study is to recover the contributions of the many mass-meeting participants, not just the leaders who delivered well-known speeches. To this end, the mass-meeting scenes in this book showcase individual and collective rhetorical participation across many locales and movement moments. The places of meetings include Sumter, Savannah, and Albany, Georgia; Nashville, Tennessee; Hattiesburg and Jackson, Mississippi; Montgomery and Selma, Alabama; Danville, Virginia; and St. Augustine, Florida. The case studies span movement years from 1955 Montgomery to 1965 Selma. Rather than following a geographic or chronological organization, the book moves according to the genres of the meeting. The first chapter approaches the mass meeting as a whole genre set, unpacking liturgy of change as a rhetorical concept. The next three chapters examine this liturgy through the faithful genres of song, prayer, and testimony—genres that collectives developed and transformed for Black freedom. I use the term "faithful genres" to denote their place in the liturgy and their religious dimensions. The final chapter takes up the complicated questions of audience and purpose: to whom this liturgy and its faithful genres spoke.

In using the years 1955 to 1965 as the temporal frame for the study, I follow standard movement periodization. This period guides my selection of civil rights mass meetings to examine, but Black activism obviously preceded and continued beyond these years.[1] While this method is standard for chronology, my expansive approach to geography is a departure from the norm. Much scholarship on civil rights rhetorics centers on particular figures or protests and is thus tightly focused both temporally and geographically (Rivers and Weber, "Ecological, Pedagogical, Public Rhetoric"; Keith Miller, *Voice of Deliverance*; Holmes, *Where the Sacred and the Secular Harmonize*). This method is true of rhetorical studies more generally, in a "move to restrictive, specialized histories" (Hawhee and Olson, "Pan-Historiography," 91). While there are numerous benefits to the narrow approach, I am interested in how mass meetings, as a recurring, repeated liturgy, operated as key sites for creating and sustaining a unified movement identity and vision across places and moments.

This study is anchored then in the contributions of dozens of ordinary, little-known individuals such as Elizabeth Burgess in Nashville, Tennessee, and a young man referred to as "big boy" in Hattiesburg, Mississippi. These figures and their rhetorical work remind scholars that one of the movement's, and the mass meeting's, greatest accomplishments was empowering "local people," to use historian John Dittmer's apt phrase (*Local People,* 1). This book uncovers not just the significance of local people to the movement for Black freedom but also their emergence as rhetors: through careful study of mass-meeting patterns and discourse, *Liturgy of Change* offers insight into a faith-infused rhetorical process that accomplished these transformations from audience member into speaker poised for action, as well as the textures of those performances. Participating in these genres at the mass meeting provided an experience of a changed world, one where Black people's dignity was recognized before God, the law, and the nation.

Beyond recovering the concrete participatory rhetorical and democratic dimensions of the meeting, the book attends to participants' descriptions of these events as experiences of faith. Here, it is impossible to ignore activists' reliance on religious imagery to explain the power of these meetings. For example, writing about the group singing "Onward Christian Soldiers," Martin Luther King Jr. observes: "When that mammoth audience stood to sing, the voices outside swelling the chorus in the church, there was a mighty ring like the glad echo of heaven itself" (*Stride Toward Freedom,* 50). The mass meeting was more than a site for political organization and rhetorical engagement: it was also a religious experience, intertwined with feeling, where activists prefigured the changes they sought by speaking and acting as though they were already true.

A core argument of this book is that the civil rights mass meeting was transformative through the rhetorical, religious experience that collective participation created. By referring to these events as rhetorical, religious experiences, I mean that they were holistic, structured encounters among people, places, and beliefs and more than discrete rhetorical moments, that is, one leader's persuasive address to the crowd.[2] As Gregory Clark writes about experience generally: "Individualized and self-sufficient, experience is always located. It is a construct made from our encounters with places— including the people and events those places comprise—that gives us essential elements of identity and purpose" ("Rhetorical Experience and the National Museum in Harlem," 116). Looking beyond the features of individual addresses, this book reveals how the mass meeting operated on a broader level as a familiar experience—it was *like* church. This familiarity was built into not just the discourse but the very pattern, space, and embodiment of events, and this resonance was rhetorically powerful on several levels. When individuals entered the meeting, they had an index for understanding what was happening and what participation looked like: singing in church, for instance, was something that many, if not most, Black people in the South had experienced. Singing, praying, and testifying might be familiar but, in the context of the mass meeting, they were also novel and exciting, and as such took on new purposes. To sing at the mass meeting was to embody with the group a desire, commitment, and vision for enacting change. Inhabiting the liturgy of the Black church tradition and its genres through their participation in mass meetings, then, enabled large groups of people to take first steps into collective activism.

This familiarity was important because stepping into the civil rights movement came with extraordinary risks and consequences. The mass meeting was not a secret space hidden away from the realities of Southern towns and cities. Rather, it signified to everyone in the community—and, through the press, to the nation—that change was happening. Simply by attending the meeting, individuals claimed greater freedom and demonstrated their will to join the movement for civil rights. Thus, the second major argument of this book is that the religious structure and genres of the meeting poised activists to move out into more public protest in unique and authentic ways. For example, the genre of prayer was useful within the meeting as an internal mode for reflection, affective renewal, and planning. Outside of the meeting, activists embodied this genre at marches, kneel-ins, and pray-ins. Such silent direct-action protest enacted Christian nonviolence collectively, signifying a unified, peaceful movement for public audiences.

By attending to the mass meeting's complex relationship to wider publics, *Liturgy of Change* reveals these events as inventive spaces unique to the movement for Black freedom. Taken together, the first four chapters show the spiritual rejuvenation, intimacy, and belonging that the liturgical structure created for those within the meeting. In the final chapter, I step back from the internal purposes of the meeting to consider how African Americans negotiated and spoke with other groups who sought to engage them and (most often) to disrupt, surveil, and thwart their collective work. Studying these negotiations illuminates the ways in which relying on the Black church for structure and vision positioned meeting rhetors to exploit outsiders' interruptions and use them to their rhetorical advantage. The mass meeting, after all, was like church, open to all, and an experience that required its participants to desire justice and treat neighbors with love. Thus, when outsiders entered, their racist interruptions, interrogations, and surveillance attempts stood in stark relief to the songs, prayers, and testimonies of activists, and indeed appeared absurd. Attempts by segregationists, local police, and members of the Klan and Citizens' Council to derail it showcase the mass meeting as a nonviolent tool similar to marches and sit-ins.

In recovering the mass meeting as a liturgy, I draw attention to religious rhetoric's capacity to form collectives; educate about democracy; and shape identity, speech, and action. Such inquiry is valuable because liturgies continue to shape, inform, and intersect with the public sphere. Jeffrey Ringer and Michael-John DePalma claim: "In gaining a deeper understanding of the roles and functions of religious rhetorics in public discourse, rhetoricians will be better prepared to recognize the inventional possibilities of religious discourses, timely opportunities for counterstatements, and rhetorical appeals best suited to our present contexts. . . . Through the study of religious rhetorics, scholars of rhetoric might be better positioned to promote pathways to mutual understanding and tolerance in the public sphere" ("Charting Prospects and Possibilities," 282). Examining the mass meetings as liturgy reveals them to be sites for social change achieved through the power of faithful genres. Other kinds of liturgical rhetorics happen seemingly out of public view but similarly position participants in particular ways toward not just religion, but society and politics. In this way, the book initiates inquiry into the interstices of faithful participation that make up the everyday rhetorical, religious experiences of so many in the United States and around the world. Paying attention to the liturgical practices of religious groups opens new avenues for examining and unpacking how they position participants toward public life and political engagements. This book tells the story of a liturgy designed to push the United States toward becoming a more just, more equitable, and more inclusive nation for Black people and reveals how liturgies promote important social change. I return to the question of liturgy, faithful genres, and contemporary public rhetoric about race in the United States in the Conclusion.

Taken as a whole, this book offers an in-depth study of the mass meeting's role in civil rights rhetorical history. It reveals how, in towns and cities across the southern United States, Black people transformed their dignity and destiny as they stood together to sing, to pray, and to offer stories of their experiences within civil rights mass meetings.

An Experience of Beloved Community:
Mass Meetings in the Civil Rights Movement

Activist Shirley Sherrod recounts praying and then feeling "such a calmness" about her decision to join the civil rights movement and remain in the South where she was born. Sherrod experienced firsthand white violence as a young person when her father was shot and killed in an argument about livestock and the white murderer was acquitted by an all-white jury (Sherrod, Interview, 15). In response to this tragedy, Sherrod developed a desire to change the violence and injustice that marked her story and her place. But this desire did not immediately translate into an activist path. She explains: "It didn't become clear to me how I . . . could carry out that commitment, until I was in my first mass meeting . . . when I saw people who had *every right* to be afraid—people who were living on Ichauwau Plantation, Pineland Plantation, and . . . other farms owned by white people in the area—not being afraid, you know. The strength we gathered from each other being in those meetings and planning and deciding to fight together, once I saw that, I knew that this was a way I could fight back" (15). Sherrod gained a sense of what her activism might look like, what it could sound and feel like to be a civil rights activist, in a mass meeting. The meeting offered a clear and concrete first step into the movement for Black freedom. These events structured people's entrance into the civil rights movement and catalyzed their shift from fearful or uncertain individual to a member of a courageous collective at work. *Liturgy of Change* recovers the rhetorical modes that enabled people like Sherrod to see themselves anew through the mass meeting and transform their worlds as well. In this way, the project extends the insights of scholars who have explored the civil rights mass meeting as a forum for significant individual addresses and who study the rhetorical tactics of the movement.

Like historians, rhetorical critics have long understood the mass meetings to be significant sites of movement activity. Kirt Wilson describes the Holt Street meetings as "part political rally, part religious revival, and part business meeting" ("Interpreting the Discursive Field of the Montgomery Bus Boycott," 304). Studies like Wilson's have amassed great insight into the strategies leaders including King, Ralph Abernathy, and Fannie Lou Hamer devised to exhort and encourage mass-meeting audiences to work toward civil rights goals.[3] Examining her address to a meeting audience in Indianola, Mississippi, for example, Maegan Parker Brooks illuminates how Hamer exhorted Black Mississippians to register and vote (*A Voice that Could Stir an Army*, 109). Brooks's analysis reveals much about Hamer's sophisticated argumentative strategies. For instance, she shows how Hamer's complex jeremiad structure "undermine[d] the plantation mentality and the white supremacist terror that bound [her audience's] potential" (109). Brooks's study explains how Hamer used the meeting as a platform for speech-making to motivate African Americans in the Mississippi Delta.

While studies like Brooks's and Wilson's offer valuable insights into the rhetorical dimensions of important speeches, they also raise new questions about how the mass meeting achieved the kinds of transformations outlined by Sherrod and others. Brooks, for instance, gestures toward a broader significance of these events: "Reflecting on audience reception to 'We're On Our Way,' in particular, and Hamer's mass-meeting orations, more generally, also provides a glimpse into the vital role mass meetings played in propelling SNCC's [the Student Nonviolent Coordinating Committee] grassroots campaign for social and political change in Mississippi" (*A Voice that Could Stir an Army,* 87). In his study of the 1963 Birmingham civil rights scene, David Holmes notes that the mass meeting was essential to African American life in the South during the 1950s and 1960s, comparable to the Underground Railroad ("'Hear Me Tonight'" 157). While both Holmes and Brooks largely focus on individual speakers, their descriptions of the entire event implicitly call for further examination of the mass meeting's rhetorical functions. As Keith Miller writes: "rhetorical critics should now examine in detail how *all* the oratory and song lyrics of a specific civil rights rally functioned together to create patterns of argumentation as sophisticated as the weave of a Persian carpet" ("On Martin Luther King, Jr. and the Landscape of Civil Rights Rhetoric," 179, emphasis in original).

Responding to these studies, this project takes an expansive approach to the mass meeting, reconstructing these events across civil rights locales. Rather than individual speaker's addresses, I instead examine the rhetorical practices of the collective. I show the mass meeting to be a mode of direct action. The most common and well-known collective tactics were the sit-in and the march. Sean Patrick O'Rourke and Lesli K. Pace's collection of essays, *Like Wildfire: The Rhetoric of the Civil Rights Sit-Ins,* recovers the civil rights sit-ins in well-known sites in addition to less studied places and moments such as Jackson, Mississippi, in 1963. Critical assessments of civil rights marches, though less cohesive than this treatment of the sit-ins, likewise understand the march as a movement tactic that functions through broadly applicable rhetorical features and with fine-grained nuances particular to the towns and cities where it was performed.[4]

Liturgy of Change provides a rhetorical history of an additional movement tactic, the mass meeting. I see the mass meeting as useful and important to the movement for Black freedom for many of the same reasons the sit-ins and the march were: it could be repeated across diverse locations as a collective, nonviolent public statement, yet it was flexible enough to be tailored to the needs of activists on the ground and across the ups and downs of the movement. Studying the mass meeting in this way highlights its distinctive role in the rhetorical repertoire of civil rights activism. Like the sit-ins and the marches, the mass meeting operated as a kind of direct-action tactic of nonviolence, providing a collective structure for protesting unjust laws and social mores. Yet the mass meeting was unlike the sit-ins and the marches in that it was not officially or spatially an out-in-the-open performative protest. Here, the mass meeting provided participants with a space for renewal and planning, functions typically associated with the behind-the-scenes space public sphere theorists refer to as an enclave. In these ways, the mass meeting, as a tactic that was carefully defined and maintained as a site to live out the vision of a peaceful, integrated world, operates as a kind of space of its own, unique among movement tactics and in the history of counterpublicity more generally.

The Movements of Civil Rights Rhetoric

This study contributes to conversations about rhetorics of social change by examining the meeting as a recurring, recognizable space in the movement for Black freedom and, in so doing, by providing insight into the *movement* of rhetoric across civil rights mass meetings, and indeed, the movement for Black freedom. Scholar Karma Chávez has argued that in studies of social movement rhetoric generally, the focus has largely been on the rhetoric of the streets—the protests, the important speeches, the most public, widely circulated moments of social movements. Calling attention to "protected enclaves," Chávez suggests the significance of "behind the scenes," off-the-radar movement spaces, where internal rhetorics are produced ("Counter-Public Enclaves and Understanding the Function," 2). These rhetorics are not necessarily intended for wider audiences and may not be accessible or available beyond the protected enclave itself. Yet these spaces are incredibly valuable for study of social movement, because, in Chávez's words, it is in these spaces where "activists interpret external rhetorical messages that are created about them, the constituencies they represent, or both" and where they "invent rhetorical strategies to publicly challenge oppressive rhetoric or to create new imaginaries for the groups and issues they represent and desire to bring into coalition" (3). Historian Charles Payne suggests that this question is especially important for civil rights scholars: "This notion of how movements maintain an internal sense of community is crucial" ("'Sexism is a helluva thing,'" 325).

In the movement for Black freedom, the mass meeting is widely recognized as the single most important site for internal community. Holmes makes this point, recognizing the meeting as a "type of hush harbor," insofar as the movement for Black freedom could create a space away from the demands of rhetorical production for public audiences ("'Hear Me Tonight'" 158). As an extensive treatment of this key internal site for civil rights activists, *Liturgy of Change* thus extends the conversation about enclaves, internal–external rhetorics, and the role of these spaces and dynamics in social movement. As I discuss in chapter 5, while the Black church was indeed a Black-owned and controlled space, this ownership did not fully protect or seal the space from outsider's attention when activists began holding meetings. Indeed, it is well documented that in many locales, holding a meeting was dangerous; thus, mass meetings cannot be thought of as protected, or wholly secret gatherings. These constraints on the space trouble a view of it as an enclave while also pointing toward the movement of civil rights rhetoric. Activists made strategic use of countermovement attention, inviting reporters, police, and members of the local community to listen in on their work, leveraging a key element of nonviolent rhetorical strategy in casting light on unjust interruptions to their peaceful meetings. Taken together, analyses across the chapters suggest that the civil rights mass meeting defies key categories of public sphere theory, disturbing distinctions between internally and externally focused rhetorics and spaces.

Liturgy of Change highlights how civil rights rhetoric moves in yet another, sometimes literal, way. I examine how meeting genres afforded groups with modes to coordinate shifts into embodied, collective protest. At the meeting, people stepped into a space removed from the demands of public performance, yet through their singing, praying, and testimony shaped identities and collective actions that resonated in public rhetorical endeavors as well. Participating in the meeting initiated a step into the movement, and participation catalyzed steps outside to more explicit direct-action performances like marches, sit-ins, and boycotts. As chapter 3 explores in detail, this movement from church building into the street was sometimes a literal spatial shift that leaders facilitated, and prayer provided a unique scaffolding for guiding people from the event into protest. The focus on the mass meeting as movement space thus recovers the ways ordinary Black women and men participated in the invention of key genres like the freedom song; explored the gestural, discursive, and silent possibilities of prayer; and mined testimony to imagine and step toward new roles in the new world they were making. These genres reveal how the mass meeting provided internal community that directly moved collectives into public rhetorical work. Through the liturgy, the mass meeting served as both a preparatory space where people had the freedom to explore their desires rhetorically and a key mechanism for coordinating and executing strategic, planned collective action.

The emphasis on liturgy as an embodied spirituality, one taken up by collectives in meetings, gives new textures to an understanding of the rhetorical vision of change that anchored the movement for Black freedom. Rhetoric moved people in mass meetings, not just because they heard about divine authority shaping their movement, but through their own participation in this faithful vision of social change. Making the freedom songs, women and men tailored the idea of civic identity as they heard about it from figures like

King and Abernathy to a particular sound, lyrical emphasis, and church-based musical vision of change. Kneeling in prayer or holding silence, collectives reflected for themselves on what they heard about their righteousness before God, the just protest they were making, and the hopes they had for their towns and cities. Through testimony, they told their own stories of what racism felt like, how things could be different, and what protests were needed. This book highlights examples of mass meetings where these practices were taken up, but the larger point is that this liturgy structured the participation at meetings beyond the scenes studied in the book, suggesting that this kind of collective participation enabled group involvement and experience with the movement's vision across the locales and years of the movement for Black freedom. More than networked circulation, liturgy is a rhetorical process tied to space, theology, embodiment, and a set of genres that turn on becoming, changing, and moving individuals and groups toward particular visions.

Genre: "Keyword" for Movement Rhetoric

Historians and rhetoricians call attention to the difficulties of recovering specifics of *how* the civil rights movement transformed people and places (Hogan, *Many Minds, One Heart;* Brooks, *A Voice That Could Stir an Army*). *Liturgy of Change* responds to this challenge using "genre" as guiding analytic, showing how the faithful rhetorics of the meeting catalyzed ordinary people's rhetorical participation as well as group formation and collective direct action. In this section, I define "genre" as a keyword for the book and for future studies of movement rhetoric. Here, I take cues from the 2018 special issue of *Rhetoric Society Quarterly* where scholars catalogue rhetoric's "keywords," or the terms that assert a vocabulary and collective identity for scholars working in the discipline. In the entry on genre, Carolyn Miller, Amy Devitt, and Victoria Gallagher theorize genre's importance for the ways it "captures large-scale patterns of symbolic interaction, patterns that are taken as meaningful" ("Genre: Permanence and Change," 270) and they define its functions as a multimodal, multidisciplinary, multidimensional, and multimethodological concept. Genre has special significance for scholars of movement rhetorics and for approaching the civil rights mass meeting because of this capacity to illuminate symbolic action and rhetorical patterns from multiple dimensions.[5] Eschewing a comprehensive, historical survey of genre, my discussion here focuses on insights relevant to study of the mass meeting specifically and movement rhetorics more generally.[6] The following five core assertions establish genre as the keyword guiding the analyses in this volume and charts a course for future studies of genre and social movement rhetorics.

Genres Shape, Enable, and Coordinate Rhetorical Action

Rhetorical scholars primarily work from and extend Carolyn Miller's 1984 definition of "genre." Genre, understood as "typified rhetorical actions based in recurring situations," Miller argues, provides rhetorical scholars with "an index to cultural patterns and . . . tools for exploring the achievements of particular speakers and writers" ("Genre as Social Action," 159, 165). Referred to as the "anchor" and "defining moment" of Rhetorical Genre Studies, this definition opened terrain for recognizing genre's influence and function across the spectrum of communication and human interaction (Dreyer, "From the Editors"; Auken, "Contemporary Genre Studies," 48). Miller elaborates on how this definition creates a major shift in understandings of genre: "What we learn when we learn a genre is not just a pattern of forms or even a method of achieving our own ends. We learn, more importantly, what ends we may have . . . We learn to understand better the situations in which we find ourselves and the potential for failure and success in acting together" ("Genre as Social Action," 163). Working from these insights, scholars continue to examine genres as characterized by recurring patterns or textual features but connect these patterns and features to the actions they enable; the kinds of responses they create and for whom; and the cultural, social, and political dynamics that inform them. Genre remains important for this capacity, to "connec[t] theory to practice, innovation and tradition, agency and structure, form and action, social and cognitive aspects of rhetorical activity," what Miller, Devitt, and Gallagher refer to as its "multidimensionality" ("Genre: Permanence and Change," 270). Genre as social action endures as the starting point for most of the varied examinations of genre that have emerged since the 1980s, which span disciplinary, professional, and public contexts.

For movement scholars, the insight that genre operates as social action accentuates the trend of critiquing leader-centered or even text-centered approaches and shifting to study a wider, more diverse range of rhetorical activity.[7] Much work has already been done on this front. As Amy Pason, Christina Foust, and Kate Zittlow Rogness observe: "scholars [have] moved beyond a single text and traditional argumentation . . . to include 'a multiplicity of voices, images, places, and events as rhetorical . . . [and] analyze many forms of agitation and organizing" ("Introduction," 12). Genre provides another conceptual tool for scholars invested in this approach, where the move is to assemble and analyze the array of genres that enable a movement to come together and accomplish its goals, and the relationships therein. In the case of the civil rights movement, for example, a genre perspective affords a view of rhetorical action comprised not primarily of leaders' speeches but also through marches, sit-ins, letters, memos, songs, prayers, testimonies, playwriting, and poetry performed by Black collectives and individual activists.[8] The point is not to situate collective and alternative genres as minor points in a narrative dominated by major leaders and their oratory, but instead to reveal movement rhetoric as multifaceted and reliant upon varied rhetorical actions, some individual and some collective. As such, genre-as-method aligns with Darrel Wanzer-Serrano's contention that movement scholars "com[e] to discourse with the assumption that *different forms intersect with each other equally*" (181, published as Enck-Wanzer, "Trashing the System," emphasis in original).

Genre as social action also pushes movement studies deeper into issues of networks or rhetorical ecologies, and of consideration of how rhetorical action is coordinated, circulated, and sustained across time and space. Nathaniel Rivers and Ryan Weber reveal the possibilities of this type of genre study in their examination of the Montgomery bus boycott. They provide an "ecological telling" of this moment, identifying how "public discourse gets enacted through a complex system of multiple, concatenated documents and rhetorical actions produced through the combined agency of rhetors, audiences, texts, objects, history, and institutions" ("Ecological, Pedagogical, Public Rhetoric," 195). They start from a critique of histories that position King and Rosa Parks as the two key actors in Montgomery and work to reveal the range of individuals and genres necessary to carry out and sustain the boycott, such as Robinson's 1954 letter to Montgomery Mayor W. A. Gayle (*The Montgomery Bus Boycott and the Women Who Started It,* 198). As theorists maintain, genres operate as sets, repertoires, and systems; thus at the level of ecology or networked action, they provide a vocabulary and set of relationships to observe and analyze (Devitt, *Writing Genres*; Bawarshi and Reiff, *Genre*).

Genres Construct Identities and Exigencies

Genres shape and coordinate social action; they also provide inventive spaces for identity-making and crafting new social imaginaries. Returning to Carolyn Miller's 1984 definition, genres may be inhabited to invent *who we may become* as much as to observe "what ends we may have" ("Genre as Social Action," 163). Genres thus help rhetors observe and *invent* possibilities, know about themselves and the world, and create new identities for the world they desire. Scholars recognize this connection to identity. For example, Anis Bawarshi writes: "Genres are both functional and epistemological—they help us shape the ways we come to know these situations" ("The Genre Function," 340). While genres can guide individuals toward appropriate, expected responses to situations, they can also suggest transformative or resistant ways of being and acting in the world.

In this view, genres are not just pragmatic tools that people use to achieve their goals; they are not just "typified responses to recurring rhetorical situations" (Carolyn Miller, "Genre as Social Action," 159). They may also serve as spaces for transformation or transcendence, for invoking a self or exigence that is not-yet. Genres may function too as frames for recognizing a recurring rhetorical situation and resisting the typified response with an unexpected one. This understanding of genre takes cues from the constitutive approach to rhetoric more generally that recognizes groups form through rhetoric (Charland, "Constitutive Rhetoric"). A constitutive approach to rhetoric, Alisse Portnoy writes, recognizes how texts may "create exigencies and identities; they generate and call forth new, sometimes transcendent or transformational, ways of being and relating to the world; sometimes they foreclose possibilities and sustain extant power dynamics" (*Their Right to Speak,* 7). Christa Olson argues that these transformational rhetorics may be observed in "collections of artifacts and acts surrounding those [important national] documents—visual elements, political performances, and the material experiences of everyday life" (*Constitutive Visions,* 26). While neither Olson nor Portnoy deeply consider genre, they reveal that it is through a range of genres and modalities—paintings, sculptures, petitions—that rhetorical actors find resources for constituting new identities and exigencies. Genres then hold the potential for remaking self and the world.[9]

On this point, genre prompts attention to another kind of multidimensionality of particular interest to movement studies, the nexus of collective identity and collective action, or constitutive and instrumental rhetorics.[10] Most social change scholars recognize the significance of symbolic change, or the ways that movement actors reconceive of themselves and their worlds, resist oppressive structures and rhetorics, and craft new imaginaries, while also attending to material changes at the level of policy and the law. Yet the different goals of social change often prove difficult to hold together and examine as different facets of activists' work.[11] Genre, viewed as identity and action, provides a tool for toggling analytically among aspects of change. Pason, Foust, and Rogness write that social change requires "interaction between various material and symbolic elements defined by and coordinated through communication, where change is about shifting power" ("Introduction," 17). Genre, as a multidimensional concept, prompts examination of how the material and symbolic work together to make change. For example, a focus on genre enables insights into the bidirectionality of action, identity, and function. Recognizing the ways that movements conceive of themselves through genres they select, scholars can probe more deeply into the study of identity, form, and action, moving among symbolic and material goals as blended rhetorics and processes enabling social change.

Genres Cohere and Constitute Publics and Counterpublics

Reflecting on the ubiquity of genre, Miller, Devitt, and Gallagher write: "No matter what we do here . . ., they will be here too—genres invoked, avoided, honored, remembered, resisted, echoed, imitated, ridiculed, transcended. . . . They are baggage we acquire along with language itself, along with rhetorical consciousness" ("Genre: Permanence and Change," 269). To participate in any community, public, or social movement, genres are necessary: they are the forms that enable individuals to become recognizable to one another and to craft relationships. If a public is understood as composed in part through discourse, then genres permit this composition and coherence (Warner, *Publics and Counterpublics,* 11–12). As Michael Warner writes: "The notion of a public enables a reflexivity in the circulation of texts among strangers who become, by virtue of their reflexively circulating discourse, a social entity" (11–12). It follows then that publics and counterpublics depend on genres; they require them to come together and to carry out their work. In Bawarshi and Mary Jo Reiff's estimation, "Publics and the performances of public life are textually embodied and mediated through genre networks" (*Genre,* 5).

Given the turn in genre studies to explore publics, it follows that genre might also help to explain and conceptualize counterpublics, a key concern for movement studies. As with publics more generally, counterpublic activity may be understood through attention to the genres most salient to its members and their relationships. Following Reiff, attention to the variability or shifts in genre use may shed light on the goals and needs of the counterpublic and the relationship to the power dynamics the group seeks to change ("Geographies of Public Genres," 101). Through attention to counterpublic formation through genre, scholars are thus poised to attend to movement organization, emergence, and action and to explore the complexity of internal/external dynamics.

Extending this point further, analysis of counterpublic genres affords opportunity to inspect how movements make use of what Jonathan Alexander and Susan Jarratt theorize as the "unruly." In their collection of essays (co-edited with Nancy Welch), Alexander and Jarratt define the "unruly" as rhetorics that "disrup[t] what appears or is taken to be the normal flow of life" ("Introduction," 7). They note the significance of the body to unruly rhetorics: particular bodies, including women, disabled people, and racial minorities, are more likely to be understood as unruly or disruptive in certain contexts. Part of Alexander and Jarratt's project is to question civility as a mode of politics, or "ideals of rationalism, stakeholders-at-the-table mediation" (16). A genre perspective might extend this project further, inviting consideration of how genres become imbued with civility or unruliness. Scholars might also ask how and why some genres disrupt and the ways these disruptions resonate with movement participants. Questions such as these offer insights into counterpublic formation and rhetorical performance.

Genres Are Dynamic, Power-Laden Sites *That May Be Adapted by Their Users*

The rhetorical view of genre focuses not only on the ways that genres open up possibilities but also to the limits they impose. Scholars including Risa Applegarth, Lindsay Rose Russell, and Mary Jo Reiff make this point in their discussion of the ways that genres are inflected by power. In Applegarth's view, "Genres frequently normalize and reproduce relations of power and stabilize the worldviews they imply—for instance, by constructing some people as knowers while positioning others as consumers or objects of knowledge and by authorizing certain versions of reality at the expense of other versions" (*Rhetoric in American Anthropology*, 16). Applegarth traces this point into the disciplinary community of anthropology, revealing the ways that the scholarly monograph, for instance, served as a site for "*disciplining* the knowledge that members of the community create" (17, emphasis in original). While this normalizing function might be expected for a disciplinary genre like the monograph, Reiff asserts that even a public genre such as the petition, with a clear social intervention to "seek redress for grievances," is "shaped by conditions that work to exclude participants and forestall change" ("Geographies of Public Genres," 101). These observations about the ways that genres delimit users' identities and actions lead to examining genre change and investigating possibilities for adaptation. What happens when genre users recognize and push against generic constraints? Or when they perceive a new exigency, or desire a different set of patterns or resources?

Attention to genre as a multidimensional concept, one that accounts for agency and structure, enables examination of the cultural positionings that open and close off actions to individuals and groups due to race, gender, or sexuality, and other factors and the kinds of genre responses that users create, particularly strategic attempts to adapt genres and craft them more inclusively. Dylan Dryer explains how this kind of study might proceed: "If genre conventions produce and reflect social responses perceived as recurring, then those social responses are changeable by deliberate changes to those conventions, even at the level of routine inscription. Perhaps Rhetorical Genre Studies is ready to return to those features of genre that have always preoccupied Formalism . . . but with an edge. Motivated genre change, as *tactical social intervention*" (Dryer, "From the Editors," emphasis in original). Studying the English Dictionary, Lindsay Rose Russell observes that scenes of genre invention are particularly ripe for examining shifts at the level of convention, and more generally, for recognizing the ways that individuals participate in genre creation and deliberate over genre needs. Russell, like Dryer, pushes for more study of agency on the part of genre users: "When we focus on genres as (temporarily) stabilized social structures that 'help do our rhetorical thinking for us' we tend to ignore the rhetorical thinking that goes into genre invention itself" ("Defining Moments," 85).

Movement scholars are well-posed to examine the ways that genres may be intentionally tailored or reconceived of for movement goals or needs. Genre selection, adaptation, and even invention thus become sites of inquiry and exploration. Across the spaces and needs of social movement, participants' deliberations over genre reveal the strategic ways they choose, adapt, and sustain modes of action and identity. This meta-discussion of genres found in alternative or little-known texts then becomes as significant a site of study as movement genres themselves.

Genres Are Embodied and Felt in Relationship to Space

Given the manifestations of power in shaping genre activity, many scholars have called for attention to the materiality of genre.[12] One vein of this scholarship invites study of embodied performance and experience of genre. Examining the film, *The Passion of the Christ,* Joshua Gunn argues: "Our more commonplace understanding of genres as names for textual patterns overlooks the important ways in which affective and bodily modalities underwrite and interact with such patterns. A genre is not merely the label for a text, but the signature of an affective apparatus that both presumes and produces bodies-in-feeling" ("*Maranatha,*" 364). Gunn points to the ways that generic features shape emotion or may provide clues for how and what to feel. Similarly, cultural theorist Lauren Berlant conceives of genre as "an aesthetic structure of affective expectation" (*The Female Complaint,* 4). Observing the material, embodied dimensions of genre means considering the feeling bodies that inhabit genres as well as the residual affects that genres acquire through recurring use.[13]

In marking this distinction between feeling/emotion and affect, I follow scholars who articulate these concepts as related but separate concerns.[14] In this view, "feeling" refers to an emotion like joy that an individual might name, define, or explain, and "affect" denotes a broader cultural category that invites feelings that may or may not be recognized as such. Christian Lundberg explains: "Where emotion describes a subjectively felt state, affect describes the set of forces, investments, logics, relations, and practices of subjectivization that are the conditions of possibility for emotion" ("Enjoying God's Death," 390). Applied to genre, this insight invites scholarly scrutiny of emotions as they are expressed and recognized by individual and collective genre users and of how genres condition certain kinds of feelings over and against others.

A material perspective on genre also assumes that bodies inhabit genres in actual *spaces,* situated in relationship to institutions and power. To understand genre as embodied means inspecting how it is spatially situated and to what ends. As Jessica Enoch avers: "Both body and space animate one another: the body and its activities help to define the space and the space helps to define the body" (*Domestic Occupations,* 17).[15] Applegarth explores this point in her study of writer Mary Austin, for whom writing a literary nature essay in the desert opened up the possibilities of the genre, particularly with regard to ethos and gender ("Genre, Location, and Mary Austin's Ethos," 50). Spatiality, then, can expand or restrict genre possibilities for rhetors, and it informs the felt experience of genres as well as the availability of rhetorical resources.

The nexus of genre, emotion, affect, and space represent new possibilities and questions for movement scholars. Lisa Corrigan, in *Black Feelings,* calls for deeper attention to the "emotional repertoires" of social movements, the ways that feelings mobilize and sustain groups and their work, create new identities and possibilities for being, and speak back to dominant perceptions of how people should feel about oppression. Corrigan examines the Black liberation discourses of figures including King, Malcolm X, and Stokely Carmichael, revealing "how black political feelings like rage, shame, resentment, disgust, betrayal, and melancholy created structural coherence in Black Power discourses to manage the increasingly narrow possibilities for black dissent and to invigorate black ontologies" (*Black Feelings,* xxiii). As a method for examining varied categories of movement activity from individual to collective, from leader to ordinary participant, genre provides a mechanism for mapping and tracing emotional valences within and across movement discourses.

In the remainder of this book, I elaborate on these core assertions, studying the mass meeting as genre—liturgy—and discrete genre set—song, prayer, and testimony. This approach enables study of the mass meeting as holistic event, where large groups formed their collective identities and learned, practiced, and performed Christian nonviolent rhetorical action. Genre enables recovery of these collective rhetorical movements, from individuals curious about civil rights to activist group ready and set for direct action, and the specific ways the Black church facilitated this transformation. Beyond the case studies of the book, this genre-informed framework offers movement scholars new ways to hold together the textures and nuance of individual performances with attention to broader patterns of collective action, affect, and power dynamics.

Recovering Civil Rights Mass Meetings: Methods and Methodology

In his essay about the first mass meeting held in Montgomery, Alabama, Wilson comments: "To experience the remarkable power of the Holt Street Address, I recommend that one travel to the State Historical Society of Wisconsin in Madison and listen to the audio copy that resides in its archive. Even then, the temporal distance of fifty years and our ideological separation from 1950s Alabama will frustrate any 'perfect' appreciation of the speech" ("Interpreting the Discursive Field of the Montgomery Bus Boycott," 307–8). One of the preoccupations of this project is to examine what Wilson identifies—and suggests is very difficult to recover: the rhetorical power and felt significance of mass-meeting rhetoric. In no way am I suggesting that a "perfect" appreciation of events is possible; my interest is in trying to get closer to the moment of the mass meeting, when religion, feeling, and collectivity animated the experience in ways that were rhetorically significant.

Liturgy of Change thus takes on the task of reconstructing the "indescribably moving" event so central to the civil rights movement, and more broadly, to African American religious history (King, *Stride Toward Freedom*, 53). Toward this goal, I draw together materials including audio recordings, photographs, memos, programs, posters, memoirs, and interviews. These materials come from physical archives like the Guy and Candie Carawan Collection at the University of North Carolina Chapel Hill in addition to digital archives such as the Eyes on the Prize Interview Collection at Washington University.

The most significant archival materials for my study are the audio recordings of meetings. I transcribed these recordings to document who spoke and what they said in addition to how the event was structured through genre—prayer, song, testimony, sermon, reports, and so on. These transcriptions offer insight into both the rhetorical textures of individual and collective performances, and they also enable me to make claims about the patterns of meetings and how they functioned holistically.

I draw on other kind of materials, such as photographs and memos, to help fill out an incomplete historical record of the mass meetings. As other scholars have observed, the audio archives of civil rights mass meetings, compared to the number of meetings that actually happened, are not as robust as one would hope (Houck and Dixon, "Introduction: Recovering Women's Voices from the Civil Rights Movement," xviii). Another trouble spot in archival collections is a focus on well-known leaders and "men of the movement." Some recordings shut off after a leader, such as King, finished speaking (Holmes, "'Hear Me Tonight'" 117). To account for these absences and omissions, then, I examine both complete and partial audio recordings, and I include photographs, programs, fliers, posters, memos, interviews, and memoirs in the corpus of texts for the study. This method expands the body of available evidence, but I am nevertheless working from a limited set of texts relative to the many, many meetings held during the time period under review here. Thus, analyses should be read as partial, descriptive glimpses of events rather than definitive accounts. Broadly speaking, the analytical perspective of this book works from the theory of genre outlined above. I inspect the materials I have drawn together to understand and explore the "felt sounds" of the meeting as a liturgy, a participatory pedagogy and an experience, and the genres that structured the pedagogy, experience, and process (Campt, *Listening to Images*, 7). This method opens up room to study the holistic rhetorical operations of mass meetings, ordinary people's individual contributions, and group performances of song, prayer, and testimony.

There are limits to what any scholar can say about the rhetorics of religious experience or a faith-infused process of becoming. Still, I take seriously the persistent and evocative claims activists make about the faithful dimensions of meetings. Toward this end, I turn to the method historians label "lived theology." In Charles Marsh's definition, lived theology "might be considered a probing and careful narration of life inside the movement of God in the social world" ("Letter from the Director," 4). Ansley Quiros adds lived theology "is the story people tell themselves and others about what God is doing in the world and how they are participating in that divine action" (*God with Us*, 9). As a method, lived theology entails attention to "the way theological convictions shape the patterns and practices of particular Christian communities" (Marsh, "Letter from the Director," 4). Lived theology, then, names the study of the intersections of religious belief and rhetorical speech and action. For me as a rhetorical scholar, this move means analyzing both the primary texts that depict the meeting scene and examining the interplay between these texts and activists, accounts of what they experienced or believe about the rhetorics of the mass meeting. These often-theological activist perspectives provide starting points for studying and interpreting the primary texts of events.[16]

THE FIRST CHAPTER of the book depicts the mass meeting as a *liturgy of change*. I overview how liturgies, rooted in religious traditions, operate rhetorically as sites for becoming through interwoven faithful genres. Extending scholarship by Raphael Warnock, Beverly Moss, Shirley Wilson Logan, and others, I situate liturgy of change in an African American religious tradition and show how Black church history uniquely supported the mass meeting's straddling of religious experience and the sociopolitical arena.

Chapters 2–4 examine the particular genres that comprised the meeting liturgy: sacred song, prayer, and testimony. In chapter 2, I argue that activists, especially women, used the sacred musical portion of the meeting to craft a genre unique to the civil rights movement, the freedom song. An emerging civil rights genre, freedom songs offered an introduction to what it felt like to belong to the movement, spiritual resources to sustain activism, and a mode of peaceful action for protest in public spaces. Chapter 3 centers on prayer at civil rights mass meetings. The freedom song's quiet partner, prayer catalyzed group formation through gesture—kneeling, bowed heads—and shared contemplative, spiritual silence as well as reflection, deliberation, and petition. Prayer provided the group with specific, coordinated means of embodying peaceful action, while it also opened space to reflect on movement progress, steel themselves for future protest, and process their feelings before God. Chapter 4 studies the most flexible of mass-meeting genres, testimony. Testimony afforded those gathered in the meeting an opportunity to stand up and speak their minds, thus empowering local people to perform as individual rhetors and cultivate rhetorical and democratic knowledge. Testimony was taught in the meeting as a loose, or "fuzzy," genre, one that has malleable boundaries and accommodates a range of features and social actions (Medway, "Fuzzy Genres and Community Identities").

The final chapter of the book steps back from examining the internal dynamics of the meeting to investigate questions of audience(s) and liturgy. Here, I consider the ways segregationists, local police, and members of the Klan and Citizens' Council attempted to surveil, interrupt, or disrupt meetings. The mass meeting served as a pedagogical forum for Christian nonviolence, using the liturgy to teach and enact this method of countermovement engagement.

I conclude by reflecting on the ways the book resonates with twenty-first-century racial justice activism. I explore Black Lives Matter as a Black queer feminist response to some of the limitations of liturgy as it animated the civil rights movement, and I close by considering the unexpected ways that liturgy and faithful genres persist as resources for advocating for racial justice.

ONE

Becoming Hopeful

The Civil Rights Mass Meeting
as Liturgy of Change

We grew up with the liturgy of the church . . . that we translated
to the Civil Rights Movement, the songs . . . and the preaching
and the testifying. All that took place in those mass meetings.

Historians, rhetoricians, and sociologists agree that the Black church
was key to the success of the movement for Black freedom. Sociologist Aldon Morris puts it this way: "The black church functioned as
the institutional center of the modern civil rights movement" (*The
Origins of the Civil Rights Movement,* 4). Morris shows how the Black
church provided meeting places, people to form a movement base, leadership, financial support, and cultural resources. Moreover, he notes, the
church was largely independent from white control. Rhetorical scholars have
extended Morris's observation by recovering and/or analyzing the speeches
of activists, revealing this church connection through appeals and biblical
language. For example, the two-volume anthology *Rhetoric, Religion, and the
Civil Rights Movement,* edited by Davis Houck and David Dixon, present
abundant discursive evidence of the Black church's central role in the movement. These two collections powerfully showcase the significance of religious language as it appears in the speeches of figures such as Mary McLeod
Bethune, Mordecai Johnson, and Benjamin Mays.

In this chapter I address religion's rhetorical role in the civil rights movement, specifically the mass meetings, from a different angle. Rather than
examine appeals or discourse, I consider the movement's reliance on the
Black church's liturgy. Quoted in the epigraph above, activist and scholar
Joyce Ladner emphasizes that the mass meeting served as the space where
activists brought liturgy to the movement's work, employing it as a recurring

rhetorical experience and malleable organizational tactic (Ladner and Ladner, Interview). As discussed in the Introduction, "liturgy" refers, broadly speaking, to the order and structure of a worship service. In this chapter, I develop the concept to name the rhetorical means by which religious experiences shape belief, action, and identity and the set of interwoven religious genres that accomplish these purposes. While liturgies comprise individual genres that can be examined discretely (as I do in the chapters to follow), they also function as genres themselves, with the key social action being collective worship.

The liturgy of the mass meeting was not an ordinary worship service. As Ladner explains, activists translated the liturgy of the Black church for movement needs.[1] The liturgy of the meeting, then, is best understood as a *liturgy of change*. Here, I mean the ways that participation in this faith-infused event constructed the group's bonds to one another, their identities, and their vision and enactment of sociopolitical work. This concept opens up the view of the meeting as training ground for activism and felt experience, amplifying both its faithful dimensions and its relationship to the power dynamics that activists sought to change.

As a liturgy of change, the civil rights mass meeting provided a recognizable rhetorical experience throughout the Black freedom movement, an experience that was at once pragmatic, action-oriented, faithful, reverent, and intimate. I examine meeting patterns from different vantage points: the interwoven set of genres that comprise liturgies, activists' reflections on how they felt while participating, and the spatial elements of events. My analysis focuses on meeting programs, memos, retrospective interviews, and a series of photographs from Savannah, Georgia, materials that taken together provide a broad view of the meeting as a holistic scene. Such a holistic view is important, because, as many activists attest, the mass meeting cannot be understood through attention to one moment, one figure, or one speech. Rather, events functioned and transformed like a liturgy—as a call-and-response pattern structured through different genres, a felt sense of unity, an experience of collective faith. These purposes of the meeting only come into view by stepping back and studying the whole.

Liturgies of Change and
African American Religious History

The word "liturgy" comes from the Greek and means "the work of the people" (Colsten, "Music in the Liturgy of African American Congregations," 10). Most simply, liturgy names the order of what happens in a worship service. Liturgies of church services are in general rhetorical as they provide invitations to people to inhabit particular faith-informed ways of being, acting, and speaking in the world. Liturgies extend these invitations through different genres of religious actions ordered to structure individual and group participation in worship. As I discuss it in this book, liturgy relates to Christian traditions, given the emphasis on Christianity in the civil rights mass meetings I study. Key genres in this tradition include prayer, song, and sermon. Like all genres that work together in a set, group, or ecology, liturgical genres share important relationships that work to coordinate action, shape identity, and enable group formation.[2] Liturgical genres, or faithful genres, are unique in that they are, first and foremost, about and for faith, and as such, sites for becoming—for stepping into a reality of "things hoped for, the conviction of things not seen" (English Standard Version of the Bible, Hebrews).[3]

Liturgies, as religious experiences structured through a genre pattern, are constitutive for individuals and groups as expressions of faith. Thus, while faithful genres do shape and enable social actions and offer responses to recurring situations, they first construct individual and group identities and are tethered to a future that exists through belief. Rhetorical theorist Dana Anderson calls attention to the constitutive nature of genres about belief, specifically the conversion narrative. He theorizes conversion narratives as sites for an intense, persuasive change in identity, showing how these experiences are rhetorical constructions of individual transformation. Conversions, or "forsaking a dark, misguided past for a brighter, righter future," are an important facet of religious experience, and one that, as Anderson argues, reveals the rhetorical formation of identity centered in a dramatic change (*Identity's Strategy*, 2).

Conversion is perhaps the most obvious site of transformation in Christian traditions, but it is not the only one. Religion, generally speaking, can be understood as an ongoing, daily experience of becoming and participation in changing one's self.[4] This everyday process is constitutive, persuasive, and rhetorically crafted as faithful individuals and groups recreate themselves continually. American theologian Thomas Merton explains this point in his spiritual autobiography *Seven Storey Mountain*: "They were saints in that most effective and telling way: sanctified by leading ordinary lives in a completely supernatural manner, sanctified by obscurity, by usual skills, by common tasks, by routine, but skills, tasks, routine which received a supernatural form of grace within, and from the habitual union of their souls with God in deep faith and charity" (62). As Merton's description reveals, Christianity transforms individuals not just through a momentary conversion, but continually, through a process some theologians refer to as sanctification— that is, the habitual participation in traditions and rituals of faith. The process is structured and enabled in part by the ordinary, weekly worship services faithful people attend and the liturgies that animate these events. In other words, liturgies, as recurring sites for sanctification, shape the ongoing transformation that characterizes Christian experience.[5]

In Christianity, as it is practiced in the United States, the relationship between liturgy and the meaning and purpose of civic engagement has varied widely. For example, in the latter half of the twentieth and into the twenty-first century, many white evangelical traditions embrace the idea of individual change, but in sociopolitical terms, they support conservative political agendas and resist social change.[6] While some may view Christian worship as an otherworldly escape that shifts people's orientations away from the civic arena, liturgy as seen through a rhetorical lens profoundly shapes people's civic and political orientations, whether this training moves in conservative or progressive directions, whether it is explicitly political or not. In his recovery of the rhetoric of nineteenth-century preacher Austin Phelps, Michael-John DePalma writes about the Christian concept of self-transformation as generally oriented toward civic ends. In the thinking of many religious leaders, self-transformation in the faithful sense can be a step toward right engagement in other spheres, the civic and political included (DePalma, "Austin Phelps and the Spirit (of) Composing").

African American religious history illustrates that liturgies may be about both individual sanctification and social transformation.[7] From its inception in the African American tradition, liturgy, like rhetoric, has been tethered to Black freedom.[8] Enslaved people met together for worship services in hush harbors, spaces hidden away from white slaveowners. These hush harbors were spaces for liturgy and often, at the same time, for planning an escape to freedom. The liturgies that structured hush harbor worship combined the genres of Western Christianity and African religion. Wolfgang Vondey writes that these events included the standard liturgical genres of prayer, sermon, and song, but enslaved people made the worship their own through "the imagination and rhythm of their African roots" ("The Making of a Black Liturgy," 154). Such adaptation entailed adding oral genres from African folk religion like narrative or testimony, songs, and plays and eschewing strict adherence to a sequence of set genres in favor of a call-and-response style for spontaneous participation.

During reconstruction and into the twentieth century, the Black church supported worship and social change by providing space for African Americans to speak freely, engage in rhetorical training, and perform literate action. In this period, African American worship liturgies retained a hybrid mix of Western religious genres—sermons, prayers, and songs—adapted in the spirit of orality, play, and freedom. Writing about African American liturgies across time, Vondey contends that they are "held together mostly by the rather broad scheme of singing, preaching, prayer, and fellowship. This is coupled with an emphasis on experience and empowerment. Dialogical style and prophetic elements, including the frequent attention to celebration, liberation, and improvisation, diversify African American churches and distinguish them from other liturgical traditions" ("The Making of a Black Liturgy," 147). Centering attention on the Black church, rhetorical scholars have studied the minister's role and the sermon, free-floating literacy and rhetorical training, and hush harbor rhetorics.[9] For example, Beverly Moss demonstrates that as cultural institutions, Black churches have long served a wide range of educational and sociopolitical needs, while also being spaces central to worship and liturgy: "The African-American church is one of the few institutions where class boundaries are deemphasized, where regions are spanned, where African Americans from almost all walks of life are accepted" (*A Community Text Arises,* 17).

The civil rights movement represents a unique moment in Black church history when these strands of political action and faithful genres, realized in the vehicle of the mass meeting, came together to transform society, churches, and individuals. Indeed, the Black church was key to organization and leadership of the movement and the rhetorical forms and discourse that animated both (Morris, *The Origins of the Civil Rights Movement,* 4). This tight link between churches and the movement can nowhere be better observed than through the mass meeting. Morris's description of the meetings mirrors his contention about the church in general: "The mass meetings were the pulse and lifeline of the movement—its information center; the occasion for inspiration, rejuvenation, and commitment by means of rousing sermons and unifying Black spirituals; the opportunity for planning and strategy session; and the financial center" (23). The late congressman and activist John Lewis makes the case more succinctly: "The mass meetings *were* the church, and for some who had grown disillusioned with Christian otherworldliness, they were better than the church" (quoted in Marsh, *The Beloved Community,* 207, emphasis in original). Lewis does not just say the mass meetings were *like* church. Instead, he makes a more emphatic point: they *were* the church. As an analogue to the Black church, the mass meetings provided important experiences of faith, and this experiential quality of events was made possible through a strategic familiarity. In meetings, the feeling of church was signaled through the pattern and order of the service, from song to prayer to preaching to story. In the context of the movement for Black freedom, liturgy provided a rhetorical means to invite people into the movement, construct individual and group identity, and step toward collective action.

The mass meeting thus drew on the history of resistance in the Black church tradition, using liturgy both for its familiarity and its capacity to signal social transformation and resistance. Yet, to return to Ladner's words that opened the chapter, this liturgy was translated—it was adapted, expanded, and revised for the civil rights movement. Pastor, scholar, and current Georgia senator Raphael Warnock provides insight into the translation process. Warnock argues that throughout the history of the Black church, pastors and laypeople alike have questioned whether church was for individual conversion and sanctification or for social and political change: "for piety or protest . . . to save souls or to transform the social order" (*The Divided Mind of the Black Church*, 3). Warnock shows how through the civil rights movement, and largely through King's nascent theological vision, the Black church adapted to hold these threads of change together. King's discussion of this duality in *Stride Toward Freedom* explains Warnock's point:

> Religion deals with both earth and heaven, both time and eternity.
> . . . It seeks not only to integrate men with God but to integrate men
> with men and each man with himself. This means, at bottom, that the
> Christian gospel is a two-way road. On the one hand it seeks to change
> the souls of men, and thereby unite them with God; on the other hand
> it seeks to change the environmental conditions of men so that the
> soul will have a chance after it is changed. Any religion that professes
> to be concerned with the souls of men and is not concerned with the
> slums that damn them, the economic conditions that strangle them,
> and the social conditions that cripple them is a dry-as-dust religion.
> (*Stride Toward Freedom*, 23)

Warnock contends that the civil rights movement represents a pivotal moment in the history of Black theology, when King's dialectical vision of Christianity emerges, one where faith called worshippers *both* to seek God personally *and at the same time* to transform society and create a more just world. Adapting the liturgy of the Black church, then, meant shifting it toward this emerging vision, where worship and social change might be held together and enacted reciprocally.

Still, in the context of the movement for Black freedom, what Warnock calls "the divided mind of the Black church" lingered. Many ministers were unwilling to open their doors for mass meetings, believing that social change was not worth the cost of violent white backlash or damage to church property.[10] For both ministers and laypeople, the question of purpose was not altogether settled: many still doubted how the Black church could effect both a personal and social (collective) transformation simultaneously, while not privileging one over the other. Even among those who wholeheartedly supported the Black church's role in the civil rights movement, not all embraced King's Christian vision—particularly regarding nonviolence—and not all saw the movement in Christian terms. Many who initially embraced Christianity and civil rights activism would come to question this vision and faith's role in social change by the mid to late 1960s.

These complexities notwithstanding, the Black church and its liturgy provided the civil rights movement with the mass meeting, a space activist Bob Moses describes as "an energy machine" and historian John Dittmer calls perhaps the movement's "most effective organizing tool" (*Local People*, 131). Through its enactment in the meeting, liturgy afforded individuals and groups a rhetorical structure for (re)creating their sense of themselves, feeling that social change was possible, and experiencing the future they desired. The liturgy's spiritual pattern centered on the key genres of song, prayer, and testimony, genres that required the collective to become rhetors. Together, the genres of song, prayer, and testimony afforded everyone gathered an opportunity to construct their identities through varied types of participation. Like the conversion narratives Anderson studies, these liturgical genres reveal "how rhetors constitute *their own identities,*" and in this case, not just on an individual level but for the group as well (*Identity's Strategy*, 14, emphasis in original). At the same time, these genres were useful within and beyond the meeting walls for direct action protest.

The rhetorical liturgy of the meeting was an available genre set situated in and connected to the space and resources of the church. It was flexible and indicated faithful hope in a new future. The individual genres that comprised the liturgy were available and adaptable, and as a set, they reinforced shared goals and themes, however a local movement might be defining its purpose at the time.

Liturgy as Participatory Readiness and Religious Experience

As a liturgy, the civil rights mass meeting encouraged people first to participate deeply in the events, and second, through this participation, to believe that the nation could be changed and that their actions could change it. This participatory element reveals the liturgy of the meeting as pedagogical, a site for learning and practicing faith-infused democratic speech and action. Scholars have observed the role that meeting leaders played as teachers. Ralph Abernathy, for instance, is figured as a pedagogue in Birmingham mass meetings (Holmes, "'Hear Me Tonight'"). The liturgical view extends this point to reveal how within the mass meeting as a forum of democratic rhetorical education, teaching occurred as much through the collective's structured participation in faithful genres like song, prayer, and testimony as through their listening to sermonic addresses. This participation in meeting genres enabled collectives to learn about democracy and hone their rhetorical capacities as civic and political agents. At the same time, they encountered the liturgy as a felt experience of faith, one shaped by the genres of the meeting and oriented toward prefiguring the changes they sought. These events operated as rhetorical spaces that assumed the future sought was not just possible, but already true: people spoke and acted in the meeting as the political agents they knew themselves to be. The felt and prefigurative elements coupled with strategic rhetorical education enabled events to move between training for political engagement through democratic-rhetorical practices and what many activists describe as ineffable, an experience of a desired world as real and possible.

Participatory Readiness: Poised for
Civic Action and Political Engagement

As a rhetorical event encouraging deep participation, mass meetings facilitated civic and political agency through providing key moments for collectives to lend their voices and bodies to the meeting agenda, cultivating their own beliefs in the changes they sought and practicing the rhetorical skills that correlated with the democratic vision they were learning about. Here, Danielle Allen's concept of participatory readiness helps demonstrate the liturgy's operations as pedagogy of social change. For Allen participatory readiness names a desired outcome of public education, where individuals are prepared to enter a world in which they are poised to lead meaningful lives across all domains—civic and political action, breadwinning, social intimacy, and world-making. In this view, education is for eudaemonia, human flourishing at the broadest level. Allen focuses her discussion of teaching for participatory readiness on civic and political agency, outlining a model that cultivates "verbal empowerment; strategic and tactical understanding of the levers of political change, broadly conceived, and the ethics of their use; and democratic, associational know-how" (*Education and Equality,* 43). Participatory readiness as it relates to civic and political agency is notably *rhetorical,* emphasizing the intersections of language, action, and democratic knowledge. As a model of a democratic pedagogy, participatory readiness helps to illuminate the ways the meeting invited groups in and positioned them for civic and political action. At the same time, the liturgy was not wholly or exclusively about civic and political engagement; rather, the participatory readiness taught through the meeting espoused social change as broadly as Allen does education—flourishing across all domains of life.

As a liturgy, the mass meeting structured moments for individuals and the group to participate and respond to the democratic vision discussed by leaders. Maegan Parker Brooks describes the rhetorical process of the Student Nonviolent Coordinating Committee's (SNCC) work in the Mississippi Delta: "Fieldworkers engaged in conversations with local people using the ballot as a symbol to persuade them; this persuasion materialized when Delta Blacks began attending movement meetings where they were exposed to more discourse in the form of speeches and songs, which taught them about citizenship and inspired them to take action" (*A Voice That Could Stir an Army,* 47). As Brooks explains, the invitation to the mass meeting was a key entrée into citizenship, where significant teaching happened. This teaching occurred not just through exposure to discourse. People also participated in *creating* the discourse, and then in turn adapted and invented new modes of persuasion and transformation through this participation. The collective genres of song and prayer required everyone gathered to join in, through voice and body, and the range of other faithful genres opened up opportunities for individuals not in leadership positions, especially women and young people, to hone their rhetorical skills, whether through testimony, leading a devotion, or serving as a song leader. In Nashville, Tennessee, for example, the pattern for this May 16, 1960, event went as follows:

Song Service
Devotions
Song
Student Speaker
Registration and Community Status
Song, "Lift Every Voice and Sing"
Speaker [Sermonic Address]
Financial Appeal
Progress Report and Financial Statement
The Economic Situation
Announcements and Benediction

As the structure of this liturgy indicates, at least four moments invited collective participation—the Song Service, Song #1, Song #2, and the Closing Benediction (see fig. 1.1). Through the genres of song and prayer, interspersed throughout the event, the group proclaimed with voice and body their participation in the meeting's goal, explained on the program as "Against Practices of Racial Discrimination in our Community." In a church filled with people singing and praying, through gesture and voice, participation begets participation. Attendees are encouraged to join in and do as others are doing, whether song and prayer are familiar or not (though for many, familiarity was likely). These collective genres encouraged everyone to play an active, and rhetorical, role in the work of the civil rights movement in Nashville.[11] Moreover, this participation poised the group for continued rhetorical action because song and prayer are not just genres practiced in the mass meeting (see chapters 2 and 3). These genres are key to direct action protest

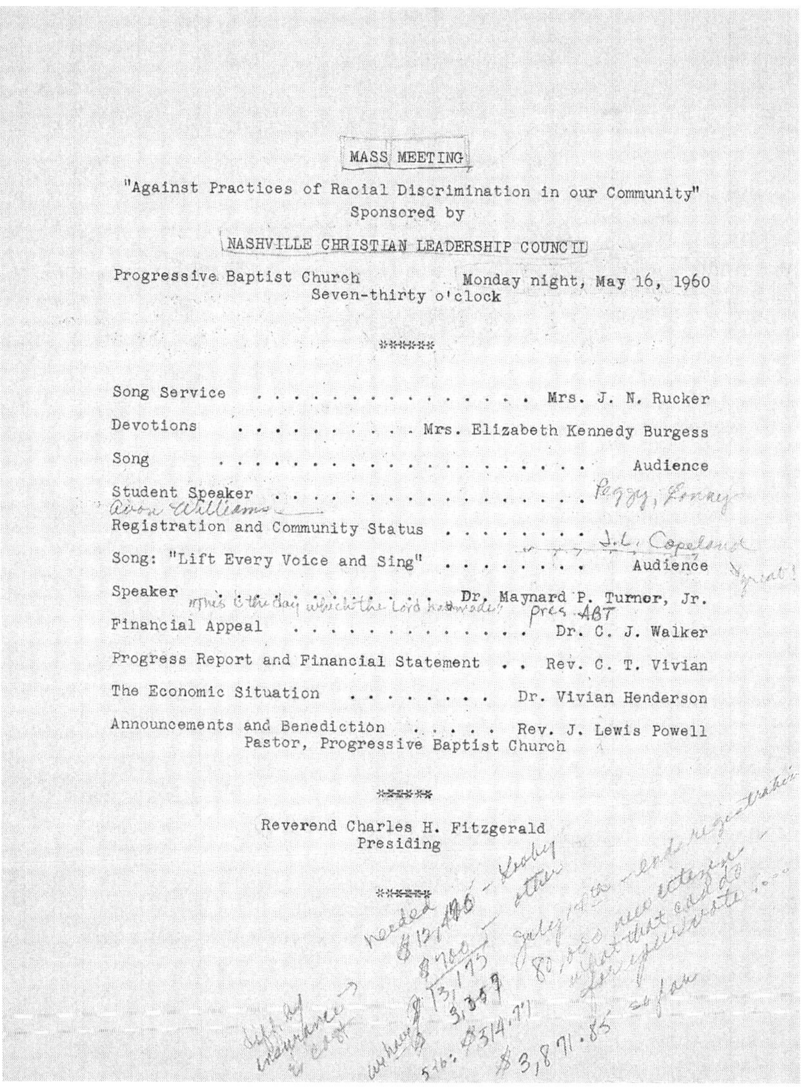

FIGURE 1.1. Mass Meeting Program, Nashville, Tennessee, May 16, 1960.
Guy and Candie Carawan Collection #20008, Southern Folklife Collection,
Wilson Library, University of North Carolina at Chapel Hill.

outside the church walls as well; stepping into them within the meeting prepared people to continue singing and praying "against practices of racial discrimination in [the] community," in public spaces. Activist A. W. Wilson makes this point explicit; after the mass meetings, he claimed, "They were ready for anything, you see. Ready for it" (Wilson, Interview, 4).

Besides structuring ways for the collective to participate as a group and respond to a vision of change, the liturgical pattern facilitated participatory readiness through rhetorical openings for ordinary people to stand up and speak. In these moments, individuals engage in deliberation, prophecy, and advocacy, and through this rhetorical engagement speak about democratic themes as well as build the new social world they are seeking.[12] According to historian Wesley Hogan, one of the key educational components of the movement was "how people learned to speak for themselves and talk to each other" (*Many Minds, One Heart*, 265). The meeting was a key space for this process, where those in the audience, the students of the meeting so to speak, practiced standing up and speaking themselves. The liturgy afforded the rhetorical participation of many who did not have credentials or ministerial roles. This rhetorical practice was an essential function of the meeting liturgy in developing civic and political agency because it cultivated people's rhetorical capacities for speaking about problems, interpreting countermovement narratives, and imagining change. As Allen writes: "Civic and political action must begin from a diagnosis of our current situation and move from that diagnosis to a prescription for a response. For these social diagnoses to become effective, one must convince others of them" (*Education and Equality*, 40–41). The democratic pedagogy of the meeting, carried out through the liturgy, then encouraged different kinds of participation, empowering people to speak and act as a group and on their own.

This varied participation was facilitated through the diverse genres that comprise the liturgy. In the Nashville meeting, for example, the genres labeled "Devotions," "Song Service" and "Student Speaker" opened up rhetorical participation for women (Mrs. Elizabeth Kennedy Burgess and Mrs. J. N. Rucker) and for young people in the community. The student who delivered a speech is unnamed in the program, and it is possible that this "Student Speaker" portion of the event invited any and all students from the Nashville community to speak if they desired. In the May 30 Nashville meeting studied in chapter 2, audio recordings reveal that the moment designated as the student speaker portion of the evening was open; the students were called upon to stand up and speak about their experiences. This kind of opening provided opportunity for young people to speak to the community about their diagnosis of the racism characterizing Nashville at the moment and to encourage the group to understand their view of changes needed. Finally, the song portions of the meeting offer yet another kind of verbal empowerment. The songs require leadership, and the individuals who hold this role are often women or young people. Song leaders often speak about the significance of singing or the importance of a particular song in helping the group to move toward their goals. Song, prayer, and testimony together provided opportunities for the verbal empowerment of everyone gathered. These genres catalyzed moments for young people, and for women and men not in leadership positions, to speak as citizens poised for continued action.

The Nashville example reveals how a tightly structured liturgy opens up deep rhetorical participation, but the opposite approach also encouraged many in the group to speak as rhetors. In some locations, a more free-form liturgy encouraged spontaneous testimony, in which individuals might stand up and speak, blending deliberation with prophecy and advocacy. This kind of blended speech catalyzes political agency. As Allen writes: "The verbal work involved in civic agency extends well beyond our usual focus on deliberation to include adversarial and prophetic speech also" (*Education and Equality*, 41). For example, in a 1964 meeting in Ruleville, Mississippi, a woman named Mrs. Irene Johnson testified and exhorted the group: "Well you're talking like you really mean it and you ain't going to let no one turn you around nohow" (Halberstam, "Negroes Meet Nightly"). Here she picked up on the singing of the freedom song, "Ain't Gonna Let Nobody Turn You 'Round" to name the group's fearlessness and to encourage them to recognize the rhetorical import of singing—to sing fearlessly is analogous to speaking fearlessly. Later in the meeting, she spoke as prophet and advocate: "We've got to go to Drew [Mississippi] and help those people loosen up. We've got to make them realize what's going on in this country because they have been living in such fear over there" (Halberstam, "Negroes Meet Nightly"). Through this spontaneous testimony, Johnson merged the prophetic with advocacy to help the Ruleville group recognize their next activist steps, to spread their fearless democratic action in a nearby town where Black people had not yet organized. Johnson's short speeches reveal how loose liturgies afforded spontaneous testimonies from the group, where individuals not on a formal program might find opportunities to speak about what is on their minds. Johnson named a problem and persuaded others to join her in responding to it through further action; she also prophesied, naming the group's fearlessness and affirming their will to continue. Through this appeal, she picked up themes from the featured speech, delivered by a minister, who preached about courage: "I'm going to talk to you about courage. The Book says, 'Be strong and of good courage.' Courage is one of the most needed things there is. God sometimes likes us to feel we can't go any further. Well that's because God only helps us with the impossible things, things we can't achieve by ourselves. So courage is that guiding light which pushes us to the narrow places we thought we could not make" (Halberstam, "Negroes Meet Nightly"). This minister's speech was the featured address of the meeting, an interpretation of the Bible's teaching on courage and a sermon of encouragement. Yet to look only at the sermon is to miss the other rhetorical openings for individuals and the group to engage with the idea of courage and to speak (and sing) about it themselves. The collective had meditated on courage as they sang "Ain't Gonna Let Nobody Turn Me 'Round," and then Johnson spoke, mining the theme of fearlessness for the very specific next steps it indicated. In this way, Johnson's performance highlights how individuals not ordinarily thought of as the key teachers or key figures found opportunity to stand up and speak for themselves within the spontaneity afforded by the liturgy of meetings like this one.

As a site of democratic education and verbal empowerment, the mass meeting also invited participants to act as deliberative political agents. The Montgomery mass-meeting scene reveals this well, as groups regularly voted in response to legislation and resolutions. The *New York Times* recounted: "A Negro mass meeting unanimously endorsed tonight the continuance of a boycott against the city's transit system. Approximately 2,000 Negroes gave a standing vote in support of a formal resolution to 'carry on our mass protest.' This was in answer to recent declarations of Montgomery city officials that bus drivers or passengers who violated state or city segregation statutes would be subject to arrest" (Popham, "Negroes to Keep Boycotting Buses"). In a November piece reporting the end of the boycott, the *Times* depicts the collective deliberation of the group to end the boycott: "Two days ago, the Supreme Court outlawed segregated seating on intrastate buses [in *Browder v. Gale*]. Montgomery Negroes voted at two mass meetings last night to end an eleven-month-old boycott of city buses when the high court's mandate reached a Federal District Court in Montgomery" ("Montgomery Firm on Bus Bias Policy"). As these examples demonstrate, the mass meeting provided opportunities for participants to act as citizens, to vote and deliberate as though they had already overcome the voter suppression that threatened their ability to participate in these processes outside the meeting. In this way, the meeting taught key methods of democratic action, voting and deliberation, while also inviting participants to *feel* the world they were working toward.

Feeling Religious Experience:
Faithful Emotions and the Mass Meeting

As a religious experience, the mass meeting can be understood in part through the pattern of genres. Religious experience cannot, however, be reduced to the program or pattern of worship; as the phrase conveys, religious experience is tethered to how faith feels and is embodied. To consider the liturgy of the mass meeting as this latter kind of religious experience, I attend to activists' and reporters' reflections on events as a felt, intimate space. Here, I bring together accounts found in two major repositories of activists' reflections, the *Eyes on the Prize* Interview Archive and the published collection

Hands on the Freedom Plow (edited by Holsaert et al.), alongside a handful of other individuals' published sentiments. These perspectives have the advantage of describing meetings across space and time but still offer only a small glimpse of the many, many experiences of the mass meetings.

Despite the growing interest in emotion among rhetoricians, the study of religious feeling remains undertheorized, a reluctance that has been mirrored across the humanities.[13] As historian of American religion John Corrigan observes: "Emotion in religion, in fact, has been defined for a very long time as essentially resistant to critical probings. It has been cast as irrational and, as such, insusceptible to scholarly analysis" ("Introduction,"1). If emotion on its own was suspect as a site for intellectual inquiry, then religious emotion was even more so. However, as Corrigan explains, religious emotion "(1) is not mysterious; (2) can be studied; (3) is about the body and not the transcendence of the body; (4) is about culture but not only about culture; that (5) the distinction between rational cognition and irrational emotion in religion is unwarranted; that (6) spirituality sometimes has to do with feeling and sometimes does not; and that (7) what we mean by religion is entwined with what we mean by emotion—and vice versa" ("Introduction," 11). To think about religious rhetoric at the mass meeting, scholars must examine the emotional dimensions of the experience. If religion and feeling are bound up together, to study the religious dimensions of rhetorical engagements means also analyzing how feeling functions and to what ends. In the case of the mass meeting, attending to emotion reveals how the liturgy prompted certain kinds of felt engagements with faith and the group while diminishing the relevance of other feelings. Participants were invited to feel moved toward action, to exchange negative emotions for peaceful ones, and to recognize their shared experience through an intimate frame and, as such, beyond public recognition.

As a felt engagement with faith and the group, the meeting invited participants to be *moved*. This theme emerges across activists' descriptions of what was important in events as they explain feeling stirred, inspired, uplifted, thrilled, energized, enthusiastic, and hopeful. Activist Jane Bond More explains: "The best moments were when I felt part of a group in mass meetings in Albany and Birmingham with the crowds, choirs, and organists. The speakers were a stirring, inspiring, and uplifting bunch, with Dr. King at the top of the list. Often, after hard and unrewarding labor, Black people of all classes came together at mass meetings; to be part of that group, working toward our freedom, was thrilling and inspirational" ("A SNCC Blue Book," 331). Jo Ann Robinson names meetings as both "a communication center and [site] for keeping up morale" (*The Montgomery Bus Boycott and the Women Who Started It,* 76). Prathia Hall observes: "I had never in my life been so profoundly moved as I was by the mass meetings that were the central rallying points of the Movement" ("Freedom-Faith," 174). As these examples convey, the liturgy of the meeting prompted individuals to feel moved and in so doing to forge bonds with one another. The emotional register that activists emphasize mirrors what historians describe as a key outcome of the meeting, its capacity to spark people to action and to sustain them (Dittmer, *Local People*; Payne, *I've Got the Light of Freedom*). The mass meeting, through the varied genres that comprised events, conditioned individuals to enter the meeting expectant of rejuvenation and excitement.

Most simply, then, the liturgy conditioned the group to feel moved toward change, and in this way, religious experience created shared, internal resources for movement creation and sustenance. As a theme of activists' accounts, this finding is not surprising; it affirms points rhetorical scholars have made before about the mass meeting. For example, Gary Selby shows how King's use of the Exodus narrative grounded activists in religious themes and provided people with a sense of hope, a narrative of "common identity and purpose—a sense of 'going somewhere'" (*Martin Luther King and the Rhetoric of Freedom*, 11). Similarly, Brooks observes: "To promote voter registration among an audience that had been exploited and intimidated for centuries, Hamer not only had to inform Delta blacks of their right to vote and encourage them to see themselves as agents of change, she also had to undermine the plantation mentality and the white supremacist terror that bound their potential" (*A Voice That Could Stir an Army*, 109). It was not just that talented speakers provided groups with powerful narratives; the liturgy as a whole prompted the group to feel energized or renewed through their participation in the varied genres, through *their own* singing, praying, and testifying. As Coretta Scott King explains: "[Meetings] would end after Martin's message with . . . a song and a prayer, a benediction, and prayer. . . . It was something about that experience that gave all of us . . . so much hope . . . the more we got into it, the more we had the feeling that something could be done about the situation. That we could change it. . . . As Christian people, they believed very much . . . in prayer and the songs of . . . the faith and all" (King, Interview, 9). By inviting people to feel moved, the liturgy of the meeting prompted participants toward action and sustained them to continue working over the long haul of the movement. The variation of "moving feelings" across genres of the liturgy helped to achieve these objectives: preaching often provided initial stirrings, while embodied genres like song and prayer were key for rejuvenation that would sustain the movement.

The liturgy was key to stirring and inspiring the group in part because, through their participation in the meeting, attendees were already making change. Mass-meeting songs, prayers, sermons, and testimonies relied, to different degrees, on the faith of the individuals inhabiting them. Faith, as an action and a feeling, claims a certain new future. In this way, the liturgy can be viewed through Tina Campt's discussion of futurity as "a performance of a future that hasn't yet happened but must . . . It is the power to imagine beyond current fact and to envision that which is not, but must be. It's a politics of prefiguration that involves living the future *now*—as imperative rather than subjunctive—as a striving for the future you want to see, right now, in the present" (*Listening to Images,* 17). In performing the songs, prayers, sermons, and stories, activists understood this rhetorical work to be important movement actions that stepped toward the changes sought outside. This dimension of faithful genres is part of how they invite feelings of excitement and renewal.

John Corrigan notes that one way to study religious emotion is to observe how key events or rituals teach participants to ignore, suppress, or forget certain feelings ("Introduction," 12). In addition to motivating, inspiring, and sustaining activists, as a religious experience the meeting sometimes conditioned groups to identify negative emotions and to exchange them for peaceful ones. By "peaceful" feelings, I mean emotions that leaders explicitly and implicitly associate with nonviolent action. As a kind of affective training, this emotional dimension of the meeting can be best understood as a felt alignment of faith, activism, and nonviolence. Meetings made space for a wide range of feelings, but liturgies were often geared toward training groups to discipline negative feelings that worked against nonviolent direct action or that might disrupt public narratives of a peaceful movement. One way to recognize this is simply through the absence of activists' accounts of negative emotional experiences at the meeting. Positive evidence of this is provided by accounts such as Prathia Hall's, where she explains expressing negative emotions to move toward new feelings: "Interspersed between the lined hymns were the fervent prayers of the deacons, the mothers, and other congregational leaders . . . That power with which those songs and prayers were infused transcended the objective reality of our situation, fashioned fear into faith, cringing into courage, suffering into survival, despair into defiance, and pain into protest" ("Freedom-Faith," 174). Hall's reflection conveys a point echoed by others (Abernathy, Interview; Sherrod, Interview; Watters, *Down to Now*). When they did express negative emotions like fear, sorrow, or pain, activists often explain how through their engagement with the liturgy, they transformed these feelings into others such as courage, faith, love, or defiance.

In light of the broader vision of civil rights collective identity, this emotive exchange appears as a strategic step toward training groups in nonviolence as a felt position. Christian nonviolence, as figures like King and James

Lawson conceived and taught it, was not just a rational argument or tool; it was defined as a way of being that encompassed how one felt and expressed emotion publicly. For example, Lawson explained nonviolence as "Christian Love" and a "radically Christian method" (quoted in Cline, *From Reconciliation to Revolution,* x). In theorizing nonviolence so broadly, Lawson sought to define nonviolence in part as centered on feelings of love and faith. The SNCC Statement of Purpose lays out nonviolence-as-emotion out even more clearly: "Through nonviolence, courage displaces fear; love transforms hate. Acceptance displaces prejudice; hope ends despair. Peace dominates war; faith reconciles doubt. Mutual regard cancels enmity. Justice for all overthrows injustice" (quoted in Quiros, *God with Us,* 84). Resonating with Hall's depiction of the meeting, this view of nonviolence makes clear that to succeed it must be felt. The statement also turns on the same type of emotional-exchange logic Hall explains, where nonviolence requires hate becoming love, and so forth.

For people like Lawson, nonviolent action to accomplish movement purposes could not be limited to partial or rational assent, and it would not work if it emerged from negative feeling. Rather, groups had to feel emotions that resonated with nonviolence—love and faith among them—and act from this felt posture. The mass meeting thus provided a space for cultivating feelings like courage, love, acceptance, peace, and faith, while diminishing the significance of feelings like hatred and rage. The liturgy of the meeting, as Hall attests, could at times catalyze peaceful emotional postures through prompting recognition or expression of negative feelings with the goal of reshaping them toward the feelings of nonviolence. The liturgy of the mass meeting, like the movement more broadly, shares a complex relationship to negative feelings. They were not altogether repressed, but they certainly are not named as central features of the experience, as far as available evidence conveys. Hall's explanation furthers the point, suggesting that the meeting at times functioned as a site for individuals to express negative feelings with the goal of shifting them toward more peaceful emotions. The emotional exchange–logic can be viewed as a way the liturgy suppressed emotions that did not resonate with public narratives of a peaceful civil rights movement.

A final theme activists discuss regarding the meeting as a site to feel faith is that it was ineffable or indescribable. Many activists suggest that describing the feeling of the meeting is an impossible task: "Oh, I don't know, I can't hardly describe" (Belser, Interview, 5); "It's rather hard to describe" (Wilson, Interview, 3); and white activist Frances Freeborn Pauley contends: "I don't think that there's any way of ever reading or seeing on television or ever getting a real feeling of what some of those mass meetings were like.

. . . It was something about that, the movement and the feeling of the movement, that was just so compelling" (quoted in Monteith, "'I second that emotion,'" 441). King takes the point even further: "I had to leave the [mass] meeting and rush to the other side of town . . . I had never seen such enthusiasm for freedom. And yet this enthusiasm was tempered by amazing self-discipline. The unity of purpose and *esprit de corps* of these people had been indescribably moving. No historian would ever be able fully to describe this meeting and no sociologist would ever be able to interpret it adequately" (*Stride Toward Freedom,* 53). As these descriptions suggest, activists often deflect opportunities to explain what they felt at meetings. This emotive deflection reveals an intimacy enabled by the meeting and its genres: the liturgy structured bonds that participants felt to be shared only among themselves and which were incommunicable beyond the group.

In this way, the mass meeting as religious experience resembles Lauren Berlant's notion of intimate publics, which are sites where individuals come together sharing "a worldview and emotional knowledge that they have derived from a broadly common historical experience" (*The Female Complaint,* vii). The space is structured largely through affective ties, "where [people] can feel de-isolated, sanctioned, held, and where they can learn about how other people survive" (quoted in Gibson, "Sentimental Education"). As participants sang, prayed, and testified, they catalyzed and developed their shared knowledge and feelings. This participation established and confirmed the intimacy of the space, such that when asked to describe what it was like, activists sometimes protect their experience through deflection. On some level, then, activists believe that religious experience offers only a limited site of study; this faithful space and its role in social change elude definitive conclusions.

Liturgy, Bodies, and Church Space:
Savannah, Georgia, 1960

The adaptability of the meeting liturgy enabled theological, organizational, and geographic complexity. As activists translated the liturgy of the church for the meeting, they accounted for the places and spaces where these genres would be enacted and the bodies that would inhabit them.[14] Photographs of mass meetings held in Savannah, Georgia, in 1960 provide an opportunity to study these material aspects of the liturgy. The image-based approach to examining mass meetings reveals how, as a genre set that shapes individuals and collectives, liturgies are intricately connected to the places and spaces where they occur and complicated by embodiment across gender, age, class, denomination, (dis)ability, and other factors. Meetings offered people an opportunity to embody a changed world, and this vision and its liturgical enactment had to be adapted to accommodate the history of the place and space. In Savannah, the city's economic prosperity and identity as a liberal, coastal town opened up possibilities for liturgies of change. At the same time, when we listen in, around, and behind the pulpit (to borrow from Lisa Shaver, *Beyond the Pulpit*), the committed, habitual presence of Black women's activism in Savannah reverberates throughout the space. In spatial terms, however, Savannah's Black churches remained gendered spaces where men and the pulpit dominate the scene. Finally, these images invite consideration of liturgy and audience.

Savannah, like other cities including Charleston, South Carolina, and Nashville, Tennessee, was characterized by racism in its more subtle forms. Whites in these cities largely avoided violence as a response to African American organizing and political activity and were willing to accept moderate change, albeit slowly. For example, when Black college students initiated sit-ins in March 1960, it was not long before civil rights activists were able to successfully negotiate desegregation of public facilities, leading Martin Luther King Jr. to praise Savannah as "the most integrated city south of the Mason-Dixon line" (quoted in Clare Russell, "Upheaval in Savannah," 779). Savannah thus became known as a site for peaceful demonstrations and a model for other locales considering taking on sit-ins. Savannahians could set their goals on practical changes and protest and believe they would succeed.

Figure 1.2 provides insight into the relationships among the liturgy of the meeting and its particular location. In this image, the focus of the photograph is on the group traditionally considered the audience of the mass meeting. Rather than showcase a well-known speaker associated with the Southern Christian Leadership Conference (SCLC) or SNCC, this photo highlights instead the Savannah collective: hundreds of African Americans sit and stand on two levels in the sanctuary of St. Philip A. M. E. Church. Men and women are dressed in Sunday best, wearing suits and ties, dresses and hats. The photograph does not center an influential civil rights figure like King or Sherrod; in Savannah, these leaders were considered unnecessary and unwanted. Meetings, as a result and in contrast to some other civil rights locales, were decidedly local affairs, and local leadership was a point of pride and intention for Savannah activists. Activist Hosea Williams asserted: "We want to keep this thing among Savannahians, we don't want to have to bring Martin Luther King here" (quoted in Tuck, *Beyond Atlanta*, 544). As this image conveys, the liturgy of meetings in Savannah did not regularly feature a visiting preacher who caught photographers' attention. The collective itself was the most significant achievement.

In Savannah, people sang, prayed, and spoke proudly of the movement they had crafted and the national attention it garnered. As a collective, they

FIGURE 1.2. Mass Meeting, St. Philip A. M. E. Church, Savannah,
Georgia, 1960. W. W. Law Photograph Collection, courtesy of
the City of Savannah Municipal Archives.

were envisioning changes, organizing protests, and remaking their city. A truly local movement like theirs, where outside leadership was not necessary, could only be accomplished through a committed base of support and a local history of Black activism. According to historian Stephen Tuck, one of the unique aspects of civil rights activity in Savannah, Georgia, was the overwhelming support for direct action in the Black community (*Beyond Atlanta,* 545). The mayor during this period, Malcolm Maclean, asserted that "it was like 95 percent of everything anybody thought about" (quoted in Tuck, *Beyond Atlanta,* 545).

People's attire in this image points to an additional place-based aspect of the meeting liturgy. Savannah was a prosperous city where African Americans, compared to other areas in the South, enjoyed a certain amount of economic advantage.[15] Social class in Savannah, like elsewhere, was connected to racial injustice, and African Americans did not experience the same level of economic success as whites in Savannah. Yet their relative prosperity enabled the movement: when African Americans embarked upon an eighteen-month boycott of downtown stores, their pressure resulted in a revenue loss of up to 50 percent for white business owners (Tuck, *Beyond Atlanta,* 134).

FIGURE 1.3. St. Paul Baptist Church, NAACP Mass Meeting, Savannah, Georgia, May 7, 1961. W. W. Law Photograph Collection, courtesy of the City of Savannah Municipal Archives.

Whereas the previous image invited thinking about the mass meeting and its connections to place, Figure 1.3 points toward the spatial inflections of rhetorical liturgies.[16] This image centers a young Black man wearing a suit and tie, standing behind a pulpit, smiling and addressing the church. Behind him, four men and two women are seated. Again, the men wear ties and women wear dresses and hats. Behind this group surrounding the pulpit, a dozen people sit in the choir loft, listening with solemn expressions.

Like any rhetorical event, liturgies shape and are shaped by space, meaning that faithful genres resonate, or do not resonate, through their (mis) alignments with objects, bodies, and buildings. Churches are designed to facilitate the delivery of faithful genres. For example, choir lofts demonstrate song as genre to be collectively performed, while pulpits dictate that sermon, prayer, or testimony are inhabited by one individual at a time. More broadly, these platforms spatially open and close off avenues of participation and leadership depending on the genre, denomination, and location. For example, Roxanne Mountford reveals how preaching is a gendered genre due in part to the space of the pulpit in churches. She argues that in many contexts the pulpit is a masculine space and shows how women preachers navigate the constraints and obstacles created in this gendered part of the church (Mountford, *The Gendered Pulpit*).[17] African American women were officially barred from preaching until the late nineteenth century, when Julia J. Foote became the first woman ordained in the AME Zion Church. Other African American denominations followed much later, with the AME Church and the Christian Episcopal Church opening up ordination to women in the 1960s (98). The choir loft offers a different example: while pulpits were historically reserved for men and coded masculine, choir lofts and by extension hymn singing have historically been open to women as spaces for church participation and leadership.

This photograph thus offers glimpses into the gendered space of mass meetings in Savannah and makes clear that the gendering of church space affects the genres of meetings held in Savannah churches, as elsewhere in the movement. The gendering of the pulpit represents and contributes to an irony in African American churches: the liberating force of the memory of Jesus historically was reserved for working on racial justice, rather than gender, sexism, or other issues (Warnock, *The Divided Mind of the Black Church,* 167). Yet Black women have remained committed and active in Black churches throughout its history, often outnumbering the men.

Given the connections among Black churches, civil rights, and mass meetings, it is no surprise that studies of mass meetings rarely feature women's contributions.[18] As historian Laurie Green advises, to recognize women's leadership and activism, it is necessary to explore the ways that the major institutions of the civil rights movement occluded their leadership ("Challenging the Civil Rights Narrative," 57). The Black church at the time largely circumscribed women's roles and limited their participation to positions subservient to men. For one thing, women's contributions in general are much more difficult to find in terms of archival evidence (Houck and Dixon, "Introduction: Recovering Women's Voices from the Civil Rights Movement"). Yet there is also a methodological problem. Warnock puts it this way: "When describing, analyzing, and criticizing the Black church, almost every eye tends to be turned toward the pulpits, pastors, and their convocations and conflicts" (*The Divided Mind of the Black Church,* 167). This overemphasis on the sermon can be thought of as a gendering of liturgy, where genres associated with male performance gain prominence and alternative, collective genres open to women and their work are viewed as less important. Warnock explains: "The work of Black women, inside and outside institutional church structures and in the worst and best of times, is not taken seriously, sometimes even by the women themselves" (167). Part of this devaluing of women's rhetorical work in the mass meeting occurs through an unquestioned emphasis on pastors and sermons, a gendered reading that should be questioned. Listening to liturgy through image provides one mode for valuing other genres of the meeting and the pathways they opened for women's participation.

The written record in Savannah does provide some evidence of women's leadership in Savannah. The local news, for example, reported: "The adage 'behind every great man is a woman' is apropos to the Negroes' fight for freedom in Savannah, for behind this great moment is the courage and the ingenuity of Negro womanhood" (quoted in Tuck, *Beyond Atlanta* 249). As an example of liturgy's embodied performance, this photograph helps fill out the record by showing *how* Black women in Savannah played visible roles in the leadership. The women sitting behind the pulpit share the spotlight with male activist leaders. In this way, the church space may have been adapted to accommodate their leadership. While there are no records that indicate whether they gave speeches at this meeting, these women's presence around the pulpit indicates their authority and leadership. As with Mrs. Elizabeth Kennedy Burgess in Nashville, women may not often be featured as speakers providing the main address, or sermon, but they do speak and lead through a range of other meeting genres such as devotions, testimonies, songs, and even prayers. To gain a sense of their participation, our focus must shift away from the pulpit and the pastors.

Savannah women also play a central role in the meeting liturgy in a more expected way: they sit in the choir loft. Like Mrs. J. N. Rucker in Nashville, women in Savannah led at the meeting through their singing. The genre of the freedom song, as chapter 2 argues, was one created by women for the movement, and church spaces enabled and supported this emerging genre. If the pulpit was an obstacle to women's leadership at meetings, the choir loft was an avenue for leadership and participation. This photograph thus fills in archival records to expand the purview of what is known about women's contributions and to reveal liturgy's gendered constraints, obstacles that women had to navigate in order to lead and speak.

A final point regarding embodiment of the meeting liturgy pertains to age. As this photograph reveals, young people were not barred from the pulpit, and by extension, from speaking at meetings. In this image, a young man takes a leadership role of speaking at the meeting, and young people from the community sit behind him, right alongside the established leaders in the community like W. W. Law, president of the Savannah chapter of the NAACP. In fact, Tuck contends that "the key to the breadth of the Savannah movement and in further contrast to Atlanta was the incorporation of youth . . . Youth were regularly placed in positions of responsibility and often led mass meetings" (*Beyond Atlanta*, 133, 134). This image thus reminds us that the meeting liturgy, as embodied spirituality, could overcome the

FIGURE 1.4. Mass Meeting at First African Baptist Church, Savannah, Georgia, May 1, 1960. W. W. Law Photograph Collection, courtesy of the City of Savannah Municipal Archives.

usual limits within the church space on the age of those who stood behind and around the pulpit.

Figure 1.4 shows a large group of African Americans departing from a mass meeting held in the First African Baptist Church on May 1, 1960. The church, a large white structure, has two entryways with double doors and stained-glass windows. Groups dressed in suits and dresses and hats crowd two doorways, waiting to walk down stairwells into the street. Cars are parked directly in front of the church, with more meeting attendees walking, standing, and talking in the street.

These final images suggest two additional points regarding spatiality and meeting liturgies. First, as this series of photographs as a whole indicates, mass meetings were events that caught public and media attention. The intensity of this attention varied but in general was considered necessary. Particularly in SCLC circles, the national news media's capacity to tell the story of the southern civil rights movement was important for putting pressure on the federal government for support and legislation (Rieder, *The Word of the*

Lord is Upon Me; Roberts and Kilbanoff, *The Race Beat*).[19] The mass meeting was open to the press and to the general public, and through this openness, the liturgy circulated to public audiences. By singing, praying, and testifying in front of news reporters and cameras, Black participants amplified their voices and created inroads for being heard widely. At the same time, this outsider presence surely must have diminished the intimacy of the meeting.

Second, and related to the preceding observation, the invitation of the public including media and reporters brought explicit dangers and risks. Besides complicating events as churchlike spaces, the opening up of the meeting brought the potential for surveillance and unwanted guests. On the back of the photograph of the First African Baptist Church meeting (fig. 1.4), activist W. W. Law notes that police were outside taking photographs as people exited the church this day. Meetings across locales were surveilled by FBI, local police, and members of the Citizens Council and the Ku Klux Klan. Since mass meetings were by design symbols to those in attendance and to the watching nation that African Americans were gathering to speak and act for freedom, they could not be clandestine events. Activists gathered to enact claims on democracy as though they were already true, and this courageous act meant that the mass meeting garnered attention from local whites, who had to reckon with the sociopolitical implications of an integrated world. In this way, the liturgy of the meeting gained an additional, complicated purpose: to challenge the perceptions of white people in places like Savannah. On a local level, inviting media attention and opening the doors of mass meetings to everyone meant that embodying meeting liturgies in fact challenged minds and enacted claims to a transformed world. This aspect of the meeting suggests a felt burden; entering the meeting knowing that it might be surveilled interrupted (or worse) surely must have been difficult. Yet as the accounts surveyed in this chapter indicate, the meeting overall was viewed as a moving experience tied to the belief that change was possible. I take up this complicated aspect of meeting space in greater detail in the final chapter of the book.

Conclusion: Liturgies of Change Across the Civil Rights Movement

Reconstructing scenes of the mass meeting, as I have done in this chapter, reveals the rhetorical and generic patterns that structured local people's first steps into activism. These patterns relied on a liturgy that invited participants to experiment with faithful genres as modes for social change. Through the liturgy, and especially the key genres of song, prayer, and testifying, Black people, along with allies, crafted identity, collectively and individually, coming together to participate in a felt experience of a more just world. This liturgy animated grand theological visions of beloved community and love-as-activism that leaders like King and Sherrod proclaimed, yet through collective participation, the group made this vision their own. One song, one prayer, one testimony at a time, people tested out Christian nonviolence and explored how it felt to be this kind of activist, working through faith toward an integrated world.

In this way, the meeting's purpose was theological, spiritual, and complex: people came together to participate in a hopeful experience, to live together for a moment in a world where their hopes were realized, while just outside the church doors the reality of white violent resistance could not be ignored. Activists insist on the meeting's felt power. They were at the same time incredibly aware of the realities of white opposition and the ever-present possibility of being interrupted or attacked. The meeting was not removed from the realities of violence. Recognizing the range of rhetorical involvement in mass meetings thus provides insight into how people were invited into activism and then supported and empowered to take first steps toward reconceiving what was possible in their place.

Church space often heightened a felt experience of faith and amplified the liturgy's capacity to spark change, while also implicating it in the realities of the Black church as an imperfect institution. The pews, the pulpit, the choir lofts: these spatial cues helped to create familiarity for people entering mass meetings for the first time, directions for where to go and how to participate as they also emphasized the theological vision of change that leaders pronounced. These spatial indicators simultaneously reinforced gendered hierarchies that were true in the Black church more generally at the time, yet women persisted in finding ways to speak and lead, through devotionals, testimonies, song leading, and other genres.

While this chapter focuses only on a handful of mass meetings, the rhetorical scenes studied here point toward the collective participation these events invited across the locales and moments of the movement for Black freedom. Beyond the individual spaces that housed mass meetings, on a broader level, churches and liturgies provided a kind of spatial network. In scope and importance, the network of churches and meetings helped create groups of people poised to participate in changing their communities and were already doing so through their attendance at the mass meeting. The liturgy of the meeting, as a recurring event, shaped and informed the direct action across the movement, from how marches proceeded to the rhetorical tone of the sit-ins.

TWO

Sounding Civic Identity

Freedom Song Invention
at the Mass Meeting

Activist Bernice Johnson Reagon recounts an incident that took place in 1961, after the first march in Albany, Georgia. Two students at Albany State College, Bertha Gober and Blanton Hall, were in prison after an attempt to integrate a movie ticket counter. Reagon, along with Annette Jones, led the march from campus to the jail as a show of solidarity. With Gober and Hall still in jail, Albany activists retreated for a mass meeting at Union Baptist Church. Student Nonviolent Coordinating Committee field secretary Charlie Jones put Reagon on the spot to lead them in a song. Reagon explains:

> I took a breath and started "Over My Head, I See Trouble in the Air."
> As I moved down that first line, I knew it would not be a good idea to
> sing the word *trouble*, even though I knew we were in trouble, but did
> not think it would help. So instead I put in *freedom*, and by the second
> line everyone was singing, with me placing a new word (*glory, justice,*
> and so forth) for each cycle:

> Over my head, I see freedom in the air
> Over my head, I see freedom in the air
> Over my head, I see freedom in the air
> There must be a God somewhere.
> ("Since I Laid My Burden Down," 149)

The exchange of the word "trouble" for "freedom" remade the song and the rhetorical situation. Through her adaptation of the song, Reagon offered the group a chance to create new terms for themselves and their place: from one perspective they might name their circumstances as trouble, but from the new vantage point of the song persona, they are free.

Reagon's description here reveals her role in the process of creating freedom songs, the genre of singing invented for the movement for Black freedom. Through her careful and strategic assessment of the situation in Albany, she used her role as song leader at this mass meeting to respond to segregation enforced through white supremacist modes of terror. Reagon led the group in remaking the situation from one where they were disempowered through extant racist structures to one where freedom, glory, and justice reign. When those gathered in the church heard Reagon begin this song, no doubt familiar through congregational singing, the sound likely brought to mind the original lyrics, "trouble in the air." By calling on this idea and then changing it, Reagon provided a new frame for the situation: she renamed what was happening, what was possible, and who this group was in the face of this oppression. The group responded to Reagon's call and leadership, and together they created a new song. Through this process, Reagon and the Albany activists sounded their new world to themselves and to the rest of the town. Later, through their creation of the Freedom Singers, a quartet that traveled and performed these songs, they circulated these sounds to the watching nation.

As the example of "Over My Head, I See Freedom in the Air" conveys, the freedom song genre was created largely in the space of the mass meeting through the savvy of song leaders like Reagon. This chapter centers on the scene of genre invention at the meeting and the collective participation this invention invited, a move that foregrounds Black song leaders like Reagon and the activist groups who collaborated in this process. Mass meetings, song leaders, and the process of genre creation remain underexamined in rhetorical studies and in civil rights history more broadly. Most studies of freedom songs focus instead on the public use of songs, narrating the genre's invention by locating its origins in African American musical traditions.[1] Historian Elizabeth Davis observes that scholars have most often treated freedom songs' emergence as inevitable—an obvious next step in the history of Black music. For Davis, the history of the freedom song is one bound up with issues of power and privilege, as the genre was shaped by cross-racial encounters and white-owned cultural institutions like the Highlander Folk School ("Making Movement Sounds," 6–7). Davis is one of few scholars to study process and power, yet even here the scene of the mass meeting, where the genre was created and circulated, is not central.[2] This chapter fills this gap and argues that while it is true that white folklorists and white institutions played key and complicated roles in shaping the repertoire, tracing the freedom song's emergence at mass meetings reveals how Black people created and cultivated the genre and how by doing so they claimed and embodied civic identity through sound.

Through study of genre making and its constitutive dimensions, the chapter also contributes to understandings of genre creation and sound as a constitutive resource.[3] I unpack and examine the process of genre invention carried out at mass meetings, a process that relied on the rhetorical significance of the song leader, often women, at these events and a strategic and felt process of selection, adaptation, and cultivation of civil rights songs and music. Through this process, activists invented a musical genre useful for experiencing their collective identity and poised to intervene in the places that denied it. In making freedom songs, activists composed this identity together, agreeing through selection, adaptation, and performance of songs like "Woke Up This Morning with My Mind Stayed on Freedom" and "This Little Light of Mine" that nonviolence, spirituality, and peace were the key actions for their group and their movement. Sound was key to the process of genre invention and for crafting identity. The scene of the mass meeting reveals activists' work to forge their identity centered on integration and coherence with the broader nation. By crafting the genre in the space of the meeting, activists created and maintained the sounds of freedom songs as their own.

The chapter examines the scene of freedom song invention across three meeting locales during the period 1955–65: Montgomery Alabama; Nashville, Tennessee; and Jackson, Mississippi. Centering attention on song leaders, including Reagon, Mary Ethyl Dozier (later Jamila Jones), Mrs. J. N. Rucker, Guy Carawan, and Matthew Jones, I inspect the ways these leaders collaborated with activist collectives and used the meeting to invent a genre together. Studying this process reveals the resources and work necessary to create a movement genre and the rhetorical advantages of doing so.

Claiming Civic Identity through Sound: Freedom Songs' History

Simply put, freedom songs are songs sung for Black freedom. As the opening anecdote reveals, many freedom songs were selected, adapted, and written in response to the oppressive power dynamics that civil rights activists sought to unsettle and remake. Activist Julius Lester offers this definition of the freedom songs: "To paraphrase . . . a minister, freedom songs should comfort the disturbed and disturb the comfortable. . . . Being a Negro is not a necessary prerequisite for singing freedom songs. Being willing to understand the Negro and his history is. It is here that the fabric of freedom songs is found" ("Freedom Songs in the North," 13). To create the freedom song genre, activists turned to various sources, some sacred like hymns, spirituals and gospels, and some secular such as the blues and labor music. Other songs were written specifically for the movement. The freedom songs *became* freedom songs through strategic teaching and singing at mass meetings, and in this process, people *became* activists, sounding out their civic identity and exploring the kinds of changes they wanted to make.

To create the freedom song genre, civil rights activists drew on and extended a longer African American tradition of merging music and resistance. During enslavement, abolition, and Reconstruction, sacred music functioned as various modes of resistance and protest for Black people in the United States. For decades, spirituals offered modes of expression, affective renewal, and communicative power to enslaved people. To sing was to redefine Black identity in a moment when before the law and the nation, enslaved people were viewed as property. Through the spirituals, enslaved people resisted this reductive view and remade their rhetorical situation, bringing African music and power to the United States and centering their identity in the sacred. Singing in this context was more than protest, however: it was culture and self-making as well as spiritual worship.[4] Abolition brought new opportunities for music to function overtly as resistance, with Harriet Tubman, Sojourner Truth, and Frederick Douglass (among others) mining the possibilities of sacred music. For example, Tubman famously used the spiritual "I'm Bound for the Promised Land" to share her plans for escape with her family before fleeing to the North (Larson, *Bound for the Promised Land,* 83). White abolitionists including William Lloyd Garrison, Lydia Sigourney, and Maria Weston Chapman also understood and employed sacred music toward ending slavery. In their case, they explored hymnbooks as resources for generating collective enthusiasm for abolition among white Northerners (Spencer, *Protest and Praise,* 42).

The relationships between African American music and protest possibilities shifted during and after Reconstruction, with sacred music becoming less common as a strategy of collective resistance. These shifts occurred as newly freed Black people accessed and created formalized church structures. In this period, gospel music emerged as a distinct form of worship, a genre not overtly concerned with protest but more about spiritual freedom expressed through song.[5] Yet African American singers continued to explore the possibilities afforded through the platform of sacred song. For example, gospel artists Thomas A. Dorsey, Salley Martine, Sister Rosetta Tharpe, and Mahalia Jackson (among others) took full advantage of their visibility and performed at public events. Jackson, for example, was involved in Chicago politics and performed at rallies and fundraisers and would become an important singer during the civil rights movement (Darden, *Nothing but Love in God's Water,* 112).

While gospel music created important opportunities for African American people in the early and mid-twentieth century, so too did the commercialization of popular music and the technologies of the radio. In the case of radio, shows including "Wings Over Jordan Choir" and "Freedom's People" circulated songs and African American history to broader audiences, demonstrating how sound technologies might afford Black people access to a national stage (Darden, *Nothing but Love in God's Water*, 95–99). However, historian Robert Darden notes that while radio made it possible for African American music to circulate, in this period white listeners were unlikely to "hear or see Black artists, whether they performed religious *or* mainstream music" (*Nothing but Love in God's Water*, 91, emphasis in original). Jennifer Stoever more pointedly argues that for the most part, radio networks operated as mechanisms for segregation. She writes that radio functioned "as a segregating industry shaped by and for the white listening ear, with little regard for Black listeners" ("Black Radio Listeners in America's 'Golden Age,'" 123). One telling example here is that radio executives catered to a so-called "Southern block" of interests. Networks culled content regarding "the Negro" that might unsettle white Southerners and worked within the logics of white supremacy (122–23). Broadly speaking, radio provides one example of the ways sound is racialized in the United States, working to create and sustain "the sonic color line." The sonic color line, according to Stoever, refers to the "process of racializing sound—how and why certain bodies are expected to produce, desire, and live amongst particular sounds— and its product, the hierarchical division sounded between 'whiteness' and 'Blackness'" (*The Sonic Color Line*, 7). This perspective on sound provides an important contextual point, as it both amplifies the importance of freedom songs' foundation in African American musical traditions and offers a reminder that segregation intertwined with sound.

In creating the genre of freedom songs, activists strategically built on and extended African American musical-rhetorical history. By employing sound as a constitutive resource for civic identity, they responded to the ways, through radio, cinema, and broadcasting technologies, that sound had become central to exclusionary practices in civic life. The freedom song genre was created both to extend latent possibilities in African American collective singing and to remake and cross the sonic color line. Freedom songs, as sonic embodiments of Black citizenship, were attempts to revise a racial soundscape that rendered Black sound separate and subjugated. Through the mass meeting, song leaders, performers, and collectives deliberately adapted songs and created new ones with sophisticated awareness of both the history of Black music and the racist soundscapes of the South and the nation. Through sonic associations with freedom, peace, interracial unity, the freedom song genre named a civic identity for the movement.

Sounding a Boycott, Creating a Genre:
Freedom Songs Emerge in Montgomery, Alabama

The night after the first day of the bus boycott in Montgomery, Alabama, protestors met at the Holt Street Baptist Church to celebrate and to consider next steps. This mass meeting, one where Martin Luther King Jr. emerged as a leader and began defining a vision of the movement for Montgomerians and for the nation, was also a chance for the group to explore and to begin to answer the question: who are we, as a group of protestors? King offered one beautiful and enduring answer through his address. As rhetorical scholar Kirt Wilson puts it, King crafted "a single identity for everyone in the audience" by "invit[ing] his audience to enact the personae of a U. S. citizen and a Christian 'brother'" ("Interpreting the Discursive Field of the Montgomery Bus Boycott," 308, 309). However, the liturgy of the meeting provided many opportunities for others to consider and speak to this question. Through the pattern of genres that comprised the event, leaders shared the spotlight with the players who made up what Nathaniel Rivers and Ryan Weber call the ecology of this moment in the civil rights movement ("Ecological, Pedagogical, Public Rhetoric"). Besides the sermonic "pep talk" delivered by the preachers of Montgomery, bus boycotters would rely too on genres that they took up together: Scripture, prayer, song. Through their collective voices and embodiment of the liturgy, night after night, week after week, they teased out their response before one another and before the nation. Singing allowed them to explore and consider this vision out loud together, and by the same turn, this singing of their vision of themselves and their goals defined the freedom song genre and its functions.

With voices raised on that first evening, Montgomerians explored their identity through music, an identity, which for King entailed "full and first-class citizenship" ("Dec. 5, 1955, Holt Street Address," 71). This term conveys both political rights and duties and more expansively the transformed social world the mass meeting and its liturgy pointed toward. Rhetorical scholars and political theorists emphasize that citizenship is fluid, contested, and far more than what legal discourse describes (Wan, "In the Name of Citizenship"; Allen, *Talking to Strangers*; Maddux, *Practicing Citizenship*). Citizenship, according to Kristy Maddux, is "a historically situated, rhetorically constituted, contextually dependent construct" and "a practice—that is, a set of repeated behaviors" (3, 4).[6] Civil rights activists understood citizenship in this practical way, as a complex lived reality, where Jim Crow laws had created tiers of citizenship. The terms "full" or "first-class" and "second-class citizenship" worked to name the ways "separate but equal" had created inequality across public spaces and dictated a code of behaviors that affected all Southern spaces, including the domestic sphere. Full or first-class citizenship entitled one to "a seat at the democratic table" and a wholly integrated society where all were treated as equals, with respect and dignity. Activists were claiming aspects of first-class citizenship like enfranchisement and democratic deliberation through a broader vision that encompassed the ordinary habits and behaviors of people's everyday lives across public and private spaces.[7] The freedom songs were invented in part to embody full citizenship through sound.

The singing at this first meeting in Montgomery reveals initial steps in crafting the freedom song genre and inhabiting first-class citizenship. Half-way through the evening, King proclaimed: "We are here in a general sense because first and foremost we are American citizens (That's right) and we are determined to apply our citizenship to the fullness of its meaning" ("Dec. 5, 1955, Holt Street Address," 71). Through their singing before and after this address, the group used their voices to test out the sounds of citizenship, experiencing and improvising this identity, making it their own. Not yet referred to as a particular movement genre, the songs for this evening included two hymns and a patriotic song. Montgomerians explored how the citizenship they wanted sounded, speaking back to the claims King made in his address. The agenda helps illustrate the point:

Hymn:	"Onward Christian Soldiers"
Hymn:	"Leaning on the Everlasting Arms"
Prayer:	Revered W. F. Alford
Scripture Reading:	Psalm 34, Reverend U. J. Fields
Address, or "Pep Talk":	Martin Luther King Jr.
Resolutions:	Reverend Ralph Abernathy
Offering:	Reverend Bonner
Closing Song:	"My Country 'Tis of Thee"
Benediction:	Reverend Roy Bennett. (Fields 70)

Singing "Onward Christian Soldiers," "Leaning on the Everlasting Arms," and "My Country 'Tis of Thee," Montgomerians tested out full citizenship as a sonic practice that centered on spiritual and national freedom and embodied Christian ideals of love and peace. The songs at this first meeting enabled the group to articulate this identity as loving citizens desiring to unite across racial lines. Through their singing, the group explored the sounds of citizenship first as an embodied, faithful identity, second as a collaborative practice dependent on young women's leadership, and third as an interracial, peaceful action. Sounding their collective identity by extension paved the way for freedom singing as a unique civil rights genre.

First, through these songs, Montgomerians envisioned themselves as Christians and as "full citizens," and as they did, their town listened in. King emphasized the spiritual aspect of their identity in his speech: "I want it to be known throughout Montgomery and throughout this nation that we are Christian people. We believe in the Christian religion. We believe in the teachings of Jesus. The only weapon that we have in our hands this evening is the weapon of protest" ("Dec. 5, 1955, Holt Street Address," 72). The lyrics of the hymns reinforced and expanded this point. Singing "Onward Christian Soldiers," the group asserted:

> Onward Christian soldiers!
> Marching as to war,
> With the cross of Jesus
> Going on before.

With the hymn "Leaning on the Everlasting Arms," the collective proclaimed:

> What have I to dread, what have I to fear
> Leaning on the everlasting arms?
> I have blessed peace with my Lord so near
> Leaning on the everlasting arms.[8]

These hymns provided sounds, lyrical images, and a group voice expanding on the identity King articulated. Moreover, these songs offered a clear collective statement on the citizenship they were after and how it would be carried out through nonviolent direct action. As Reagon writes: "The Negro community articulated their convictions in several ways on the first day of the boycott. First, they stayed off the buses; second, they attended the mass rally; and third, they made a statement at that rally, not only in their response to the speakers but also through what was said in song" ("Songs of the Civil Rights Movement 1955–1965," 93). Through the songs, Montgomerians asserted their identity for the protest, one where they would march with the strength of a solider, lean on faith and community, and lay claim to their country.

The liturgy of meetings fostered and enabled collective singing as identity formation. Through the genre pattern and its familiarity, the meeting liturgy invited the group to participate, both in singing and in recognizing their singing as a collective statement. Meeting liturgies centered the congregational style of singing, where the group would sing as a collective, often in response to a song leader. Sociologist William Roy explains that the congregational style of singing is especially participatory, emphasizing the significance of music as action rather than music as something to consume through watching a performer (*Reds, Whites, and Blues,* 184).[9] Thus, the liturgy primed Montgomerians to recognize freedom singing as an active genre dependent on everyone gathered. The freedom song genre, from the beginning, was rooted in the familiar practice of congregational singing, and the mass meeting with its liturgical pattern was key for teaching large groups how this worked. At the same time, the mass meeting's connection to the boycott and purpose in garnering full citizenship signaled that the songs also transformed civic identity.

Singing at the meetings enabled activists to use music to experience collective identity. Using music for genre invention created intimacy and belonging *within* the group. Activism was extremely demanding in Montgomery, as it was in many other southern locales. Group unity and solidarity was an ongoing process during the boycott, where class, gender, and age differences meant that Black people had diverse experiences with their city and its racism (Wilson, "Interpreting the Discursive Field of the Montgomery Bus Boycott," 309). As King put it that first evening: "Unity is the great need of the hour (Well, That's right), and if we are united we can get many of the things that we not only desire but which we justly deserve" ("Dec. 5, 1955, Holt Street Address," 73). By singing the songs and laying a foundation for freedom songs, the group experienced the new possibilities they heard King describe and explored sound as a resource for making and feeling this new identity. The songs provided Montgomerians with a mode for coalescing as a group and stepping toward their new future, a process uniquely facilitated through embodied sound and music. As sound studies scholar Michael Morrison writes: "Music is processed by a listener as an arrangement of sounds into recognizable patterns and structures; importantly, to translate vibrations into frequencies that yield a constellation of sounds, which might be interpreted as music, is an embodied process. By embodied, I am suggesting that sound *literally* travels through the body, as it activates many of our human faculties and senses, while we make sense out of sound(s) from our cultural experiences" ("The Sounds of Subjection," 16, emphasis in original). Like rhetorical scholar Steph Ceraso (see "Sounding Composition"), Morrison defines sound, here music, as a fully embodied experience, in which listeners and singers engage with sound physically on multiple levels. While individuals would bring a range of cultural backgrounds to bear on their engagement with the music and sounds of songs, joining voice and bodies together for singing, the group cultivated their unity and agreed in the moment on their identity. This felt processing of music and song made use of sound to experience a sense of belonging to one another through shared music. The songs played a key, perhaps the key, role in experiencing this unity and belonging together.

Second, the Montgomery scene reveals the integral role young women played in sounding the boycott and composing civic identity. The congregational style of singing depended on a song leader to motivate the group to sing, and these song leaders were often women, sometimes very young women. In the case of Montgomery, the Montgomery Improvement Association (MIA) recruited three teenage girls to serve as song leaders. These young women—Mary Ethyl Dozier (later Jamila Jones), Minnie Hendricks, and Gladys Burnette Carter—became the three individuals tasked with laying a foundation for a key movement genre. Once this trio was selected, they were in charge of the songs—selecting them, adapting them, and leading groups in singing. Dozier explains how their leadership came about: "Pretty soon after the first mass meeting in 1955 we started singing for the Montgomery Improvement Association. We were doing songs of the Movement, 'This Little Light of Mine,' 'I'm Gonna Let It Shine.' 'We Shall Overcome' came later. We would make up songs. All the songs I remember gave us strength to go on, like 'We Are Soldiers in the Army.' It was kind of spontaneous; if somebody started beating us over the head with a billy club, we would start singing about the billy club, or either that person's name would come out in a song" (quoted in Reagon, *Voices of the Civil Rights Movement*, 97). Like Reagon, Dozier participated in creating the freedom songs through a process of adaptation. This leadership, as she points out, was key to shifting from the singing of hymns and church music, like in the first Holt Street meeting, and actually making this type of singing into the genre that came to be known as the freedom songs. Song leaders like Dozier selected, adapted, and taught the songs, demonstrating how music might function in specific, strategic, and unique ways in the civil rights movement.

Dozier, Hendricks, and Carter defined the way music worked in the Montgomery movement, shaping the genre and the identity it created. Looking to the program for the meeting held a few weeks after the boycott began helps make this point:

Opening Hymn:	"Lift Him Up"
Reading of Scripture:	Rev. R. W. Hilson
Report of Transportation Committee:	Mr. Rufus Lewis
Acknowledgment of Visitors:	Mr. Pierce
Progress Report and Instructions:	Rev. M. L. King
Appeal for Funds:	Rev. R. J. Glascoe
Closing Remarks:	Rev. M. L. King
Closing Hymn:	"Bless Be the Tide"
Benediction:	Rev. E. H. Mason

("Program for MIA Mass Meeting," 84–85)

In this program, women's role in this meeting was behind-the-scenes, reiterating the commonly held (and often true) belief that the civil rights movement was a hierarchical enterprise, dependent upon the male reverends of Montgomery. Yet through the lens of genre creation, the leadership of Dozier, Hendricks, and Carter demonstrates that when the music played—in the meeting and across the city and nation—(young) women were often in charge. Through their leadership these young women were inventing a new genre—one where to sing for the movement, whether hymns, gospel songs, or labor or patriotic music, was to participate in making political identity and sounding this identity to the nation. In fact, Dozier, Hendricks, and Carter were invited to perform at Carnegie Hall, where they did this very thing, and at the end of the trip, they recorded their songs for the album, *The Montgomery Story*, and the album continued the circulation at the national level.[10]

Third, in these ways, the embodied, faithful identity crafted through sound enabled singing to function as an interracial, peaceful action and mode of response to racism. Just as the congregational style of singing embodied a new identity of peaceful, spiritual action, singing was, from the beginning, thoroughly integrative, as it showed how the sonic color line might be crossed and remade. For example, the selections for the first meeting were not specific to Black churches or the Black community in Montgomery. The hymns were found in standard hymnals that would be in the pews of any church in the city and in churches across the South and the nation. As songs shared with Christians across the nation regardless of race, "Onward Christian Soldiers" and "Leaning on the Everlasting Arms" sounded a peaceful identity centered in the idea that the nation belonged to Black people in Montgomery as much as anyone. "My Country 'Tis of Thee" affirmed and extended the point, as another selection that would be shared across racial lines.[11] Choosing songs that were well-known to white people through church or singing in public schools thus emphasized interracial unity as the vision—and sound—of the movement. Collective identity sounded like songs shared by all, whether through church or school. Freedom singing at the meeting, from the beginning, was thus about crossing and remaking the sonic color line with songs that signified both resistance and peace, both a new civic identity for Black people and interracial unity.

Through their singing, activists in Montgomery were laying a foundation for the musical genre of the civil rights movement, freedom songs. Singing together invented an identity and a genre at once, and these processes were reciprocal and mutually reinforcing. NAACP meetings in Montgomery relied on singing as part of their programs as early as the 1940s, but in places like Montgomery and Birmingham in the 1950s and then later in Nashville, Tennessee; Jackson, Mississippi; and Albany, Georgia; in the early

1960s, activists tethered freedom songs to particular activist goals and protest events, expanding and codifying the genre for collective direct action like boycotts, marches, and sit-ins. In the case of this first Holt Street meeting, the hymns "Onward Christian Soldiers" and "Leaning on the Everlasting Arms" were being developed into freedom songs through the group singing at the mass meeting. These songs resonated in new ways, sonically and lyrically, with thousands singing at the church that evening after walking to work or carpooling rather than riding the buses. Writing about "Onward Christian Soldiers" in particular, Reagon observes: "The lyrics of this song stood in a new light when sung in the MIA rallies . . . it came to life as a marching song in a struggle against evil and oppression" (*Voices of the Civil Rights Movement*, 94). Through their singing, the collective crafted an identity centered on peace and spirituality, and these actions remained key as the genre developed in the coming years.

Expanding the Repertoire, Owning the Genre:
Mrs. J. N. Rucker and Guy Carawan in Nashville, Tennessee

In the early 1960s, civil rights activists continued composing civic identity through sound, and as they did, they self-consciously developed the freedom song genre in new ways. In this moment, singing for civil rights is named "freedom singing," marking a crystallization of the genre as a key mode of sonic civic identity and action. The scene of the mass meeting remained central for extended explorations of sonic citizenship and the expansion of the genre. While song leaders had been leading collectives in congregational singing at mass meetings from the beginning, in the 1960s many of these same song leaders expanded the reach of their roles, moving between adaptation, selection, songwriting, and rhetorical performance to codify, cultivate, and teach the genre of freedom songs.

Song leaders also worked to respond to new movement exigencies, including the entrance of college students in key activist roles and the resulting fractures and fissures that emerged between younger and older groups in the movement.[12] Black song leaders also led and partnered with white folklorists including Guy and Candie Carawan, Pete Seeger, and Alan Lomax who sought to encourage, support, and ultimately shape the freedom song repertoire.[13] Studying the project of genre creation at mass meetings reveals the complexities of cross-racial genre engagements.

To inspect this key moment in the creation of the freedom song genre, I turn to a Nashville mass meeting held in May 1960. At this meeting, the key white figure in freedom song history, Guy Carawan, performs as song leader to teach activists to embrace song selections like "It Could Be a Wonderful World," and "The Ink Is Black, The Page Is White." Carawan is respectfully treated as a visitor, and Mrs. J. N. Rucker, the local song leader, remains in charge of the familiar congregational singing that opens and closes the meeting and scaffolds the period of music Carawan leads. While Carawan encourages activists to expand the freedom song repertoire, Rucker keeps the singing rooted in liturgy, church, and the familiar congregational style of worship. This scene reveals the continued significance of Black women song leaders, the range of strategies and practices Carawan attempted to bring to the movement and the repertoire, and the way in which the forum of the mass meeting enabled Black activists to reframe, and sometimes resist, the song leading of white figures like Carawan. Ultimately, this cross-racial engagement reinforces peaceful resistance as the key action of the genre.

The spring of 1960 was an exciting time in the Nashville movement and a key moment for freedom songs' expansion. Working under the Nashville Christian Leadership Council (NCLC), minister Kelly Miller Smith and other longtime Nashville residents initiated their work around three objectives: to increase voter registration, to raise Black employment, especially in the Police Department, and to desegregate lunch counters and restrooms at downtown stores. The NCLC attempted to draw white clergymen into their plans, imagining they might be sympathetic to the NCLC's project. This effort was unsuccessful. The NCLC then initiated dialogues that took place at two local stores, Harvey's and Cain-Sloan. At one of the dialogues, a resident claimed desegregation might happen "but not in our lifetime" (quoted in Houston, *The Nashville Way*, 80). The NCLC turned next to local students, almost "as an afterthought," in an attempt to get more volunteers to help as they turned to more direct means of protest (81).

This serendipitous strategy altered the Nashville campaign and the course of the civil rights movement broadly. Key to my analysis here, it also had important effects on the identity created through freedom songs. Historian Ben Houston writes: "It is no exaggeration to say that the Nashville sit-in movement proved to be a model for activism as much as the Montgomery Bus Boycott. In 1961 these same students would rescue and extend the Freedom Rides, capturing the attention to the entire world" (*The Nashville Way*, 107). In Nashville, the student activists successfully desegregated lunch counters in downtown stores in the spring of 1960. The Nashville scene of civil rights, while imperfect, demonstrated a harmonious interplay of students and local Black activists. The students embodied and enacted the strategies of Christian social action the NCLC believed in, and the NCLC board and longtime Nashville residents provided structural leadership, infrastructure, and economic support. For instance, after students were arrested and imprisoned, the NCLC raised $50,000 to support the rest of the campaign (Houston, *The Nashville Way*, 90).

The May 1960 mass meeting marked the desegregation of downtown establishments. This event was a "victory meeting," and singing the freedom songs was part of the celebration. Nashville activists had accomplished the first of their goals, and leaders faced the challenge of keeping the students and the rest of the community united as they sought to work toward new objectives. The mass meeting had to celebrate the students' achievements and spark new campaigns. As in Montgomery, the songs worked to unify the group across age, gender, and class. The established Black community in Nashville was solidly middle-class, while many of the students came to Nashville from rural or blue-collar backgrounds. This success, attention, and need for unity provides the backdrop for the mass meeting held before Nashville's student activists left the city for the summer break.

Practically speaking, this long event sought to showcase the students' achievements, to consider the group's next goals, and to keep everyone motivated and unified. The program below (Nashville Mass Meeting Recordings; also see fig. 2.1) reveals an expanded liturgy, one that retains standard features and includes some new ones:

Opening Hymn:	"Leaning on the Everlasting Arms," Mrs. J. N. Rucker
Hymn:	"We Are Climbing Jacob's Ladder," Rucker
Scripture Reading:	Ephesians 6, Rev. Jr. C. Johnson
Prayer:	Rev Jr. C. Johnson
Introduction of Visiting Song Leader:	Rev. Vivian
Period of Singing:	Selections led and taught by Guy Carawan
Hymn:	"Lift Every Voice and Sing"
Opening Remarks:	Rev. Vivian
Four Testimonies:	Alexander Looby, Mrs. C. M. Hayes, Mrs. Burgess, and unnamed student
Introduction of Visiting Speaker:	Rev. Vivian
Pep Talk by Visiting Speaker:	Ralph Abernathy
Hymn:	"Lift Every Voice and Sing"
Prayer:	Rev. Vivian
Reading of Letters:	Rev. Vivian
Exhortation:	Jim Lawson
Encomium:	Dr. C. J. Walker; Mrs. Ezelle
Discussion:	Collective

MASS MEETING

"Against Practices of Racial Discrimination in our Community"
Sponsored by
NASHVILLE CHRISTIAN LEADERSHIP COUNCIL

STUDENT RECOGNITION NIGHT

Clark Memorial Methodist Church   Monday night, May 30, 1960
Seven-thirty o'clock

* * * * * * * * * * * * * * * *

Song Service . . . . Mrs. J. N. Rucker

Scripture and Prayer . . . . Rev. Julius C. Johnson
(Pastor, Seay-Hubbard Methodist Church)
Music   Guy Carawan
Tribute to Students . . . . Attorney Z. Alexander Looby
. . . . Dr. Matthew Walker
. . . . Mrs. C. M. Hayes

Presentation . . . . Mrs. Landry Burgess

Student Response . . . . James Bevel

Introduction of Speaker . . . . Rev. C. T. Vivian
(Vice President, Nashville Christian Leadership Council)

Song: "Lift Every Voice and Sing" . . . . Audience

Speaker . . . . Rev. Ralph Abernathy
(President, Montgomery Improvement Association)

Special Report . . . . Rev. James Lawson
(Projects Chairman, Nashville Christian Leadership Council)

Offering . . . . Dr. C. J. Walker

Announcements . . . . Rev. C. T. Vivian

Benediction . . . . Rev. Grady Donald
(Chaplain, Nashville Christian Leadership Council)

-ooIoo-

Reverend Andrew White, Presiding

-ooIoo-

FIGURE 2.1. Mass Meeting Program, Nashville, Tennessee, May 30, 1960.
Guy and Candie Carawan Collection #20008, Southern Folklife Collection,
Wilson Library, University of North Carolina at Chapel Hill.

Through this meeting liturgy, the songs continued to offer key moments of collective voice, moments for the group to experience solidarity and unity with their voices raised together. As was the case in Montgomery, the meeting opened with familiar hymns, songs everyone gathered is expected to know how to sing because of experience in church, and these songs are guided by local song leader Mrs. J. N. Rucker. Unlike in Montgomery and unique to this moment of genre expansion, however, the program also includes a designated period of singing, guided by the visiting song leader, Carawan. Carawan is introduced by the moderating minister, Reverend Vivian.

Taken as a whole, the genre of freedom singing, across these two distinct musical portions of the meeting, scaffolds the ongoing project of crafting their civic identity and deliberating over next steps in the movement. The period led by Carawan attempts to expand the genre to encompass working closely with white people and white-led institutions, secular visions of social change, and interracial folk sounds—like the guitar and the banjo. The hymns led by Rucker speak back to these inflections in the genre, reframing and in part resisting the newer sounds to continue anchoring freedom songs in Black experience and churches. This scene of freedom song invention offers insight into the rhetorical work of song leaders to carefully craft the genre and maintain its associations with the Black church. It also helps reveal the power, agency, and deliberate rhetorical strategy of women like Rucker, who led along with figures like Carawan. As Lindsay Rose Russell writes, genre users do "not simply register[r] societal wants; they attempt[t] to build expectations and invite repetitions by rhetorical means" ("Defining Moments," 95). In the case of Carawan and Rucker, they are attempting to build different expectations for freedom songs and thus different repetitions. In this way, the Nashville scene demonstrates dissonance in freedom song genre creation and the identity the genre was helping to craft.

Through his song leading in the meeting, Carawan invited the group to explore interracial, secular, and folk songs. To introduce Carawan to the group, Reverend Vivian explained: "And now, Mr. Brother Guy Carawan, who has been with us in these meetings before, will lead us in singing" (Nashville Mass Meeting Recordings). Carawan, a white man from California, was and continues to be a key and well-regarded figure in histories of freedom songs and the civil rights movement.[14] In the winter and spring of 1960, Carawan occupied the role of Director of Music at the Highlander Folk School, located in Monteagle, Tennessee, and he had been visiting Nashville to work with activists on music and to help develop the freedom song repertoire. Highlander, well-known as an institutional support for the civil rights movement, provided Carawan with opportunities to meet and exchange musical resources with civil rights activists from the beginning of the movement. Carawan saw one of his key roles to help document and circulate the freedom songs: for example, when Dozier and the Montgomery Trio began traveling and singing, it was Carawan who created an opportunity for them to record their music and then helped put out their album, *The Montgomery Story*. He would go on to do the same in all major civil rights locales, including Nashville. In the context of this Nashville meeting, Carawan's leadership brings to the fore an important tension in freedom song creation as a site of identity. Because making the freedom song genre was also making civic identity, Carawan's leadership is complicated by his ties to the white folk world—including Lomax and Seeger—and the institutions like Highlander and Folkways Recording that both supported and circumscribed the genre.

Through the selections Carawan brought to this meeting, he attempted to expand the freedom song repertoire to be spiritually inclusive, drawing from secular sources in addition to religious ones. His wide range of song selections moved the genre beyond the sacred music of the Black church to encompass protest songs from the labor movement, children's songs from the United Nations, Quaker hymns, and Black spirituals from enslavement, which many Black activists shied away from using. Carawan taught the following song selections at this meeting:

"We Shall Overcome"
"We Shall Not Be Moved"
"It Could be a Wonderful, Wonderful World"
"How Can I Keep From Singing"
"Michael Row the Boat Ashore"
"The Ink Is Black, the Page Is White" (Nashville Mass Meeting Recordings)

The first two selections, "We Shall Overcome" and "We Shall Not Be Moved" had already been accepted by the students as freedom songs. Carawan attempts to teach the group the next four selections, and they provide insight into the activist practices Carawan believed were important to build into the genre. "It Could be a Wonderful Word" and "The Ink is Black, the Page is White" are selections taken from secular sources. "How Can I Keep From Singing" and "Michael Row the Boat Ashore" represent sacred song selections; "How Can I Keep From Singing" is a Quaker hymn, and "Michael Row the Boat Ashore" is a spiritual sung by enslaved people in South Carolina.[15]

In this meeting, "It Could Be a Wonderful, Wonderful World" and "The Ink Is Black, the Page Is White" provide sounds, lyrics, and musical histories that support secular activist habits. For the first song, Carawan asserts:

> I'll teach you a children's song if you don't already know it. It's called "If we consider each other a neighbor, a friend, or a brother, it could be a wonderful, wonderful world, it could be a wonderful world." It comes out of an old book put out by the United Nations of children's songs called *Big Subjects for Little People.* Y'all see if you can't pick this up and go home and teach it to your children. (Nashville Mass Meeting Recordings)

Carawan recognizes that this song is unfamiliar to the group, and he attempts to argue for its usefulness. A children's song provides Nashvilleans with a new resource for activism across all ages—connecting not just the older local people of the meeting with the students but unifying the group with an even younger group of local children, presumably absent from this event. The adults are tasked with learning the song and then sharing it at home. This selection and rationale demonstrate the interracial, spiritually inclusive collective identity Carawan understands the freedom song genre to be about: freedom singing is something that adults, students, and even children can do, and the identity it embodies is not distinctly Black or Christian, but rather, one that is interracial and spiritually inclusive with secular appeal. The lyrics and sound of the selection extend this point. The first stanza of the song goes:

> If each little kid could have fresh milk each day
> If each working man had enough time to play
> If each homeless soul had a good place to stay
> It would be a wonderful world, oh yes
> It would be a wonderful world. (Nashville Mass
>   Meeting Recordings)

As these lyrics convey, the song imagines a more "wonderful world" and not just one that changes the racist structures of power in the United States; rather, the song represents investment in class shifts as well. Referencing hungry children, overworked laborers, and homelessness, through the singing of this song, the group sings about class issues, creating economic inflections in the identity they are crafting. This selection shows Carawan as a song leader with a global vision of the freedom songs. Through music, activists take on labor issues; they can be shared with the very young and are not limited to the history of Black church music.

Through his performance, Carawan also modeled cross-racial engagement and its role in freedom singing. His leadership did not consist simply of standing at the front of the meeting and singing; like other song leaders in this phase of freedom song development, he used music as a platform to speak to audiences. In the case of this meeting, he sought to explain and teach the songs, narrating their histories and advocating for their significance. He attempted to persuade the group to accept the songs by showing why particular songs might be useful for the identity of the movement.

With the next two selections and a shift back to religious themes, Carawan argues for songs with interracial histories. Here, Carawan sought to cultivate interracial collaboration as part of the identity of the movement through his very presence and teaching, but also, more specifically and overtly through these song selections and narrations of them. These two selections, the Quaker hymn and the spiritual, are reminiscent of Black–white collaborations in working against injustice. To introduce the first song, the Quaker hymn, "How Can I Keep from Singing," Carawan says: "Now I'm gonna sing you a song that is a very old Quaker hymn. This goes way back to the days of the British Isles when the Quakers were being persecuted for their religion and many of the first colonists who came to this country from the British Isles were Quakers seeking religious freedom. This song is about how their leaders were all put in jail and their faith that [they] would still find a land and time when everyone could worship God the way they pleased. It's called 'How Can I Keep From Singing'" (Nashville Mass Meeting Recordings). Carawan draws in Quaker history, from both Britain and the United States, to make a case for singing one of their hymns. The parallel he points to is an understanding of unjust persecution from the state and using music to find endurance. While Carawan does not mention it, the Quakers are well-known as abolitionists, thus a symbol of white people supporting Black freedom. They are also celebrated as a pacifist group, refusing to turn to violence no matter the cost. The lyrics of the hymn reveal the significance of music as a resource for remaining resolute in response to violent persecution:

> Thro' all the tumult and the strife
> I hear the music ringing;
> It finds an echo in my soul—
> How can I keep from singing? (Nashville
> Mass Meeting Recordings)

As these lyrics indicate, the hymn reinforced the identity expressed through freedom songs as fundamentally peaceful and about spiritual freedom. This hymn also expanded these sounds to encompass an interracial history, one inclusive of a white pacifist group well-known for their sacrifices to end slavery.

The next selection turns explicitly to slavery in the United States, again attempting to expand the freedom song genre through historical resources. This move works to expand the genre to include spirituals, and like the Quaker hymn, is a reminder of the successful interracial work of abolition. Carawan explains the significance of the third new song: "Here's a song that comes from down in the Sea Islands of Georgia and South Carolina way back in the days when the only way you could get out to those little islands was by [a] long boat driven by slaves. Known for their beautiful singing. This is a spiritual, and this is a hymn which they used to row by. You'll have to learn it" (Nashville Mass Meeting Recordings). Carawan's introduction emphasizes that singing was powerful for enslaved people and that they were known for their singing. The lyrics of the song offer visual details of this scene:

> Michael row the boat ashore, hallelujah
> Michael row the boat ashore, hallelujah
> Sister help to trim the sail, hallelujah
> Sister help to trim the sail, hallelujah
> The river is deep and the river is wide, hallelujah
> Green pastures on the other side, hallelujah
> (Nashville Mass Meeting Recordings)

Like "How Can I Keep From Singing," this selection looks forward to a peaceful future. The lyrics tell of a gendered partnership, with Michael being "helped" by Sister. This image thus dovetails with the collaborative gendered dimension of freedom singing's leadership. However, as a song imagining how men and women work together, the relationship in the song is more reflective of gendered hierarchies and women serving in less powerful roles. In addition to the subservient image of Black women, the tone and lyrics of this song convey happy enslaved people, content to sing beautifully and work hard. Considering this selection for its joyful image of enslavement and less-than-equal depiction of Black women's role as "helper," it is not hard to see why many activists were not sure about spirituals as freedom songs.

The final selection, "The Ink Is Black, the Page Is White," is not introduced by Carawan but is perhaps the most explicit in its interracial vision, as the title of the song makes clear. Versions of this song, composed by Earl Robinson, circulated on albums released by Robinson and Pete Seeger during the 1950s, so perhaps Carawan believed it to be familiar to the audience. At the end of this selection, Carawan returns to working in a documentary capacity, as the person responsible for the audio recording of this meeting and many others. This song reinforces the point implicit in Carawan's leadership at the meeting; as a song leader, he models a Black-and-white-better-together approach to Black freedom. As the selections and his introductions above convey, this approach is laced with white-and-secular inflections in the sounds of citizenship. The selections, as a group, also work to cultivate the sounds of the freedom songs as "folksy" because of Carawan's musical choices. At this meeting, he led the songs with his guitar (see fig. 2.2). At other events, he sometimes brought a banjo. Most Black song leaders, by contrast, relied on the type of musical accompaniment used in local churches where meetings were held. In this Nashville meeting, for example, the hymns are accompanied by a piano. Other civil rights locales forwarded voice as an instrument foregoing accompaniment altogether: for example, in Albany, Georgia, acapella was the most common style of singing

FIGURE 2.2. Guy Carawan leads music in Nashville mass meeting,
April 21, 1960. Nashville Public Library, Special Collections.

in church and thus also in the mass meetings. These sounding choices are important for how the genre was created and codified, because singing with the accompaniment of an instrument created a need for a musician and the material support of the particular instrument. When Carawan came in with his banjo or guitar, he shifted the sound of the genre and taught activists to sing sounds associated with white folk genres of the time. This practice called on important labor history around protest and song, but it deviated from the familiar sounds of singing in Black churches. While Carawan continued to carry his guitar to meetings, eventually Bernice Reagon suggested that the instrument was inappropriate for freedom singing, saying "Lay that guitar down, boy!" (quoted in Davis, "Making Movement Sounds," 91).

Rucker's work as the local song leader speaks back to Carawan's teaching and song selections and the concomitant questions of genre ownership they evoked. Black song leaders in the movement were savvy to the mass meeting as a site of genre creation, where their choices defined the genre. As Russell asserts, genre invention "is not simply the 'natural' or 'lucky' outcome of some fortuitous contextual shifts but crucially also the result of rhetorical choices made by genre inventors" ("Defining Moments," 85).

Rucker's choices and deliberate leadership in this key moment in Nashville offer insight into these shifts. Here, Rucker worked to root the singing of the civil rights movement in the Black church and in so doing to protect its ownership.

As a local song leader, perhaps even the regular song leader for the church where the meeting was held, Rucker continued defining freedom songs through church singing. Her leadership echoes the sonic civic habits cultivated in Montgomery, centering women leading, faith and freedom, and peace. Her song selections open the meeting and extend the spiritual tradition of congregational singing from Montgomery. The first song, "Leaning on the Everlasting Arms," was frequently sung in Montgomery, including at the first mass meeting. The next song, "We are Climbing Jacob's Ladder," reinforces the genre as an identity rooted in congregational singing and familiar styles of music. These selections return freedom songs to the Christian democratic spirit of Montgomery and the sounds of hymn singing.

While Rucker's selections and leadership work with the generic threads present in Montgomery, her song leading creates subtle dissonance with the musical leadership of Carawan. She speaks far less than Carawan, and her leadership occurs largely through her singing of the songs. Her silence on the rationale for the songs suggests that extensive arguments for musical selections are unnecessary. Rather, selections should come from familiar sources like the church and fit into the congregational style of singing well-known to Black people in the South. Song leaders like Rucker, with experience and expertise in the Black church tradition, may have been wary of building the freedom song genre to be too broadly inclusive.[16] Rucker leads as much through her songs as through her silence. By not offering extensive arguments about songs, she reminds the group how powerfully simple church singing functions to sound freedom.

Still, she does use her leadership to make a claim about the significance of singing. After the opening hymn she asserts: "May we sing . . . 'We are Climbing Jacob's Ladder.' I noticed there are a quite a few who were not singing . . . But I contend that everybody who has a soul can sing. Now, sing a little bit. Now, so we all join and help sing this [song]" (Nashville Mass Meeting Recordings). Rucker understands the context of the church singing to encourage the participation and collaboration of everyone gathered. Making the movement sing and crafting identity through sound is a project that rests on the group, not her singing as performance or the singing of a few gifted soloists. To the contrary, "everybody who has a soul can sing." Reagon discusses this dimension of the Black church song tradition: "People who went to church went to get something from that experience. In order to get it, they had to participate in creating it. There was no such thing as coming, sitting down in your seat, and having something come to you from the stage. . . . And without any real conscious work, this was definitely the way I saw music working in the civil rights movement." (Banfield, "The Music Kept Us from Being Paralyzed," 195). As Reagon explains, the church was key to the invention of the freedom song genre. It shaped the sound of the identity, and through it song leaders built participation into the genre's core actions and features. Black churches, through their liturgies, were about structured participation and the "work of the people"; they demanded a reciprocal call-and-response interchange of audience and speaker, whether song or prayer or preaching. Turning traditional white rhetorical modes on their head, the improvisational and interactive dimensions of the Black church made it possible to foster the freedom songs as shared, collaborative, and collective statements of movement identity. Local song leaders like Rucker and Reagon had the background and experience with the church and with music to see that the freedom songs needed religious connections to function as a truly collective, collaborative genre for the movement. Recognizing this significance and building it into the genre through repetition at the mass meetings night after night and week after week, these song leaders owned their genre, shaped identities, and set themselves up to serve as experts as the genre became nationally known.

Songwriters' Role in Genre Invention: Jackson, Mississippi, 1963

By 1963, freedom songs were the most well-known and clearly articulated genre of the civil rights movement. Through their regular, repeated singing at mass meetings, Black people across the South defined the genre and used songs to craft collective identity. Turning now to Jackson, Mississippi in 1963, I analyze the role of songwriter Matthew Jones in expanding the genre to respond to persistent white violence and terror. At this meeting, Jones performs the song, "The Ballad of Medgar Evers," a song written after activist Medgar Evers's murder and the murder of four young girls in the bombing of the 16th Street Baptist Church in Birmingham. This performance shows how figures like Jones explored through songwriting the commemorative functions and capacity of freedom songs as responses to recurrent violence. Jones's song expands the genre to encompass an additional practice, remembering the lives lost to white supremacist terror and using these memories to inspire continued activism.

Evers was an active and influential leader in the Mississippi Movement beginning in 1954. When his attempt to integrate the University of Mississippi's law school in 1954 was unsuccessful, he began working with the National Association for the Advancement of Colored People (NAACP) in

Jackson. In this role, he was influential in James Meredith's successful attempt to attend the University of Mississippi in 1962 (Payne, *I've Got the Light of Freedom*, 285). After Meredith's campaign, Evers and the rest of the NAACP began work in Jackson to desegregate public places and to end discriminatory hiring practices. The Jackson movement was initially slowed by the NAACP's conservative leadership. Leaders such as I. S. Sanders, Sam Bailey, and Reverend R. L. T. Smith were not eager to encourage or support direct action campaigns, even after the Southern Christian Leadership Conference's success in Birmingham in May 1963. These leaders argued for more negotiations with Jackson's Mayor Allen Thompson; on the other side of the strategy table, Charles Jones, Ed King, and John Salter advocated for massive demonstrations. The two groups came together in a compromise, agreeing to begin direct action protest after one more attempt to negotiate with Thompson (Dittmer, *Local People,* 157–60).

Evers composed a telegram to Thompson, alerting him that should he reject their demands, they would demonstrate. In spite of this clear message, Thompson refused all demands. The next morning, African Americans initiated a sit-in at the Woolworth's lunch counter in downtown Jackson. This sit-in devolved into mass chaos as crowds of white people beat and kicked demonstrators. While initially it appeared the demonstration had convinced Thompson to give in, by the end of the day he stood firm. Movement leaders decided to move forward with more demonstrations. For the next few days, protestors marched and sang in huge numbers. On Friday, May 31, for instance, hundreds of young Black protestors marched on Farish Street in downtown Jackson. By the end of this protest, policemen had arrested 450 of the marches. These young activists were taken to a temporary prison at the state fairgrounds (Dittmer, *Local People,* 163).

Despite growing momentum, national NAACP leaders and local conservatives called for an end to mass demonstrations. While this move angered many, including Dave Dennis and Jerome Smith of the Congress of Racial Equality, the Jackson movement shifted the focus from mass demonstrations to voter-registration campaigns. This strategy would serve as the movement's focal point throughout the rest of the year. Shortly after this shift to voter registration, Evers and others attended a mass meeting on June 12, 1963. Upon leaving the meeting and arriving at his home, Evers got out of his car and was shot and killed in his driveway by a member of the White Citizen's Council. Historian John Dittmer writes that the Jackson movement never fully recovered after Evers was killed (*Local People,* 169).

Even in their grief and disillusionment, activists did continue working. In fall 1963, The Council of Federated Organizations devised plans for a voter-registration protest to carry on the success of the Freedom Vote held statewide during the summer. The council's strategy was to participate in the regular election by having a separate registration and running candidates who represented the interests of African Americans. This protest was designed with two goals in mind: to demonstrate that large numbers of African Americans did indeed want the vote and to mock the regular election by showing that the candidates on the official ballot failed to represent African Americans. Aaron Henry was the candidate for governor, and his running mate was Ed King (Payne, *I've Got the Light of Freedom,* 295).

To rally African Americans around Henry and King and to encourage them to participate in the election, mass meetings were held in Jackson and throughout the state. Even as spirits ran high for the protest, meetings in Jackson were both determined and mournful. For example, at the meeting held the Friday evening before the election, the meeting program includes rally songs as well as Jones's ballad, his commemorative song of lament. Throughout this November event, meeting speakers frequently reference Evers, reminding those gathered of his absence and his legacy. Jones' vocal performance provides the moment in the meeting for expressions of grief, as his song narrates Evers's life and laments his untimely and violent death.

Together this meeting liturgy provided participants opportunities to explore different felt associations with freedom songs. The program is as follows:

Songs:	"This Little Light of Mine" "Set on Freedom" "Everybody Wants Freedom" and "Keep Your Eyes on the Prize"
Introduction of First Speaker:	Dave Dennis
Speech:	Allard Lowenstein
Speech:	Ed King
Introduction of Special Music:	Dave Dennis
Song:	"When All the Votes Come Rolling In"
Musical Performance:	Matthew Jones, "The Ballad of Medgar Evers"
Speech:	Sam Bailey
Song:	"We Shall Overcome" (Jackson Mass Meeting Recordings, Tapes N57-58)

As the program shows, by 1963 the freedom song genre was well-defined, and all of the songs on the program are accepted and known in the repertoire. The freedom songs echo the genre initiated in Montgomery and worked out in Nashville, singing that centers peace, inclusive leadership, and interracial unity. Through the musical selections, activists continue singing about these themes as they also renew their energy for continued activism. Songs like "Set on Freedom" and "Everybody Wants Freedom" provide moments for joy and enthusiasm, with upbeat, forward-looking, and hopeful lyrics and melodies. The song that begins the second segment of music, "When the Votes Come Rolling," also upbeat, is set to the tune of "When the Saints Come Marching In." The lyrics look forward to a large number of African American votes to celebrate after the upcoming demonstration.

Jones's performance of the "The Ballad of Medgar Evers" shifts the tone of the meeting, the function of the singing, and the emotional range of the genre. Through strategic repetitions and careful circulation, freedom songs overall had been working to signal peaceful collaborations with white people and a desire for interracial unity; the "Ballad," however, attempts to reconcile this function of the genre with ongoing white violence. As a songwriter, Jones recognizes the freedom songs as a way for him to speak to activists and to use music to expand the civic practices they are taking up. His song reveals memory and lament as important actions of the genre.

Since Jones is visiting Jackson, leader Dave Dennis introduces his performance to the group. Dennis explains to the Jackson meeting participants the connections between the song, Jones, and the memory of Evers. He says: "Now we have somewhat of a special occasion. Tonight, a person to dedicate to us, to the Mississippi people, in memory of a great man who lived here and who fought here, who died here. A man whom we all knew, and a man whom we all loved. A man who might not be able to walk with us physically but shall forever live within our hearts as long as we do. This man who is going to dedicate this particular song is a man . . . who has worked with the SNCC [Student Nonviolent Coordinating Committee] in Danville, Virginia, all of us have heard of what happened there. He has been abused and has been scorned too. Praise be to God, he is still here to talk to us about it. Without any further ado. I'd like to present to you, Mr. Matthew" (Jackson Mass Meeting Recordings, Tape N58). Similar to the work of Carawan in Nashville, Dennis persuades the audience to reflect on the past to understand the music they are about to hear. In this case, however, Dennis is reminding Jacksonians of their *own* history and memories to persuade them to accept the song. In this way, Dennis prepares activists to consider how the freedom songs of the movement might function as sites for remembering their loved ones lost to white supremacist violence. After Dennis's introduction, Jones prefaces his performance of the song by making this connection more explicit. He claims: "This song tells you exactly how the death of Medgar Evers affected the whole United States. I think I was in Danville at the time. And I thought about the song. But the song really became a reality when [four] kids in Birmingham died. I knew that something had to be done. I hadn't done enough. Going to jail is not enough. We have to lay our bodies on the line continuously" (Jackson Mass Meeting Recordings, Tape N58). For Jones, the song offers a way to remember together and to use the memories to inspire continued work for Black freedom. As he puts it here, the murder of Evers is part of a larger, ongoing pattern of white violence against Black bodies. He argues that their response is to remember and to continue using nonviolent direct action, "lay[ing] [their] bodies on the line." In this way, he connects memory with peace as actions of the freedom song genre.

The song offers lyrical images and sounds that thread together peace, memory, and activism with Black freedom. Toward this goal, it presents Evers's life and death and depicts the violence of Byron de la Beckwith, Evers's assassin. The first stanza narrates Evers's life and death, and the next three stanzas tell the rest of the story. The final stanza moves to describing his life on earth and in his "heavenly home":

> Medgar had some company in his heavenly home,
> Those little children from Birmingham,
> Like Christ they died for you and for me,
> They died for you to be free (van Rijn, *Kennedy's*
> *Blues*, 101)

Through the song as a whole, Jones commemorates Evers and connects his murder to the bombing in Birmingham and the four young girls lost. The song offers two intertwined themes toward shaping memories of Evers. The first is that he did not die in vain; though he was brutally murdered by a "high-powered rifle" that "tore out his heart," Evers now lives in "his heavenly home." Evoking the image of Christ as necessary sacrifice, the song prompts listeners to associate the deaths of Evers and the children with meaningful, powerful sacrifices. This theme encourages a second: these sacrifices are calls to action. The final line makes this explicit: "They died for you and for me, They died for you to be free" (van Rijn, *Kennedy's Blues*, 101). Through these interlaced themes—Evers's new life in his "heavenly home" as a call to action—Jones draws listeners into the shared experience of contrasting these movement tragedies with the life of Evers.

This song includes some features of the traditional murder ballad, such as the naming of Evers's killer. However, scholar Minrose Gwin notes it seems more strongly composed in the African American tradition: "Its sonorous, mournful rhythms, deep seriousness, and appeal to human dignity and freedom all seem to derive from African American music traditions going back to slavery" (*Remembering Medgar Evers*, 141). Jones was not the only one to compose a song in response to Evers's death. Bob Dylan, Phil Ochs and Bob Gibson, and Dick Weissman also composed and performed such songs. But it was only Jones, and the Freedom Singers with whom he would later perform the song, who were in the trenches as activists (Gwin, *Remembering Medgar Evers,* 126). Jones's performance thus uniquely evokes the memory of Evers: he sings as an activist with other activists.

In writing new songs in response to movement tragedies, songwriters like Jones made it possible for freedom songs to express the complex emotional dimensions of civil rights activism and to commemorate friends and loved ones. Performing these songs in the space of the mass meeting offered the group the opportunity to feel the lyrics and music together, remembering Evers and reflecting on what his life means for the Jackson movement. In so doing, this song provided a moment for grief, sadness, rage, and fury—the felt dimensions of walking the long, hard road to freedom during the civil rights movement. This ballad expands the emotional register of the freedom songs and conditions participants to express sorrow or rage through music. Yet given its overall emphasis on continued love, peace, and faith, and situated in the larger liturgy of the meeting, the song can be viewed to function in line with the emotional-exchange logic described in chapter 1, where difficult emotions are expressed with the purpose of shifting them toward key nonviolent feelings. Overall, the purpose of "The Ballad of Medgar Evers" is to create memories of Evers's death that urge activists to keep working even as they remember the tragedy that can await anyone who fights for Black freedom in a place like Mississippi. This civic sounding, like the cross-racial partnership of Carawan and Rucker, creates another dissonance in the freedom song genre. In composing "The Ballad of Medgar Evers," Jones explores the capacity of freedom songs to remember lives lost to ongoing white violence, yet through repetitions and careful cultivation, the freedom song genre continues to center interracial unity and peace.

Conclusion: Freedom Songs as Faithful Genre

Examining the ways in which Jones used the freedom song genre to explore responses to persistent, systemic white violence points to a tension that the genre ultimately could not expand to accommodate. Night after night, week after week, song leaders and groups met in the mass meetings, building, practicing, and codifying the genre. This chapter highlighted three specific moments in the genre's history that can be viewed as examples of rhetorical work happening repeatedly and recursively over time to create conventions and expectations for the freedom songs. Through the scene of the mass meeting, with its spatial cues and familiar liturgy, everyone attending these events was invited to participate in inventing and maintaining the freedom song genre. The result of this work was a well-defined genre and identity. To sing the freedom songs was to enact a peaceful, faithful approach to Black freedom and a desire for interracial unity. Indeed, Dozier, Rucker, Reagon, and Jones were so successful in creating the genre of freedom songs as cohesive identity and set of peaceful activist practices that as visions of activism shifted, so too did the need for the genre that activists had so carefully cultivated (Elizabeth Miller, "Remembering Freedom Songs").

As a genre centered on peaceful action, the freedom song genre ultimately could accommodate the need for new forms of activism in the wake of Black Power. Black Power activists sought to demarcate their movement from civil rights ideas of faith, peace, and love. Lisa Corrigan offers this assessment: "As both a slogan and a political orientation, Black Power was nothing if not an articulation of changes in *both* feelings *and* politics, away from hope, accommodation, and moral suasion and toward electoral and community power" (*Black Feelings,* xvi, emphasis in original). As a faithful genre, the careful refining and clearly defined purpose of the freedom songs worked against its malleability as a Black Power mode of activism. Freedom songs meant certain songs, specific types of singing, and a codified set of nonviolent civic behaviors. This identity and purpose, resting on ideals of faith and peace, did not align with new ideas about Black justice that took hold as the 1960s wore on. Writing in 1964, Julius Lester puts it this way, "The days of singing freedom songs and the days of combating bullets and billy clubs with love are over" ("The Movement's Moving On," 221). Rather than try to adapt the freedom song genre, activists instead largely abandoned music as collective protest. Performers like Nina Simone continued to use music to define their individual activism, and freedom songs circulate in the twenty-first century as sites for remembering civil rights.[17] Yet as collective modes of activism, the freedom songs fell out of use. In this way, Lester's comment was remarkably prescient, foreshadowing the slow and gradual shift away from the genre that occurred over the remainder of the decade.

THREE

Embodying Peace

Prayer as Reverent Resistance

The date February 1, 1960, marks a turning point in the movement for Black freedom. In Greensboro, North Carolina, Ezell Blair Jr., David Richmond, Franklin McCain, and Joseph McNeil staged a sit-in at the Woolworth's lunch counters, ushering in a new wave of civil rights activity, one where college students were key players. Historian William H. Chafe writes: "The Greensboro sit-ins constituted a watershed in the history of America" and with these protests, "the 1960's stage of the freedom movement had begun" (*Civilities and Civil Rights*, 71). In fifty-four cities across nine states, students resisted segregation and revealed their will to change it. The nation looked on as battles over citizenship took place in downtown establishments across the South (71).

In the *New York Times* reporting of the Greensboro sit-ins, the account includes a detail frequently left out of contemporary depictions of these protests. After the students spent the day sitting in at the counter, they went together to a busy street in downtown Greensboro. Standing quietly in a circle, with hands raised toward the sky, the group recited the Lord's Prayer, a key prayer in the Christian tradition ("Negroes in South in Store Sit-Down," 28). On the first day of this protest, the students performed the sit-in; later, they prayed together as a show of their commitment to one another, the goals of the sit-ins, and peaceful social action. This portion of the protest expands the embodied nonviolence of the sit-ins to include a genre perhaps not obviously "activist": prayer. Through this public enactment of prayer, the Greensboro Four inhabited the genre to display peace, and in the same moment, they disturbed the flow of traffic and unsettled segregated space.[1]

The example of the Greensboro Four highlights prayer as an understudied yet ubiquitous genre in the movement for Black freedom.[2] In this chapter, I recover prayer as a key civil rights genre shaped in the liturgy of the mass meeting and theorize its importance as *reverent resistance*. An embodiment of the paradoxes of spiritual nonviolence, prayer occupied a significant and unique role in the activist repertoire through its capacity to hold together contradictions. In public spaces like the city street described above, prayer signaled peace through reverent gestures and speech, while in the same moment, disrupting the status quo and resisting white supremacy. In the mass-meeting scenes reconstructed in this chapter, groups crafted this reverent resistant identity and posture through their collective participation in prayer. Praying together, activists constituted themselves as a peaceful group insistent on change and rehearsed reverent ways of speaking and acting for immediate protest in streets and other public sites. They also prayed to persevere, to press on, and to hold on to faith that in an ultimate sense, their bodies were valued and safe.[3] Here, prayer fostered what scholar-activist James Melvin Washington, riffing on Adrienne Rich, refers to as "revolutionary patience" (*Conversations with God*). To embody prayer in the civil rights mass meeting was to steel oneself before God for the long road of social change and to emerge from the event as dignified political agent poised to perform immediate disruption.

For this chapter, I follow theorists and practitioners who define prayer, most simply, as "conversation with God" (Washington, *Conversations with God*, xxxii; FitzGerald, *Spiritual Modalities*, 5). From this broad definition, I identify and explore a range of prayers significant for the liturgy of the mass meeting. These prayers include directed prayer, or the formal discursive prayers delivered by individuals, most often ministers, where people listen in and follow along, perhaps expressing Amen or another kind of spoken response, and silent collective prayer, where everyone in the group might be participating individually while sharing silence. These kinds of prayer rely on gestural responses—kneeling, bowing the head, closing one's eyes. In the meetings analyzed here, prayer expresses and embodies both the complicated act of spiritual nonviolence and a rationale and experiential support for it. Activists reveal their faith in God and their will to make change in the world; they practice embodying reverent postures of nonviolence; and they rehearse these postures to shape and enact coordinated, collective protest.

Studying the reverent resistance of prayers across mass meeting sites brings into view the "unruliness" of faithful genres generally and prayer particularly. Unruly genres, as I discussed in the Introduction, "disrup[t] what appears or is taken to be the normal flow of life" (Alexander and Jarratt, "Introduction," 7). The unruly, according to Jonathan Alexander and Susan Jarratt, is a productive counterpoint to civility, understood as rational deliberation, and a lens for accounting for the ways certain bodies are more likely to be read as disruptive than others. The prayers examined here reveal another side both to civility and to the unruly. Black bodies praying, in the towns and cities in this chapter, imaged civility through reverent speech and postures, and through this very image, disrupted, shocked, and startled many who encountered the faithful enactment of nonviolence. Prayer served as an unruly genre in part because activists violated racialized norms regarding what spaces Black bodies should inhabit and because they unsettled religious norms for where prayer should occur. Disconnecting faithful genres from their expected (private) contexts imbues them with unruliness; this unruliness, in the civil rights movement, modelled civility as a peaceful response to violence no matter the costs. This complexity is ideologically central to prayer, and as this chapter will convey, the mass meeting was the scene for rehearsing the genre's capacity for peace-and-unruliness simultaneously.

To examine the paradox of peace and the unruly embodied in Black prayer, I pay particular attention to the interplay of genre, gesture, and theology. Here I read the prayers delivered aloud in meetings while also attending to the bodies silently participating, heard through quiet gestures or responses. In the call-and-response rhythm of the meeting liturgy, prayer coordinates peaceful action through the group's deliberate gestural participation in the genre. To examine the functions of the words and embodied performance, I turn to activists' theological inflections that animate the genre and the African American religious tradition that supports the work of prayer in the movement for Black freedom. The texts for this chapter, then, include discursive prayers, descriptions or verbal cues for how and when to pray, and activists' accounts on the felt effects of prayer.

The chapter opens with an overview of prayer in African American religious and rhetorical traditions. Next, I examine the role of prayer in a 1963 mass-meeting scene held in Greenwood, Mississippi, where through directed prayer, activists collectively imagine and enact their identity as dignified protestors characterized by reverence, honesty, and peace. Moving to a mass-meeting scene in St. Augustine, Florida, in May 1964, prayer provides a genre to rehearse, and then perform, reverent disruption. This group uses the mass meeting as a platform to initiate a prayerful march to a dangerous, downtown area. The final mass-meeting site considered is Americus, Georgia, in 1963, where the group engages in silent, collective prayer to reflect on a protest that had gone poorly, and then takes up "revolutionary patience" to respond to failure and disappointment and to steel themselves for continued nonviolent protest.

Prayer as Reverent Resistance:
An African American Religious Tradition

Beginning in the eighteenth and nineteenth centuries, many African American rhetors observed and enacted prayer's capacity for reverence and resistance. Reverence refers to "a discerning and gracious acceptance of one's subordinate, contingent place within an ordered and hierarchical cosmos" (FitzGerald, *Spiritual Modalities,* 82). Enslaved men and women prayed to communicate with a divine God, to find strength to endure, and also at times to resist the institution of slavery. These functions of prayer were deeply intertwined: for an enslaved person to pray to God after being forbidden to do so by a slaveholder could be both a pure act of faith and a mode of resistance. Albert Raboteau describes this aspect of religious life in slave communities. He suggests that the act of prayer was itself an act of power, particularly when an enslaved individual was reprimanded for participation in a hush harbor gathering or prayer meeting. At times slaveholders allowed these types of gatherings, and at others they forbade them. As Raboteau writes: "Christianity, as slaveholders had all along suspected, was a double-edged sword. . . . Practicing religion could be for slaves an act of resistance—an assertion of independence that sometimes required defiance of the master's commands. . . Beatings did not stop slaves from praying, and these prayers were symbols of resistance" (*Canaan Land,* 58). Prayer meetings in slave communities engendered hope for enslaved people, and in so doing, they provided a new orientation toward the bondage of slavery, one that could both provide strength for disobeying in the present and the possibility of a new and different world in the future. In the long history of oppression against African Americans, prayer has served as an important mode of responding to that oppression by seeking God's help. As such, it has also offered African Americans a means of engendering rhetorical power, resisting injustice, and claiming freedom.

For enslaved people, prayer's reverence provided agency and opened up paths of subtle and overt resistance. These prayers are complicated by the entanglement of Christianity and colonialism, but still they help to show prayer as an important rhetorical resource.[4] One example that reveals this complexity and significance is "A Slave Woman's Prayer," written down in 1816 by Stephen Hays, a minister visiting upstate New York. In this prayer, the woman repents of wishing evil upon a slave holder and petitions the divine for joy in spite of her circumstances. She prays:

> O Lord, bless my master. When he calls upon thee to damn his soul, do not hear him, do not hear him, but hear me—save him—make him know he is wicked, and he will pray to thee.

> I am afraid, O Lord, I have wished him bad wishes in my heart—keep me from wishing him bad—though he whips me and beats me sore, tell me of my sins, and make me pray more to thee—make me more glad for what thou has done for me, a poor Negro. (19)

Contemporary readers may bristle at the woman's request for blessing the slaveholder or her contrite depiction of wishing him evil. Even so, for this woman, prayer can be seen as a spiritual help and a kind of subtle resistance. She positions her own voice and perspective as superior to the male slaveholder, and she uses her prayer, spoken aloud in a site that denied her humanity, to enact her dignity and wisdom before God, while also asking for her situation to be changed. In so doing, she resists and refutes the power dynamics at play between her and the slaveholder and claims divine power as her authority.

As enslaved people gained freedom and abolition gained traction, African American rhetors turned to prayer to advocate for justice on public platforms and in widely circulated texts. Rhetors such as Frederick Douglass and Maria Stewart capitalized upon the rhetorical powers of prayer to persuade others to help end slavery and to recognize the human dignity of Black people in the United States. For Douglass and Stewart, hybrid written and spoken prayers provided important avenues for appealing to the religious conscience of their audiences while also offering them, as marginalized speakers, a source of religious power from which to craft their ethos. In his *Narrative in the Life of An American Slave, Written by Himself,* Douglass weaves prayer into his story to prompt readers to think about how God feels about slavery and the enslaved individual. In the following passage, Douglass emphasizes that when he was a slave, the only audience to listen to his grievances was God and the ocean. He writes: "I have often, in the deep stillness of a summer's Sabbath, stood all alone upon the banks of that noble bay, and traced, with saddened heart and tearful eye, the countless number of sails moving off to the mighty ocean. My thoughts would compel utterance, and there, with no audience but the Almighty, I would pour out my soul's complaint in my rude way with an apostrophe to the moving multitude of ships" (37–38). In this passage, Douglass describes watching ships pass by and feeling compelled to speak with no one to listen but the Almighty or the ships. At this point in his narrative, Douglass is enslaved; for the slave, he suggests, imaginative speech to objects, the ships, and to God, provides an important mode of frank speech or *parrhesia.*

In a hybrid apostrophe-prayer, Douglass next calls out first to the ships and then finally to God: "You are loosed from your moorings, and free. I am fast in my chains, and am a slave! O, that I were free! O, that I were on one of your gallant decks, and under your protecting wing! Alas! betwixt me and you the turbid waters roll. Go on, go on; O that I could also go! Could I but swim! If I could fly! O, why was I but born a man, of whom to make a brute! The glad ship is gone—she hides in the dim distance. I am left in the hell of unending slavery. *O, God,* save me! God, deliver me! Let me be free! Is there any God! Why am I a slave? I will run away. I will not stand it. Get caught or get clear, I'll try it. . . . I had as well be killed running as die standing. . . . Try it? Yes! God helping me, I will" (38, emphasis added). This pivotal moment in Douglass's narrative shifts from apostrophe, shouting to ships in the distance, to prayer, crying out to God. He marks this shift out with the trademark generic feature of prayer, an invocation of address, "O, God" (FitzGerald, *Spiritual Modalities,* 53). Through the passages excerpted above, Douglass communicates with God and draws audiences into his brief moment of prayer. The prayer, woven tightly into the narrative, provides a turning point for Douglass's movement toward freedom. After asking God to save and deliver him, Douglass chooses to run away, thus positioning his prayerful plea to divine power as a source of his resistance and act of rebellion against the institution of slavery.

Like Douglass, abolitionist and women's rights advocate Maria Stewart relied on prayer's posture of reverence as rhetorical strategy. Also like Douglass, Stewart employed prayer in her abolitionist writings. Her spiritual narrative, *Meditations,* collects both prayers and speeches together to narrate her spiritual life. Besides these written prayers, Stewart also used prayer to bolster her ethos on the public platform. During her short speaking career in Boston, Stewart wove prayer into her public addresses regarding both slavery and women's rights. One example is her 1854 address, in which she calls women to activism through a speech laced with prayer. Her speech, like Douglass's *Narrative,* shifts into prayer somewhat unexpectedly with the call to the divine, "O, my God." She opens with directives to women before turning to prayer: "O woman, woman! Your example is powerful, your influence is great; it extends over your husbands and your children, and throughout the circle of your acquaintance. Then let me exhort you to cultivate among yourselves a spirit of Christian love and unity, having charity one for another, without which all our goodness is as sounding brass, and as a tinkling cymbal. And *O, my God,* I beseech thee to grant that the nations of the earth may hiss at us no longer! O suffer them not to laugh us to scorn forever!" (Stewart, "Productions of Mrs. Maria Stewart," 62–63, emphasis added). Prayer emerges in the middle of this passage, shifting from exhortation to women to petition to God. Through the petition, Stewart seeks the help of God for her cause. This prayerful appeal bolsters Stewart's ethos by positioning God on her side and by providing her a posture of reverence, a move that would have heightened her credibility before her audiences. This passage offers an example of a much larger pattern in Stewart's addresses. She turned to prayer often at the beginning and end of her speeches. Her *Meditations* include seven prayers in a collection of fourteen meditations (Bassard, *Transforming Scriptures,* 62).[5] By weaving lines of prayer into her speeches and texts, Stewart crafted her ethos by inhabiting the posture of reverence.

Prayer remained important to many African Americans in the early twentieth century as the Black church was institutionalized in the United States. Writing in 1927, for instance, James Weldon Johnson writes about the role of prayer in Black church services: "One factor in the creation of atmospheres I have included—the preliminary prayer. The prayer leader was sometimes a woman. It was the prayer leader who directly prepared the way for the sermon, set the scene, as it were. . . . These preliminary prayers were hardly less remarkable than the sermon" (*God's Trombones,* 8). As Johnson notes, as formal African American church services became a recurring genre, roles such as "prayer leader" developed to describe congregants who would compose and deliver prayers. While Johnson marks prayer's function as a lead-up to the preacher's performance, he views these moments in church services as equivalent to the sermon and underscores the ways this genre opens up possibilities for women.[6]

Some prayers in this period continued to explore the intersection of eternity and the social causes of the day. Written by W. E. B. Du Bois in 1910, the following prayer brings together the idea of conscience and activism:

> Give us grace, O God, to dare to do the deed which we well know cries to be done. Let us not hesitate because of ease, or the words of men's mouths, or our own lives. Mighty causes are calling us—the freeing of women, the training of children, the putting down of hate and murder and poverty—all these and more. But they call with voices that mean work and sacrifice and death. Mercifully grant us, O God, the spirit of Esther, that we say: I will go unto the King and if I perish, I perish–Amen. ("Give Us Grace," 105)

Summoning the power of biblical character Queen Esther, Du Bois prays for collective strength to act in response to the "mighty causes" of the day: women's rights, education, and racism. Like Reagon, Douglass, and Stewart, Du Bois recognizes prayer as a support for social change and mode of rhetorical activism.

As this brief survey indicates, by the mid twentieth century, Black activists had been turning to prayer for encouragement, strength, and a reverent identity for public protest since enslavement. Minister and scholar James Melvin Washington summarizes this tradition of Black prayer through a discussion of Adrienne Rich's concept of revolutionary patience (*Conversations with God,* xlvi). Through this term, Washington observes how prayer affords Black people a mode to express the tension between divine justice and worldly oppression. In this way, he writes, prayer fosters a revolutionary patience, one where people "assume that God is just and loving, and that the human dilemma is that we cannot always experience and see God's justice and love. We pray for faith to trust God's ultimate disclosure" (xlvi). At the same time, however, this revolutionary patience is not passive. Rather, it pushes prayers back out into the world to make change as they are able. Defining this circular nature of prayer, between a patient acceptance of the world as is and a revolutionary will to change it, Washington explains: "Prayer is an attempt to count the stars of our souls. Under its sacred canopy, an oratory of hope echoes the vast but immediate distances between who we are and who we want to be. This peculiar trek sentences its devotees to an arduous discipline. Prayer demands focus and obedience, as well as intimacy and faithful nurture. A certain civility is inherent in this transaction" (xxx). Washington emphasizes that African American prayers must be read against the historical racism and oppression of Black people in the United States. A universal, abstract understanding of Black prayer is impossible; rather, African American prayers express and explore what it means to live in a racist nation and "trus[t] that the Lord would make a way somehow" (xlviii). An extension of this tradition, the prayers of the mass meeting are remarkable examples of activists' creative, civil, and unruly engagement of a longstanding faithful genre.

"This thing is too big for Kennedy": Collective Dignity in Greenwood, Mississippi, in Winter 1963

In Greenwood, Mississippi, in 1963, collectives used the mass meeting to explore and practice taking up prayer as reverent resistance fueled by divine guidance and power. Through directed prayer, the group refined their identity as dignified political agents ready to disrupt peacefully. Prayer, like song and testimony, is a genre of spiritual transformation, and as such, to inhabit it is to "see[k] to become what [one] performs, recognizing that only through performance is transformation achievable" (FitzGerald, *Spiritual Modalities*, 75). In prayer, gesture is crucial to this constitutive work, for activists are transformed through the embodied reverence they perform. Rhetorician Cory Holding writes that gesture occupies the "shared spaces of action and invention," is "rhetoric-in-formation," and is both "fully embodied and fully relational" ("The Rhetoric of the Open Fist," 415). The gestures of prayer functioned as peaceful social actions and inventive enactments of identity. Through collective prayers, meeting participants sought to cultivate their identity as characterized by dignity, honesty, and peace. They developed and practiced this identity by listening to the speech of the individual delivering the prayer and responding with gestures, spoken prayerful refrains (for instance, "Amen" or "Mm-hm") and silence.

In 1963, Greenwood, Mississippi, was marked by intractable racism and coordinated, sustained white violence. Historians debate the core issues in play but agree that the state ranked first in white violence and stubbornness to change in the middle decades of the twentieth century (Dittmer, *Local People*; Hogan, *Many Minds, One Heart*). The Student Nonviolent Coordinating Committee (SNCC) moved into Mississippi in 1960 with considerable enthusiasm and hope for change. Just three years later, some fieldworkers, quite understandably, had worn down. For instance, SNCC organizer Bob Moses wrote to his Executive Committee: "The Mississippi monolith has successfully survived the Freedom Rides, James Meredith at Ole Miss, and the assassination of Medgar Evers. The full resources of the state will continue to be at the disposal of local authorities to fight civil rights gains. The entire white population will continue to be the Klan" (quoted in Hogan, *Many Minds, One Heart,* 144). Moses expresses his dismay at the depth of corruption in the state. This waning enthusiasm was not limited to SNCC leaders. Local activists too were discouraged. After three years of hard work, white violence against civil rights activists was worse than ever, and national attention to the Mississippi problem was lackluster.

At this crucial moment, in the fall of 1963 Moses and Allard Lowenstein devised the "Freedom Vote." The Freedom Vote was a mock election "designed to dramatize, especially to the federal government, that disenfranchised Black Mississippians would cast a ballot if given the opportunity" (Brooks and Houck 3).[7] This strategy also gave Black people and other activists a much-needed victory, as the campaign offered activists something they could *do* even as federal help was limited or nonexistent. Such a strategy proved extraordinarily effective: the campaign was an outright success and gained traction across the state. To keep momentum high, mass meetings focused on rallying people to go out and vote.

Speaking about Greenwood, Mississippi, Maegan Parker Brooks claims (in *A Voice That Could Stir an Army*) that one such meeting provided the context for Fannie Lou Hamer's first important address. While these addresses offer much insight into the rhetorical work motivating the Freedom Vote, the prayers in these meetings also illustrate how Black Mississippians continually developed their collective self-respect, rejecting ideas that they were unworthy of citizenship and replacing them with embodied discussion of their value and dignity before God. At this meeting held that fall, the directed prayer was delivered by a minister, Reverend Redd, and in response to his prayer, the collective rehearsed reverent postures and reflected together on the divinely inspired goals they sought.

The liturgy for this meeting emphasized freedom singing. The event thus begins and ends with several songs, with the only speeches including a brief sermon by the moderator, a local unnamed minister, and the prayer by Reverend Redd. The program for this meeting is as follows:

Songs: "Keep Your Eyes on the Prize" "Ain't Gonna Let Nobody Turn Me Around" "This Little Light of Mine"

Sermon: Moderator

Prayer: Reverend Redd

Songs: "Lord Hold My Hand" "If I Had a Hammer" "Freedom Train A-Coming" (Greenwood Mississippi Mass Meetings, Tape N60)

During the middle portion of the meeting, a moderator calls upon Reverend Redd to come and "open up like we always we do with a prayer." Before Reverend Redd prays, the moderator reads Galatians 6:7, "No man wants to reap what he sows." This verse, he claims, offers the crowd a way to respond to their white opposition. He says: "See our white brother have sowed so many bad seeds. And he don't want to hear it. That's why he's worried, trying to lock up a few people, but you tell him that I said to stop this movement he got to lock up God, and he can't do it. (Laughter.) . . . You know Negroes started this stuff two thousand years ago. . . . Don't worry yourself. This thing is too big for Kennedy. This is God's movement." Through this short Scripture lesson, the moderator establishes the purpose of Reverend Redd's prayer and sets the tone for it. With humor and references to the Kennedy administration, the moderator suggests that what is happening in Greenwood is "too big for Kennedy" and too powerful for white men to stop.

Reverend Redd picks up the themes established by the moderator. Through his prayer, he emphasizes the strength and will to freedom he has observed among Greenwood African Americans. He begins: "Let us bow our heads. Our Father in Heaven as we come humbly again before thy holy throne. We come with thanksgiving; we come thanking thee, Heavenly father, for the many blessings that Thou have granted unto us from our early existence in life up until this present moment" (Greenwood Mass Meeting Recordings, Tape N60). Continuing with the thread, "this thing is too big for Kennedy," Reverend Redd describes how God has been present to the Greenwood African American community since the beginning of the movement. His prayer reinforces a view of the movement as belonging to God. These first words also instruct the group to assume a position of reverence. Here, Reverend Redd defines the group's character: they are humble, thankful, and blessed. By naming these qualities of the group before God, he establishes the collective character of the group as dignified, reverent Christian people seeking God's help. As meeting participants listen in and pray along, they remember who they are *together* before God and agree with Reverend Redd's assessment of who they are. Through collective prayer, they reaffirm their commitment to the principal strategies of the movement: Christian nonviolence blended with democratic ideals.

Reverend Redd extends this opening image of the Greenwood group's character as he petitions God for help. Through his discussion of Greenwood activists' efforts and enduring service to civil rights causes, he speaks to God about their collective dignity: "Father in Heaven, bless these who are here tonight who came for freedom who are putting in every effort, trying in every way to achieve what is rightfully theirs. Have mercy on us tonight. Do not leave us, Heavenly Father, I don't care how hard the struggle gets or how hard the fight may be, stand on our side. We attempt to serve you in all ways. Help us to fight this battle. Give us the courage to continue. Don't let us stop until the victory has been won. In Jesus' name we ask these blessings and for his sake" (Greenwood Mass Meeting Recordings, Tape N60). Reverend Redd continues emphasizing the collective dignity of those gathered together. Through plural pronouns "us" and "we," Reverend Redd imagines how the group appears before God. He highlights how they are "putting in every effort," and they "attempt to serve" with all they have and demonstrates how they are indomitable fighters for justice and freedom. They love mercy, and they believe that their struggle is one that requires constant work, even as they believe it is God's struggle. Reverend Redd's prayer reveals how speaking to God serves to define the character of the group, shaping their ethos and fostering their political agency.

William FitzGerald describes this character formation aspect of prayer as a "space of rehearsal." He writes: "One can regard prayer as having this precise purpose: to shape character by orienting performers to present and future action by manifesting a communicative self" (*Spiritual Modalities,* 23). In this way, we see "prayer function as a space of retreat and recalibration in which aspects of communication and performance (such as *ethos* and agency) are 'worked out' through *practice.* Prayer is a space in which rhetoric is tested and true" (23). Through the retreat and recalibration that prayer avails, the group in Greenwood inhabits prayer to practice how to speak, act, and be in a state infamous for persistent racist corruption and violence. In enacting their collective identity as blending qualities of reverence and resistance, Reverend Redd and meeting participants practice postures of peaceful unruliness. The discussions of their humility and subordinate position before the divine emphasize peace and reverence. Through petitions for God's help, they look forward and affirm their will to resist injustice through necessary disruptions and unruliness as they participate in the voter-registration drive.

Prayer on the Move: Rhetorical Perseverance
in St. Augustine, Florida, May 1964

So far in this book, the mass meetings I have examined have taken place in a designated space, most often a church. Yet these events were not always discrete or hidden from view. At times, the meeting provided the starting point for a collective to move out into the streets for a public march or other performative protest, or the group would return from a protest into a church building and then initiate a mass meeting. The tension between meeting-as-intimate-activist-space and meeting-as-protest-event is the subject of chapter 5 and will become important in chapter 4 as well. Here, my focus is on a mass meeting that transitions into a march in St. Augustine, Florida, and the role that prayer plays in facilitating this fluid movement from church to street. Indeed, prayer functions as a way for the collective to coordinate their protest, in this case a "night march," and to assert the nonviolent, reverent terms for the demonstration to one another and segregationists waiting in the streets. Analyzed alongside the Greenwood example, St. Augustine activists' performance of reverent resistance reveals the unruliness of prayer on the move and the radical civility of nonviolent action.

Civil rights marches, as public protests, performed the new world activists were seeking. According to Lisa Corrigan, the marches functioned as "both chronopolitical and spatial challenges to segregation. . . . The march, as a movement tactic, put the *move* in *move*ment as a way of embodying a different kind of chronopolitics that moved from (white) nostalgia for a calcified past to a newly emergent, dynamic (black) future" (xxi, emphasis in original). An embodiment of a more just future, the civil rights march, like the mass meeting, was often framed by activists through the lens of theology or faith. For marching, prayer often provided the frame. The clearest example here is the 1957 Prayer Pilgrimage for Freedom, the national prayer march held in Washington, DC, led by Martin Luther King Jr. The mass meeting studied in this section offers a smaller scale example of prayer-as-march, in which the mass meeting provides the rhetorical scaffolding that supports this public protest. Prayer, as a genre dependent on gesture and a clear image of reverence, was well-suited for coordinating movement, embodying peace, and signaling a new future. One could march and pray at the same time, captured well in Abraham Heschel's recollection of marching at Selma: "My feet were praying" (quoted in FitzGerald, *Spiritual Modalities*, 115).

In the case of the St. Augustine march studied in this section, prayer described and informed the march, designed to disrupt racist practices in the town and bring national attention to white supremacist violence. This meeting-to-march occurred in an especially volatile moment in St. Augustine. In spring 1964, the Florida city became the site for the next major campaign of the Southern Christian Leadership Conference (SCLC). St. Augustine received the SCLC's attention because of its economic position. One of the nation's oldest cities and a site of tourism, St. Augustine was a site of excitement and planning as white community leaders looked toward summer 1965, a moment intended as a quadricentennial celebration for St. Augustine. Officials expected festivities to bring significant economic gains for white business owners. These hopes for a successful tourist season provided civil rights leaders with leverage for negotiations. White leaders, however, continually refused their demands, and the Ku Klux Klan (KKK) escalated tensions through organized meetings and threats to National Association for the Advancement of Colored People (NAACP) leaders. In the midst of these negotiations, a member of the civil rights community shot and killed a Klansman as an act of self-defense (Fairclough, *To Redeem the Soul of America*, 179–82).

Responding to this chaos, the SCLC targeted St. Augustine. Given the recent shooting, the SCLC's planning included a strategic push to re-center nonviolence. Writing to activist Hosea Williams, Andrew Young of the SCLC explained: "I share with you very strongly that the St. Augustine movement must visually pull the nonviolent thrust of the Negro back on center . . . Somehow we must re-capture the moral offensive so that it cannot be suggested that the nonviolent resolution has become surly, irresponsible, and undisciplined" (quoted in Fairclough, *To Redeem the Soul of America*, 182). Prayer would play a central role in a "moral offensive." Tactically, the plans included workshops, weekly mass meetings, and the boycott of white businesses. From this plan, the SCLC along with local leaders initiated a series of night marches. In the event studied here, the night march operated as a prayerful protest launched directly from the mass meeting. The night marches were a particular tool that "magnified the likelihood of a violent confrontation," "designed to provoke the white militants, draw attention of the media, and bring outside pressure on St. Augustine to desegregate" (Fairclough, *To Redeem the Soul of America*, 184; Colburn, *Racial Change and Community Crisis*, 3). Given the extreme danger of participating in this type of protest, it makes sense that leaders sought to center the march in prayer and harness its peaceful postures and spiritual power. One activist claimed, we "feared for our lives every time we went" (quoted in Colburn, *Racial Change and Community Crisis*, 4). Prayer, as reverent resistance, enabled work toward the twin purposes of anchoring the group's identity in nonviolence and offering extra measures of courage and strength for enduring a violent response.[8]

For this meeting-to-march in May 1964, the group began the prayerful night march from their meeting in St. Paul's African Methodist Episcopal (AME) church, with the portion of the event in the church building focused on learning how prayer would inform the march. In the church space, the moderator opened the meeting by explaining the purpose of the march. He exhorts the group to see the march as a performance of their dignity, strength, and righteousness: "Stand up in dignity . . . march on with a sense of strength and fortitude . . . hold your head high and show the world the power of righteousness" (Recording of Mass Meeting and March). The moderator works to inspire and motivate the collective to participate in the dangerous night march. Reminding the group of their dignity, strength, and righteousness, the speaker echoes the themes heard in Reverend Redd's prayer in the previous section.

After the moderator's opening exhortation about the significance of the march, Young begins a pedagogy of prayer, a moment within the church space where he provides explicit instruction that spells out how they will be marching and praying at the same time: as they march, they will all pray. These instructions emphasize prayer as a mode of rhetorical perseverance, a discursive and embodied resource for pursuing nonviolent action no matter the costs. Similar to directed prayer, this prayerful pedagogy functions to teach about prayer's capacity to shape nonviolent action and then closes with an "Amen," indicating that people joined their faith with Young and agreed with the terms he sets out. Young explains that prayer offers a mode of response to violence and a way to embody reverence through posture and gesture: "I don't care what happens. We want you all to remain nonviolent. I don't know how often you pray, but I want you to pray tonight. I want you to pray especially for anybody that looks mean at you or anybody that curses you or spits at you. If somebody throws something at you, it doesn't make any difference. Hold your head straight ahead. Utter a prayer in your heart for them. And let's stay very silent. Let's stay nonviolent. Let's have a quiet and very dignified march" (Recording of Mass Meeting and March). Since the march was designed to provoke white opposition, leaders like Young sought to teach protestors how to use prayer to steel themselves and respond peacefully. Prayer's flexibility and clear ties to nonviolence made it well-suited for this function: people could silently pray, close their eyes, or simply put their head down. This range of possible ways to pray and march promoted nonviolent action and embodied reverence at once.

The embodied reverence performs a kind of radical civility, a performance Young explains must be motivated by love. The night march by design served as a disruption to the logics of white supremacy and thus was intended to initiate unruliness in the streets. Yet defining the march as a prayer, the group agreed their responses would be loving and nonviolent. Continuing his instructions, Young expanded the moderator's description of the purpose of the march and its relation to prayer: "We believe that we shall overcome. But we won't overcome by trying to be as mean and hateful as . . . as our enemies. If we overcome, it will be overcoming through love. Now I want you to walk quietly, and I want you to pray. If anybody curses you, you walk straight ahead, and say a prayer for them. If anybody says any kind of mean word to you, I want you to pray for them. If anyone should throw something at you or spit at you, pray for them. If anything happens, don't even look evil at them. All right, let everybody say, Amen for me. (Amen) Amen! (Amen!) All right" (Recording of Mass Meeting and March). Explaining how prayer embodies what he referred to elsewhere as the "moral offensive," Young teaches the group to expect hatred and violence from the white people gathered but to see prayer as a mode of peaceful resistance. Prayer performed in this way gives rhetorical texture and power to nonviolent action. Rather than encourage the group to say or to do nothing in the face of violence, Young teaches them to use prayer's discursive and gestural resources to steel themselves against oppression.

Continuing his role as prayerful pedagogue, Young leads the group out into the streets to begin the prayer march. Here, the group prays collectively and silently and then also prays along with Young's directed prayer. Out-in-the-streets, Young leads the group in two kinds of prayer. First, he leads them in silent, collective prayer, where activists are prompted to use prayer to deliberate about their decision to participate in the march. Second, he leads them in directed prayer performed before continuing the march into the targeted area, a slave auction block, where a KKK group had already gathered. Young begins: "I'd like to ask that we all bow our heads for a minute. I'd like to ask again if we could be perfectly quiet. If each person could pray silently in his heart whether or not you are ready to go on. Let us pray" (Recording of Mass Meeting and March). The group turns to prayer, out in the streets, to deliberate about their will to continue marching in the protest. They use the resources of prayer to explore their convictions about proceeding. In the quiet of shared prayer, and their remaining together, they reaffirm their group identity and their will to mine prayer's capacity for peaceful disruption.

Next, Young leads the remaining group in directed prayer. This prayer, performed in the street immediately before the group marches together toward the slave market, brings together all the threads of prayer as reverence and resistance. Young prays:

You have called us to be thy sons and thy daughters. We come before thee like empty pitchers before a full fountain, confessing our fears, confessing our doubts, and yet knowing dear God that Thou has ordained us to be sons and daughters. We ask you this evening for courage, we ask you for strength, for wisdom, we ask you dear Father, melt our hearts, mold them in thine image, give us the strength of the prophets of old. Give us the strength and courage of children and adults in all ages who have stood their ground in order that man might be free. We would pray, dear Father, for those that would stand between us and our freedom. For we know they are not to blame, we know that they are only saying and repeating those things which they have heard for generations and which we have silently adhered to. (Recording of Mass Meeting and March)

As Young prays, the marchers listen in and affirm together their commitments to their identity: courageous, strong, wise. Before God, and before a violent white community, the St. Augustine marchers remember they are claiming freedom and their pursuits are not in vain, even if they are not realized immediately in the march they perform. Rather, through prayer, they position their marching in a different temporal frame, one that looks back and lays claim on Christian and democratic promises to demand change now and looks forward to a certain changed future. In looking forward, as they march, they call on King's assertion that "marching feet announce that time has come for a given idea. When the idea is a sound one, the cause a just one, and the demonstration a righteous one, change will be forthcoming" ("Nonviolence," 132).

Young's prayer not only images reverent resistance and demonstrates how prayer enables the group to persevere, but it also saps spiritual power from the white supremacist opposition. By praying for "those that would stand between us and our freedom," Young creates a moral arc of justice to describe their literal and figurative movement: activists march toward justice and freedom with white supremacists serving as unjust and unwise obstacles. This narrative move reiterates the spiritual end of the march and its certain victory, while also claiming righteousness before God and rejecting white opposition's claims to faith.

Overall, prayer enabled a fluid transition between the intimate space of the mass meeting and nonviolent protest in the streets, while also centering events in language, tone, and gesture that conveyed the collective as peaceful and spiritual. If through prayer in the meeting a group rehearsed their dignity, honesty, and righteousness, then the genre could resonate in these same ways as they moved out into the streets. This aspect of prayer might be seen as a kind of felt payoff for rehearsal, where a group garners emotional effects from prayer as the genre also helps coordinate bodies and position them to be read as reverent, dignified, peaceful protestors. Generally then, the meeting-to-march made rhetorical use of prayer's capacity to demonstrate reverent resistance and to offer spiritual terms for interpreting the violent response that occurred in the streets. As a strategy of a moral offensive, prayer held the group together as it also provided an undeniable, yet still resistant, image of peace.

Prayer's Reflective Capacities: Americus, Georgia, 1963

Turning to the final mass-meeting scene of the chapter, Americus, Georgia offers another look at the relationship between prayer in the mass meeting and prayer in public protest, but in this case, an unsuccessful moment in this local movement. On August 17, 1963, Black citizens and civil rights workers in Americus, Georgia, staged a march from the church where mass meetings were usually held across the town to the City Hall. Similar to St. Augustine, prayer in Americus was intended to play a central role in this protest. A meeting leader instructed the folks gathered to the plan: "This is what we're going to do now. We're going out the back door . . . and you're going to City Hall, you're going to kneel and pray, and you're going to pray until they carry you in. All right, all right, so walk in twos down to City Hall and pray and stay there" (Americus Mass Meeting Recordings, Tape AM 1.2). The desired goal was demonstrating to white Americus officials and residents that their civil rights activism had not waned, and prayer was the intended strategy for carrying out this campaign. Despite this clearly laid out plan, this protest did not go well. Very few people attended the protest after they had assured the leaders they would be there. Because few people marched, the campaign that day was executed poorly. In the mass meeting held directly after this march, the event centered both on reviving prayer as a protest tool and instructing the group in how to employ prayer effectively. Toward this aim, the meeting is structured around songs, discussions of prayer and its relationship to protest and freedom, and periods for both silent and discursive prayers.

The political objectives for civil rights organizing in Americus were in line with the other 1960s campaigns studied in this chapter: exposing white supremacist terror and violence, promoting voter registration, and fully desegregating public spaces. In Americus as elsewhere, activists understood these goals through a broader, spiritual vision of justice. As historian Ansley Quiros puts it: "In marching down the streets of Americus, protestors claimed they were children of God. In waiting in registration lines, they fashioned themselves as the children of Israel wandering in the desert before entering the Promised Land. In enduring beatings and humiliations, they took on the mantle of Christ at Golgotha. In languishing in fetid jail cells, they imagined the sufferings of Paul and Silas in a Roman prison centuries earlier" (*God with Us*, 81). In the weeks immediately preceding the mass meeting studied here, Americus activists' beliefs were tested as their city became the subject of national dialogue. After leading direct action protests, four civil rights workers were jailed on charges of insurrection, a capital crime according to Georgia law. Georgia's Anti-Treason Act dictated that "anyone arrested for attempting to incite rebellion against the state could be put to death" (Quiros, *God with Us*, 101). Don Harris, Ralph Allen, and John Perdew were arrested on this antiquated charge after leading a nighttime march, and then a week later, the group became four when Zene Aelony received the same charge after initiating a prayer demonstration at a police station. Referred to in news coverage as the "Americus Four," this group remained in a Georgia prison until a federal trial in October. They were eventually cleared of the charge, and the intervention through the federal courts was a win for civil rights activists over the longer term. However, Quiros explains: "The harsh indictment succeeded in impeding the movement by taking away its leaders and instilling fear" (*God with Us*, 109). In the words of SNCC fieldworkers, after this ordeal "the many big and little pieces of the movement drifted apart and a lot was lost in the immediate effect of the August demonstrations and in the long range strength of the movement in Americus" (quoted in Quiros, *God with Us*, 109).

Occurring shortly after Harris, Allen, Perdew, and Aelony were charged, this August 17 mass meeting offers insight into the role of prayer in this difficult moment in the Americus movement. As African Americans and allies coped with obstacles familiar to civil rights activists across the South—cruel and obtuse law enforcement, white hatred and violence, and waning energy to keep the spirit of the movement going—they turned to prayer as a resource for reflecting on what to do next when their movement was in trouble and a protest had failed. It made sense for the mass meeting to center on prayer given its role in the failed march and its centrality to the Americus movement generally. Quiros observes: "Prayer was 'vital' to the theological Civil Rights movement in Americus" (*God with Us*, 101). Those gathered together in the meeting were the very activists who did not show up for the prayer march, and no doubt, many were afraid to protest after recent events. At this meeting, the moderator (unnamed in archival records) sought to persuade participants to continue enacting prayer as activism. Then, through the times of silent prayer, he sought to provide opportunities for them to look back and understand what had been happening in the Americus movement.

In the silent prayers, the group reflects on the protest and why it failed. The reflection here, in line with Frierian praxis, was geared toward renewed action (Friere, *Pedagogy of the Oppressed*, 87). As both a means of fostering deeper awareness of oppression and taking steps toward changing their situation, the moments of silent prayer provided participants with a site for reflection on movement goals and strategies, even as it functioned too as their contrition for failing to act in ways consonant with those ideals.

After the songs that opened the meeting, the crowd grew silent for a few moments, waiting for directions on how to proceed. The meeting leader began his instructions by connecting prayer to larger movement goals. He suggested that their march failed because too many of them are still afraid: "We really need some bodies. We need you. We need some bodies. We *really* need some bodies. Like the people that just left here . . . they proved that they weren't scared of nobody. That they really wanted their freedom. Sing louder, 'Do we really want our freedom?' It won't be long brother, before men like you, decide to put your body on the line like those children did. It won't be long. This is no joke. Everybody in this church really means business" (Americus Mass Meeting Recordings, Tape AM 1.2). These opening instructions emphasize that the Americus movement depends upon courageous activists who will enact embodied, prayerful protests. The moderator wanted them to be present with him praying on the steps. As he makes clear that embodied protest is crucial to enacting freedom as their goal, he also gently chastises those who did not choose to participate in the protest held earlier that day. In this opening discussion the group is reminded of their overarching goal—freedom—and the strategies necessary to achieve it—courageous, embodied protest in public. At the same time, they are prompted to begin reflecting on why some of them fell short of their goal and did not attend the protest.

This initial discussion of their goals and strategies paved the way for scaffolded instructions on how to pray to change the direction of the movement and to revive activist participation in direct action. The leader moves from reflection on the failed prayerful protest to calling for the crowd to shift into a time of prayer. He suggests that praying now, in the meeting, will change how they act in public. The leader continues: "You gotta act like you want freedom . . . You know prayer changes things. (Yes it will.) Prayer changes things. Sometimes we can see ourselves when we're praying and after our prayer. We can sometimes see ourselves. It's time we look at ourselves now. We point at other people; it's time we look at ourselves now. I think we need prayer in this church bad, and we need it now . . . That's everybody here, kneel down" (Americus Mass Meeting Recordings, Tape AM 1.2). In this instruction, the leader explains how they can mine prayer collectively.

Participants probably recall the hymn "Prayer Changes Things" as they listen and reflect. The leader defines prayer here as a means of contrition and rhetoric of collective transformation. As the "we" pronouns indicate, the leader is calling for everyone present to sit in silent reflection on their failure. This silence then must prompt their collective change in action. Through prayer as contrition, they renew their commitments to courageous public protest. Where traditionally contrition operates as an individual's confession and repentance for sin, in this meeting contrition provides the group with an opportunity to reflect on their collective failure to move toward greater freedom in their town through their marching. Prayer creates an opportunity to repent together and to turn away from the day's ineffective protest. It is a chance to "change things" by "seeing themselves" as they really are. In this way, the leader has framed prayer as a type of praxis, reflection that must inspire further action. This praxis-prayer time enables the group to parse out what past actions show their desire for freedom most clearly and which past actions might have distorted or impeded their quest for that desire.

The leader's directions are important in shaping the prayers of the group toward continued action. Rather than simply move to silent prayer, the leader continues speaking and instructing the crowd while they are kneeling down. He walks them through what they should contemplate in their prayers. In this way, the time of prayer works through the silence and contemplation of the group in conjunction with the leader's promptings. For example, after the leader directs the crowd to kneel down, he claims that they must first address God to request forgiveness: "Ask God to forgive you, to help you, to make you stronger . . . ask God to help you make up your mind that you want to be free, help you to say it like you mean it, you want to be free, help you to fight" (Americus Mass Meeting Recordings, Tape AM 1.2). This instruction in how to move from contrition to petition reveals how the leader scaffolds the crowd's prayers. He directs them in how to go to God and find spiritual strength for failure and to find further strength for future embodied actions. This direction prompts the group praying to see contrition as a step toward renewal and repentance—toward new modes of action.

The prayer time at this meeting fosters silent contemplation as a resource to be leveraged toward movement goals. Scholars Tina Campt, Cheryl Glenn, Anne Ruggles Gere, and Gesa Kirsch have written about the powerful possibilities that silence, quiet, and contemplation avail. Glenn and Gere, for instance, argue that silence operates in reciprocal relationship with speech and offers significant rhetorical resources (Glenn, "Unspoken," 7; Gere, "Revealing Silence," 207). Glenn puts it persuasively: "I argue for silence as a rhetorical art, one that can be as powerful as the spoken or written word. . . . As a constellation of symbolic strategies [silence] serves many functions" (18). Kirsch agrees, writing that silent contemplation, coupled with spirituality, enables rhetorical agency. For Kirsch, contemplation and reflection provide important modes of engaging with "complex social, political, and ethical problems" ("From Introspection to Action," W11). In the Americus meeting, prayer is the genre that enables silence and quiet to foster spiritual engagement with the most pressing social, cultural, and political issues facing African Americans in southwest Georgia.

Periods of silence punctuate the pauses between the leader's instructions. In these silences, it is likely that many in the group, kneeling in the church, offer up prayers to God. Drawing on the work of Richard L. Johannesen, Glenn names twenty functions of silence; number eleven, "The person is in awe, or raptly attentive, or emotionally overcome," offers insight into the meaning of the group's silences during this prayer time ("Unspoken," 16–17). The silence affords space for attention to feelings about the movement, whether fear or discouragement or desire. The leader periodically interrupts the silence to interject more instruction. After a period of quiet, he begins: "Just think, all those kids went down on the mall. And yesterday, Thursday night, you knew, I told you. . . . I asked how many people want their freedom? Who is willing to go out [on the] town now? Everybody jumped up. Everybody was willing to fight then, everybody was willing to go downtown" (Americus Mass Meeting Recordings, Tape AM 1.2). Creating moments for contemplation on what happened that day, the leader reminds the group that they had promised to march and pray with him, subtly calling to mind the fact that they broke their promise. During this time, activists encounter what Campt writes about as "a form of quiet where gnawing questions simmer and send one searching for more complicated answers" (*Listening to Images,* 18). Quiet pauses afford the group space to contemplate before God and one another why they were not willing to participate and seek divine help for continuing activist work in Americus.

In providing direction for the group's silent prayers, the leader at times punctuates the silences with layered questions and statements that instruct meeting participants to feel shame and guilt. Shifting from questions the group should direct at God, he directs questions at them: "We're supposed to be freedom fighters, I mean freedom fighters! Ask yourself, Are you a freedom fighter? I don't know, Do you feel guilty? Do you feel bad seeing those people walk down there and you not being with them? Do you feel bad? (Yes) You should feel bad. (Yes sir.) You should feel bad" (Americus Mass Meeting Recordings, Tape AM 1.2). In this moment, the leader prompts the group to use the prayerful silence to experience shame and guilt.[9] He repeats the questions to reinforce his disappointment in their actions and to prompt them to move into a specific "bad" emotional state before God. The image of the group kneeling silently as the moderator speaks to them brings to mind the power dynamics of prayerful rhetorical situations in the meeting and beyond. All of the directed prayers in this chapter have been delivered by men with church titles or authority within the movement. The silent prayers of groups in response to authorities' direction can be read as, to a certain extent, imposed upon them. As Glenn writes: "The question is not whether speech or silence is better, more effective, more appropriate. Instead, the question is whether our use of silence is our choice (whether conscious or unconscious) or that of someone else" ("Unspoken," 13). While in this Americus meeting the leader does not explicitly tell the group they must be silent, as moderator he has the authority to make decisions about how the prayerful portion of the meeting unfolds. Overall, he uses this power to encourage them to mine prayer's resources for a path forward for their movement. In this moment, however, his instructions veer into prompting the group to feel ashamed and guilty and serves as a reminder of how silent prayer can shift from source of spiritual power to imposition.[10]

After creating moments for silent prayer to consider the day's events, the leader exhorts the group to turn from contemplating the past to silent prayers about how they might begin to act in new ways. Interjecting another exhortation, the leader shifts the group's thinking to how they might move from reflection on their fear and failure to how shared suffering and equality provide strength for their actions: "Never turn back. Actions speak louder than words. Those kids were willing to go to jail. If others can go, I can go. One person suffers, I can suffer. How many people think they're better than those kids? None of us. We're equal. It was God who created all of us to be equal. We gotta realize it. All these boys over here. All the girls over here. Right there, right there" (Americus Mass Meeting Recordings, Tape AM 1.2). In the silences, the crowd considers how collectivity—shared action and suffering—provide spiritual strength. Moving away from ideals of divine protection, the leader instead urges everyone to consider how equality offers them a resource for action even while protection from harm cannot be guaranteed. The knowledge that before God all people are equal should encourage their willingness to suffer together if necessary. At this point in the Americus movement, the leader realizes that contemplating protest may call to mind the Americus Four being held in jail under threat of the death penalty. Instead of asking to be spared suffering, the leader suggests that the group must expand their spiritual understanding to embrace it as part of their activist philosophy.

Once the leader finishes exhorting the group in how to pray and think about prayer as inspiring their action, the remainder of the meeting moves through more silent and also sporadic or extemporaneous prayer. The leader structures this portion of the meeting by instructing everyone to kneel and encouraging all types of prayer: silent and spoken. If an individual wants to speak (or sing) prayers, that's fine. The others should just pray along silently: "Everybody kneel and pray. Whoever want to lead a prayer, lead. Somebody's going to lead a prayer, lead. Just really pray. Now you can really pray. Prayer changes things. Let us kneel. On our knees" (Americus Mass Meeting Recordings, Tape AM 1.2). As the first example in the chapter indicated, in many meetings ministers or other individuals lead a formal, directed prayer while everyone listens and silently prays along. This Americus meeting, however, functions differently. The leader never moves from instruction in prayer to actually praying; instead, he offers everyone an opportunity to pray, whether silently or aloud. While he does provide significant direction for their prayers, the leader does not speak the prayers himself and instead urges the meeting participants to voice the prayers of the group. A woman responds and sings a prayer to God, and then the group sings a hymn-prayer together. These musical genres close the meeting.

Conclusion: Prayer as Faithful Genre

In an interview, Ralph Abernathy was asked to describe his response to the bombing of the Sixteenth Street Baptist Church in Birmingham, where four little girls—Addie Mae Collins, Carol Denise McNair, Carole Robertson, and Cynthia Wesley—were murdered. Abernathy explained that he stepped away from his pulpit at West 100th Street Church in Atlanta to take a phone call when he received the news. He recounts his dismay and sadness and then having to resume his preaching and leading of worship: "I returned to the congregation and called for prayer, prayer for the families of these beautiful young girls who had been slain, prayer for their slayers in the spirit of love and the spirit of nonviolence" (Abernathy, Interview, 15).[11] Abernathy's prayerful response to the Sixteenth Street Church bombing reveals a complicated aspect of love and nonviolence as an activist identity: the turn to reverence in the very face of violence and terror. Reverence, understood as acceptance, is perhaps most difficult to grapple with, no less perform, in the wake of unspeakable tragedy (FitzGerald, *Spiritual Modalities*, 82). Abernathy's recollection is a reminder, however, that civil rights activists returned again and again to prayer to persevere and hold on to faithfulness, as an identity and a movement belief. The meetings reconstructed in this chapter offer insights into the ways collectives of civil rights activists rehearsed and performed prayer as peace and resistance at once. Prayer provided a step into a reverent posture of faith and love regardless of circumstance or the action of their oppressor. In this way, many believed prayer's reverence resisted not just through social or public disruptions to racist structures and ideologies, but also, on a theological level as a move toward a different ontological and kairotic reality: in prayer as response to terror, activists entered "a different time zone, a different realm of existence," and they did so through body, speech, and silence (Washington, *Conversations with God,* xxxiii). In this sense, the genre is unruly not just as a disruption to racial norms but also a disruption to public, secular space and time. Prayer afforded activists with a genre useful for rehearsing and enacting peace regardless of circumstance and performing faithful resistance. This capacity for paradox was also a useful way to facilitate rhetorical movement. As the example of St. Augustine indicates, prayer tactically functioned as a gestural transition from the mass meeting into protest in the streets. In public spaces, prayer offered collectives felt resources of resolution while also serving a clear image of embodied peace.

Civil rights prayers, like the freedom songs, diminished in activist power over the course of the 1960s. Activists began to interrogate prayer as a mode of protest by 1966, and indeed for others no doubt these questions had been simmering all along. For example, in the 1963 Greenwood meeting examined in the chapter, after Reverend Redd's prayer, the moderator of the meeting speaks at length, telling jokes and Bible stories to get audiences ready to sing. Toward the end of his remarks, he closes the speech by recounting a conversation he had with someone in the community: "And another one said I tell you, you ought to tell those young folks not to pray. And I say no let us old folks pray. Let those young folks fight" (Greenwood Mass Meeting Recordings, Tape N60). This remark is brief, and he offers no context, but still, it is telling. Even in 1963, prayer's function as resistance was being called into question. As a genre associated with "old folks" on the sidelines, some activists saw limited possibilities for prayer as protest. The moderator's words suggest that prayer as a mode of resistance may not have ever received unilateral acceptance among civil rights activists in Greenwood. By 1966 Stokely Carmichael urged activists to abandon the genre altogether: "No more long prayers, no more Freedom songs, no more dreams—let's go for power'" (quoted in Carawan, *Freedom Is a Constant Struggle,* 8). The turn to Black Power meant leaving behind not just the freedom songs, but also prayer, two of the genres most important to the mass meeting's liturgical structure and to performance of nonviolent direct action. Like the freedom songs, prayer was so closely associated with Christian nonviolence that a turn away from this activist ideology meant a turn away from the genre as well.

FOUR

Speaking Truth in Love

Testimony in Hattiesburg, Mississippi, and Danville, Virginia

annie Lou Hamer is remembered as one of the most outstanding civil rights orators. In her first speech on record, Hamer tells her story. As a Black woman in the Mississippi Delta, she experienced intimidation after her first attempt to register and vote and violence in Winona, Mississippi, while traveling with other civil rights activists. These experiences, she asserts, will not stop her from working for Black freedom, and fear of retaliation should not stop others either. She charges her audience to join her in remaking the Delta, offering her own life as an example of the possibility and the risks. As she puts it: "It's no easy way out. We just got to wake up and face it, folks. And if I can face the issue, you can too. . . . It's poison for us not to speak what we know is right" ("I Don't Mind My Light Shining," 4). Hamer urges the Black people gathered at the Williams Baptist church to recognize that they can, like her, "wake up and face it," and speak and act for justice, a pursuit that according to Hamer should improve all areas of Black life in the Delta: poverty, the Black church, policing, and enfranchisement. At the heart of this vision and this charge is Hamer's testimony, her experiences of injustice, activism, and the consequences of speaking out for Black freedom.[1]

Significantly, the mass meeting provided the setting for Hamer to testify to these experiences and to cultivate her speaking career; after all, it was at a meeting just a year earlier that she joined the civil rights movement. These events by design offered opportunities for local people, like Hamer, to take these first steps into collective participation and rhetorical performance, and testimony played a key role in this process as an opening for ordinary individuals to test out and refine their rhetorical skills and democratic knowledge before one another. Activist and leader Bob Moses explains the importance of testimony at the meeting in this way: "People learned to stand up and speak. . . . The meeting itself, or the meetings, became the tools. . . . People were feeling themselves out, learning how to use words to articulate what they wanted and needed. In these meetings, they were taking the first step toward gaining control over their lives by making demands on themselves" (quoted in Polletta, *Freedom Is an Endless Meeting*, 69–70). Moses points out that through their standing up to tell their experiences, people explored language that named their situations and created collective stories about their desire to create change. As his description conveys, the meeting opened opportunities for everyone to participate in this kind of rhetorical praxis, not just featured or outstanding speakers.

This chapter takes up the question of testimony's role in the meeting liturgy and explores how individuals and collectives understood and inhabited this genre to divergent ends. While Hamer's testimony is certainly remarkable, her example is a reminder that the meeting was intended to encourage all those gathered to stand up and speak, to share their stories with one another, and in so doing, to catalyze their identities as agents of change in their communities and to encourage one another to do the same. The meeting liturgy often included a dedicated time for testimony, taught as both a sacred and a free-form genre for story and experience. This portion of mass meetings might feature a sequence of planned testimonies or might include a time for extemporaneous testimony, where anyone can stand up and testify, tell their story, and explain what is on their mind. The time for testimony thus invited individuals to take turns participating in the liturgy through sharing stories or naming experiences. Through their testifying, local people like Hamer narrated their sense of God in their lives; they shared what it was like to participate in direct action for the first time; they found words for the problems they saw and explored possible solutions; and they observed together how interlocking systems of oppression operated in the places where they lived and worked. Broadly, they explored word and story as sites of transformation and experimented with their own language and narrative frames for their places and experiences. Testimony thus relied on a shared platform, where all people who attended meetings were encouraged to speak.

Toward these ends, the mass meeting capitalized on testimony as a "fuzzy" genre to provide space for people to speak truth and describe experiences, feelings, and perceptions, spiritual or otherwise, and then through this speech to gain sacred and faithful frames for making sense of them and piecing them into a collective story about loving Black people in pursuit of justice. Fuzzy genres are understood as genres with permeable boundaries and a range of possible social actions (Medway, "Fuzzy Genres and Community Identities"). Testimony, as it is practiced in the meeting, is highly flexible and usefully imprecise in terms of its features, functions, and its relationship to faith and liturgy.[2] For individuals standing up to explain a desire for change or an observation related to white supremacy, the openness of the genre empowered speakers to feel their way toward language that suited their experience; whether that language turned on faith or ignored it was no matter. In the meeting, people could shape testimony for themselves, dialing up the faithful dimensions or minimizing them in favor of other generic features, and this flexibility expanded the genre's activist potential and its heuristic and transformative power. It encouraged people of all ages to speak up because it was not difficult to learn or navigate; one could not get it wrong. The constitutive power of testimony as well as its generic endurance can be located in its continued malleability.

For individuals delivering testimony, the genre's features, functions, and actions are helpfully fuzzy. Yet through the liturgy and the framing around testimony, civil rights leaders taught and modelled testimony in a tradition that Hamer exemplifies, testifying as telling the truth in love (Brooks and Houck, "Introduction"). On the individual level, then, testimony affords openness and flexibility, while on the collective level, truth-telling (*parrhesia*) and love hold it together. Testimony thus functioned as a genre for individuals to forge their activism on their own terms and for the group to craft themselves as a collective of truth-tellers motivated by love. While the textures of the individual stories people shared varied widely, their delivery in the mass meeting enabled them to be woven together into a collective account oriented toward these broader aims of the civil rights movement. Testifying as truth-telling demonstrated resolve and courage as a way to create evidence of a different kind of world, one exemplified through the mass meeting where spiritual love bound the community together and violence had no place. Testimony structured a transformation from meeting audience member to civil rights activist speaking truth to power in a loving collective.

This chapter attends to testimony as a fuzzy faithful genre through attention to its role in two mass-meeting scenes. In Hattiesburg, Mississippi, in 1964, Charles Sherrod and Lawrence Guyot guide the portion of the mass meeting allotted to testimony, during which some twenty local African Americans of all ages and a few visiting white ministers offered testimony. The next mass-meeting scene I examine is from Danville, Virginia, in 1963. In this meeting, leaders address diminished participation in organizing and action, inviting those gathered to testify to their experiences.

Testimony in African American Rhetorical History

Scholars of rhetoric have explored the rich history of testifying and testimony in the African American rhetorical tradition, and their work provides the groundwork for the investigation I take up in this chapter. Since Geneva Smitherman's work in the 1970s, rhetorical scholars such as Jacqueline Jones Royster, Shirley Wilson Logan, and Rhea Estelle Lathan have defined and analyzed how testimony operates as a genre of activism. Smitherman viewed testimony as an important mode of Black communication and provides important insight for defining the genre and considering the actions it enables. For Smitherman, testifying entails

> a ritualized form of black communication in which the speaker gives verbal witness to the efficacy, truth and power of some experience in which all blacks have shared. In the church, testifyin is engaged in on numerous symbolic occasions; newly converted ex-"sinners" testify to the church congregation the experience of being saved, for instance, or on Watch Meeting Night, New Year's Eve, when church folk gather to "watch" the old year go out and the new one come in—they testify to the goodness of the Lord during the past year. A spontaneous expression to the church community, testifyin can be done whenever anybody feels the spirit—it don't have to be no special occasion. (*Word from the Mother*, 58)

As Smitherman points out, testimony emerged as a faithful genre, "a spontaneous expression to the church community." The Black church supports and enables testimony because of its long history as a space where congregants are encouraged to tell stories. As she also observes, testimony, while historically encouraged by the church, also takes place in broader contexts.

These two key insights are important for my work here: first, the mass meeting affords activists a churchlike space to speak up about their experiences—ordinary and extraordinary—in the movement for Black freedom. Walking down the aisle of the church to speak up at the meeting was not so different from walking down the aisle to confess one's sins or to testify to "having the Spirit." In this way, the mass meeting works as an important catalyst for the testimony of local individuals not accustomed or experienced in speaking up about racial injustice in front of audiences. Second, as Smitherman argues, testimony is not always overtly religious even as it is supported and rooted in the context of the church. Thus, while the churchlike space and meeting pattern helps foster testimony as a faithful genre, the mass meeting also provides the context for individuals to deliver testimonies not specifically or apparently about faith or issues of religion.

Smitherman's definition serves as the foundation from which much other work follows. Rhea Estelle Lathan builds on Smitherman's work and argues for understanding testimony at the intersections of secular and sacred and to see its central purpose as naming solutions. According to Lathan, testimony "is a communicative, literate practice with nonmaterial dimensions including faith, hope, courage, willingness, humility, unconditional love, perseverance, open-mindedness, awareness, vigilance, self-discipline, sharing, caring, and service" with its key purpose being "to empower by communicating valuable, life-giving, life-changing solutions" ("Testimony as a Sponsor of Literary," 41, 34). Taken together, the definitions of Smitherman and Lathan show that testimony operates broadly, across secular and sacred spaces, as a mode of making meaning from Black experience, rooted in the church tradition.

Historians and religious scholars emphasize that what Lathan describes as the purpose of testimony—the creation of a life-giving solution—resists white supremacy in two significant ways. First, according to Rossetta Ross, testimony "cast(s) everyday life as sacred by asserting divine intervention in ordinary circumstances" (*Witnessing and Testifying*, 13). Ross uses the term "the ritualized mundane" (13) to describe the way that testimony asserts divine intervention in ordinary life. The ritualized mundane names the way that people suffer daily, ongoing oppression and remake their trying experiences into narratives that are shared, meaningful, and powerful. Put differently, testifying provides a mode for reseeing one's experience as a resource for rhetorical action as it also makes this experience shared and thereby validated. Historian Kidada Williams speaks to the second way testimony fosters resistance through an emphasis on witnesses. She writes: "Testifying about racial violence was a crucial factor in African Americans' individual recovery and their collective resistance to white supremacy because whenever victims related their experiences of this violence, they created witnesses to their trauma" (*They Left Great Marks on Me*, 5–6). Williams notes that testimony has played a crucial role on the individual and collective level for African Americans resisting white supremacy. As she emphasizes, people generally first turned to family members, friends, and neighbors to deliver testimonies about experiences with violence, but others sometimes turned to other forums. In the civil rights movement, the mass meeting was one such forum. As a context similar to the church service, the mass meeting provided the space for individuals to inhabit testimony and testify to God and everyone present about their experiences in the movement and the prejudice, violence, intimidation, and other forms of racism they experienced.

From the beginning of the African American rhetorical tradition, Black rhetors have inhabited testimony to the powerful, memorable, and efficacious ends described by Lathan, Smitherman, Ross, and Williams. For enslaved African Americans in the eighteenth and nineteenth century, testimony forcefully spoke to the state's legal subjection of them and denial of their humanity. The narratives of Olaudah Equiano, Mary Prince, Harriet

Jacobs, and Frederick Douglass, among others, created an important counterargument through their testimony: by circulating the testimony of the violence and inhumane treatment they received as enslaved African Americans, they participated in abolishing slavery by drawing attention to their experiences with the cruelty and injustice that permeated the institution. For instance, Logan recounts how William Lloyd Garrison often whispered, "Tell your story, Fred," as Douglass walked to the podium (quoted in Logan, *Liberating Language,* 73). Logan writes that the effect of these testimonies was "in creating a *presence* of slavery" (73, emphasis in original). She argues that for Douglass as well as Sojourner Truth, personal testimony coupled with enactment "becomes a major source of appeal" (73).

Besides these rhetors' testimonies against slavery, other African Americans leveraged testimonies toward resisting forms of white oppression that emerged in the aftermath of the Civil War, as well as arguing for women's rights and education. Many of these rhetors took to the platform to deliver their testimony. Exemplary here are Sojourner Truth, Ida B. Wells, and Nannie Helen Burroughs. Still others wrote essays in which they drew on the significant power of testimony to create a sense of self and truth. Royster writes: "These writers have a particular regard for testimony and bearing witness, acts that blur in provocative ways the lines between logical arguments and pathetic and ethical ones. Testimony, for example, as it credits proximate experience, sets in motion the opportunity and obligation to actually give the testimony, or as it is typically phrased, to bear witness" (*Traces of a Stream,* 67). Royster is concerned with how testimony helps writers fashion themselves for audiences in authentic ways; such self-fashioning, she writes, provides epistemological resources for these writers as well. By focusing on testifying to an experience, African American women created avenues for powerful truth-telling as a mode of activism.

As this overview illustrates, the African American tradition is rich with examples of how testimony serves as a genre widely useful for rhetorical activism. This overview also points to one of the unique functions of testimony as a faithful genre—unlike freedom songs and prayers, its religious dimensions can be muted. It is a flexible genre that is rooted in and shaped by the African American religious tradition but that is not always overtly or explicitly religious. Extending and adapting this tradition, civil rights activists inhabited testimony to explore word and narrative as steps into the movement and a group identity. In the mass meeting, leaders helped participants to shift from audience members in seats to activists standing up and speaking out about their experiences with police brutality, disenfranchisement, poverty, and the evils of life under segregation. This shift further affected change in the listeners: as they saw their fellow community—ordinary men and women, boys and girls—stand up and testify, the rest of the group gained deeper awareness of the ubiquity of white oppression and their collective will to resist it through agreed upon campaigns. Through testimony, they forged their group as truth-telling people speaking up for justice because of their deep love for one another and those around them.

Hattiesburg, Mississippi, 1964: Truth, Love, and the Fuzzy Edges of Testimony

Reflecting on his vision for Black freedom, minister and Student Nonviolent Coordinating Committee (SNCC) leader Sherrod quotes the book of Romans in the Bible: "Nothing can separate me from the love of God in Christ Jesus, our Lord" (English Standard Version of the Bible, Romans 8:38–39). Sherrod explains: "What it meant was that nothing but death could stop me from the mission that I had of developing our people. . . . If they could promote violence among us, then they could break us. But these young people they could not break . . . if we confronted them with love" (Sherrod, Interview, 2, 4).[3] The 1964 Hattiesburg, Mississippi, mass meeting studied in this section reveals testifying as an important mode of loving confrontation. Here, Sherrod teaches those gathered in this meeting how to engage these ideals through the practice of testimony. Confronting with love simply means speaking the truth about experiences and telling stories about injustice. African Americans and allies take turns responding to Sherrod's invitation to stand up and testify to what they have seen. As a collective, they practice using testimony to confront in love, speaking the truth before one another. Individually, this testifying offers each speaker an opportunity to explore language and narrative that catalyzes agency and forges civic identity. For everyone gathered, they gather deeper knowledge of the widespread and varied forms of oppression shaping their places and lives and their sense of the courage and strength found in the collective they have cultivated.

While Sherrod's teaching reveals testimony as a mode of confronting with love, the testimonies delivered make clear the openness of the genre, the fuzzy edges that enable divergent features, functions, and uses. Fuzzy genres, according to theorist Peter Medway, are genres characterized by malleable boundaries and varied purposes. Medway's study, "Fuzzy Genres and Community Identities," focuses on the architectural sketchbook, and he finds that while the genre has shared functions, it resists typical generic status in key ways: it does not have a definitive name or a recurring social action, and it is only loosely connected to the community and institution. Like the sketchbook, the features, functions, and social actions of testimony are imprecise. Its clearest and most significant purpose is crafting one's self, and its self-making capacities are heightened by its fuzziness. Because of, not despite, the flexible nature of testimony, people found ways to explore how to speak as a truth-telling activist. Through their testimonies, activists dial up the spiritual inflections of the genre to share their belief in God's power in their work. However, they also mute these explicitly faithful features to narrate their daily, sometimes mundane, experiences while protesting or to explain their own sense of and experience with entrenched racism in their town. Across the varied testimonies in the meeting, people feel out and compose their activism, exploring language that names who they want to be and the injustice they have experienced across their lives. They experiment with truthful language and narrative that coalesces with the loving vision of change that leaders like Sherrod set out. Testifying, practiced in this way, creates a collective of activists who speak both truth and love, possess deep awareness of the realities of racism, and are committed to change.

In the early 1960s, Hattiesburg was an important site for the work of the Council of Federated Organization (COFO) in Mississippi. SNCC workers viewed Hattiesburg as key to creating change in race relations in the southern area of the state, a region where many rural counties went unaffected by civil rights gains made elsewhere. Located near the coast, Hattiesburg differed from the Mississippi Delta towns of Greenwood and Greenville. Where Greenwood and Greenville were marked by intransigent racism and stark economic disparity between impoverished African Americans and white plantation owners, Hattiesburg Black people were less poor, and whites' resistance less strident. Perhaps the presence of universities such as the University of Southern Mississippi and William Carey helped combat the vitriolic racism that characterized so many other areas of the state (Dittmer, *Local People*).

These qualities notwithstanding, Hattiesburg was far from a beacon of racial equality. In John Dittmer's words: "Still, Hattiesburg was a segregated city, and blacks suffered from lack of economic opportunity, poor schools, and inadequate city services. Above all, in denying blacks the right to vote, Forrest County circuit clerk Theron Lynd put his Delta counterparts to shame" (Dittmer, *Local People*, 179). An investigation by the Justice Department found that Lynd had allowed no Blacks at all to register in his first two years as circuit clerk. Lynd was subsequently the target of several federal suits, including *United States v. Lynd* in 1962 (United States of America vs. Theron Lynd).[4] This suit required federal courts to protect Black voters from Lynd's efforts to keep them from registering (Dittmer, *Local People*, 179–80). Such federal attention further drew the interest of SNCC organizers to Mississippi's southeastern city.

In Hattiesburg, like Albany and other cities in the South, organizers made major gains after securing the support of a local church, St. John's

Methodist Church. As one activist puts it: "That's really where the Hattiesburg movement started. It started for all practical purposes in St. John's
Church in Palmer's Crossing" (quoted in Dittmer, *Local People,* 181). St.
John's Church provided the institutional base as the site for mass meetings
and signaled support from local African Americans.

In January 1964, a new wave of COFO activity took this organizing to
the next level. Inspired by new federal injunctions against Lynd as well as
the success of the Freedom Vote in other parts of the state, Bob Moses and
Lawrence Guyot planned a Freedom Day demonstration to call national
attention to Lynd's refusal to comply with court orders. The Freedom Day
was planned for January 22. This demonstration was designed to extend the
voter-registration efforts already taking place. The idea was that on this Freedom Day, rather than having one or two African Americans go to the courthouse to attempt to register to vote, large numbers of local Black people
would march to the courthouse together and try to register. At the same
time, other supporters would set up a picket line outside the courthouse
to protest the unjust practices of the circuit clerk (Dittmer, *Local People,*
219). This strategy confronted Hattiesburg whites as it also would serve as
a symbol to other local African Americans: "such a show of strength would
'give heart to other blacks' who were afraid to make the registration attempt
alone" (220).

The evening after the first day of the Freedom Day protest, some 250
people gathered for a mass meeting that included songs, prayers, and (most
notably) a lengthy period of testimony. The group included some fifty white
ministers from states outside Mississippi; COFO had invited outsiders to
Hattiesburg to garner attention from the national media. At this invitation,
the National Council of Churches recruited a delegation of white clergy
to join the protestors. Other important civil rights leaders also joined the
group from other parts of the movement. Hamer, Sherrod, John Lewis, and
Ella Baker all came in for Freedom Day and some were present to help lead
this mass meeting. During the period of testimony, twenty people—Black
and white, male and female, ages 12 years to elderly—stood up and delivered testimonies. Some of these individuals took the opportunity to speak at
length; others spoke for only a few minutes. People described their feelings,
their hopes, their ideas, their fears; they testified to the significance of what
they saw happening in their city. In so doing, they forged and catalyzed
their activism and created a diverse, vibrant collective story of the loving,
truth-telling activists gathered in Hattiesburg. To highlight the divergent
functions of the genre in the meeting and its fuzzy edges, the remainder of
this section will focus on the use of testimony in the event, beginning with
Sherrod teaching and leading testimony.

Speaking Truth in Love

In the January 23 meeting, Sherrod and (later) Lawrence Guyot carefully structure and guide the time for testimony. Sherrod opens the audience speaking part of the program as gentle pedagogue, empowering the audience to see how telling a story is both easy and significant, both truthful and loving. Then he scaffolds the testimony, designating times for different groups to stand up and speak; he begins with Black student activists, moves on to the older Black Hattiesburg residents, and finally invites the white ministers to speak. This instruction is key, for through it Sherrod models and teaches testimony as a mode to speak truth and love, and he helps make the genre feel cohesive, even while people use it for different ends. The framing keeps the genre familiar, and this familiarity is important for self and group making. As Medway writes: "Others can understand us—we can understand ourselves—because we recognize as familiar the sort of thing that is being done" ("Fuzzy Genres and Community Identities," 149). Sherrod and Guyot also draw the diverse group together around the shared goal—continuing demonstrations in Hattiesburg—and pulling meaning out of the personal narratives shared to show how through their truth-telling, each individual contributes to the larger goal and is part of the story they are making. In this way, each Hattiesburg participant learns to see themselves as one activist participating in a collective, interracial group protest that is changing their town. Sherrod's moving instruction invites the crowd to "start talking together" and to listen to one another:

> Let's talk together. The only way we can be successful in this movement is to be together. And they are saying now, what we are gonna do, is let 'em demonstrate a couple of days. Let 'em get it out their system. They don't know how long we've had it in our system. It's gone take a *long* time to get it out of our system. One thing we've got to do. That is, to start talking together. How many of us live in Hattiesburg? Raise your hands. All right. Now I'm going to ask you to do something easy. Raise your hand one more time to one other question.
>
> How many of us were downtown today? Beautiful. Now take about 3 people over here, 3 people here in the back. And I guess about 2 people here. Come up, those who feel strong enough, to stand up and come up here and tell what you saw downtown today. Just tell what you saw downtown. And if you want to say anything else. Say it. If you want to say what you think we ought to do, you say it. Say what you feel. Now what we got to do, listen. I don't want no talking you know. Everybody got to listen to what *this* person gonna to say.

Now can we get a volunteer from the first three. Who over here want to stand up and tell what you saw. Just tell what you saw.

Speak up loud and clear like you ain't scared of nobody 'cause you want your freedom. (Hattiesburg Mass Meetings Recordings, Tape N74)[5]

"Talking together," Sherrod explains, is key for sustaining their protest over the long period of time that will be necessary to create the changes they seek. Through his instructions, Sherrod encourages the group to see testimony as a flexible, accessible genre with a simple, clear feature: telling the truth about what happened that day. This emphasis on a direct, clear feature for their speeches is a helpful cue to the young people that they all have something they can say simply because they participated in the protest, as indicated by their show of hands. While Sherrod emphasizes the simplest feature, he opens the genre up to "anything else." If there is something someone wants to say, they should say it, whatever it might be. This framing thus simplifies the genre to an accounting of the day's events but also accommodates infinite other features. If the speaker wants to share memories, hopes, or dreams or practically look forward to what the collective will do next, Sherrod teaches the speakers to tell this truth too and the audience to listen and to understand.

Throughout the remainder of the evening, Sherrod helps the entire crowd learn what it looks and feels like to talk together. As the collective testimonies make clear, the activists gathered are keen to tell their truth and not just the simple version about what they saw during the day's protest. Indeed, the group takes Sherrod at his word that they can say anything and speak their minds about not only their experience of the day's events but also why they need to protest, what it means to protest, and a range of other kinds of stories, including one older woman who shifts her testimony into preaching and exhorting the group. Sherrod and Guyot do not cut anyone off or direct them back to just describing their experience of the day. Rather, they encourage everyone to listen to one another, and through their framing, work to validate and draw together the variety of ways people inhabit testimony.

Ritualizing the Mundane

After instructing the audience on what to say and how to listen, Sherrod cues the first young person to stand up and speak. This move generates energy for the rest of the evening; many student activists are eager to stand up and share. Eight young people, including a sixth grader, respond to Sherrod's teaching and invitation to stand up and explain how it felt to march downtown. They talk about being afraid at first, or even remaining afraid, but they see the protest as exciting and worth the discomfort. Here, for instance is the sixth grader who leads off the evening, whom the audience cheers for (referring to him as "Big Boy"):

> I was in the bed this morning. Some fellows came by [the] house. They said, "Are you going downtown today?" I said, "I don't know man. I been planning on it, but I'm scared." And, really, I was scared.
>
> I went by the office and saw everybody getting picket signs. I said, "Where you going?" [They said] "I'm going downtown." I said, "Well, I will wait and see how many more go."
>
> [Someone said], "Come on let's register." [I said,] "You know, I mean, sign my name and tell where I'm located before I have to go to jail or anything." He said, "Naw man, I'm fixing to go, come on, let's go." So I went and registered and got my sign.
>
> I started downtown, and I got halfway. I turn around. . . . I saw another group of people coming uptown. So I went uptown. I got uptown and I saw the cops. Cops said, "Where you going?" and I said, "To the courthouse." They said, "You can't go this way. You gotta turn around and go back." So I turned around and went back. I came up that way. The cops said "Where you going?" and I said, "To the courthouse," and they said, "You can't come this way. You gotta turn around and go back." Bob [Moses] said, "Come on, and I'll take you to the courthouse." I got to the courthouse and I saw cops standing on every corner, a lot of people marching and singing.
>
> I joined in and I marched and sang too. I think everybody feels the same way. (Hattiesburg Mass Meeting Recordings, Tape N74)

Big Boy's testimony, full of humor and excitement, sets the tone for the testimonies of the students. He speaks simply, telling the truth about what happened during his day of protesting. The crowd offers hearty laughs as Big Boy recounts the police's attempts to thwart their marching. Testimony serves Big Boy as a way to catalyze his rhetorical potential. Through his marching, he took a public stand for freedom and his desire to act as a citizen in his town, and then through his testimony before the meeting audience, he explores the rhetorical capacities of citizenship that are analogous to this public stand—speaking the truth about who Black people are in Hattiesburg in this moment. To testify about his day, Big Boy dials down the religious dimensions of testimony in favor of pure narration that moves quickly from one event to the next without analysis or interpretation.

This testimony exemplifies the dominant feature of the first few student speeches: simple narration of the day's protest. Like Big Boy, the first several speakers do what Sherrod instructed, delivering straightforward accounts of their experience in the campaign. These speakers describe encounters with policeman, feelings of fear, and other struggles. They also celebrate their pride in standing up for freedom in their town together and call attention to the excitement of the day. These plainspoken, direct accounts of the day enable the young people to take advantage of testimony as "ritualizing the mundane." Through telling their stories, they recognize the significance of quotidian civic participation and mine its extraordinary potential to change their place and their lives. They parse out what might seem ordinary: marching and picketing. Rather than just sitting and listening to leaders like Sherrod tell them that their actions matter, they inhabit testimony to name this significance themselves in language that resonates with their experience. This invitation to testify, then, helps them to recognize that the day was in fact very important as a step toward freedom, particularly enfranchisement, and then to hone their rhetorical competencies for speaking the truth about their will for citizenship.

Consciousness-Raising

Other students' testimonies move beyond simple narration of the day's events and reveal another feature of testimony: naming the ways segregation restricts their civic opportunities and relies on an unjust code of behaviors that affects Black life in Hattiesburg. In this way, testimony functions as consciousness-raising, or speech that generates new awareness about how deeply entrenched racism is in their town. In rhetorical history, consciousness-raising is a practice often associated with second-wave feminism. As Karlyn Khors Campbell defines it, consciousness-raising is to "make the personal political: to create awareness . . . that what were thought to be personal deficiencies and individual problems are common and shared" ("The Rhetoric of Women's Liberation," 79). One important site for this practice is the speak-out, where individuals stand up and share stories, and others recognize themselves as part of the collective. For example, Tasha Dubriwny writes about the Redstocking's speak-out, an event that centered on abortion, and reveals "a collaborative process of persuasion based on individuals' lived experiences" ("Consciousness-Raising as Collective Rhetoric," 398).[6] This time of testimony in the meeting might be viewed as similar to a speak-out, as people not only narrate their experiences protesting, but they also, as in the example that follows, reflect on their experiences with segregation and injustice. Through their testimonies, individuals bring these experiences before one another, deepening everyone's understanding of the breadth of racial oppression in their place. Through their will to tell the truth about it, they also catalyze their agency and refine rhetorical modes for remaking their lives through collective direct action and civic participation.

One young woman, for example, delivers an eloquent testimony explaining how she is beginning to see her own problems as part of a bigger narrative:

> Today after school I went downtown. The main reason was I wanted to see what a real demonstration was. When I got there, what I saw made me almost cry. I had been reading a book on Frederick Douglass, the father of the protest movement. I remember how he had been beat by these people. For nothing. Only because his skin was dark. This made me feel very bad. And so I said, if my friends can do it, so can I. These people are here to help me, so why don't I join in too. I wasn't permitted to go until after school. Even after school, I went. And to me, I saw William Lloyd Garrison, Frederick Douglass, and John Brown all marching. (Hattiesburg Mass Meeting Recordings, Tape N74)

Like Big Boy, this young woman describes her marching downtown, highlighting the emotional experience of protesting. At first, she was curious and even a little afraid of protest, but then once she tried it for herself, she was moved by the collective power of their group and the strength she felt with others. She astutely draws connections for the audience too with references to her reading, further dignifying the work of the marchers and picketers by comparing them to William Lloyd Garrison, Frederick Douglass, and John Brown. In taking Sherrod up on the invitation to speak, she adds another dimension to the accounts of the day's protest as she imbues their work with meaning and significance.

Yet this young woman also goes beyond direct narrative of the day to speak about racism as she has seen and experienced it. Here, she reflects on her family's experiences with discrimination across domains of life. Speaking about the white domestic sphere, she explains to the audience how segregation and discrimination inflect her mother's work:

> The things that have been said to my people. My mother, she works in a white man's kitchen. This woman talked to my mother like she's just anybody. I dislike this. I work myself after school. I am trying to get an education because I really want one. . . . I want people to talk to me like I talk to them. And the only way that I think that I can ever achieve this is by joining in and trying to help my people instead of laughing and saying, "I'm kinda scared." I will be [there] tomorrow. I can't go down until after school, but after school, I'll be there. (Hattiesburg Mass Meeting Recordings, Tape N74)

In this portion of her testimony, she tells the truth about how white people treat and speak to her mother. She names this treatment as a systemic and perpetual problem, one that will surely mark her life and work. As she explains, unless they collectively intervene, she will continue receiving this kind of treatment and condescension herself, and other Black people can expect to as well. Through this speech, then, she finds language for the racism she has seen and experienced, and she begins connecting it to the work of the movement in Hattiesburg, recognizing that through her participation, she can make change in her town. This testimony and others like it take advantage of story as a frame for renaming and thus reclaiming experiences with oppression and discrimination. As Dubriwny writes: "one way oppressed groups rename—and hence create new meaning from—their experiences is through the articulation of those very experiences" ("Consciousness-Raising as Collective Rhetoric," 396). In finding language for the day's protest and the experiences that motivate it, this young woman forges her identity and participates in the creation of their collective story.

Like Big Boy, the young woman participates in the meeting as a speaker, standing up before her community and testifying to what she has experienced. For all the young people, the performance of testimony cultivates their rhetorical repertoire: speaking up about what they see happening in their communities. These testimonies in the meeting, as the group delivers and listens to them, refine and expand the civic practices they are acquiring through the movement in Hattiesburg. Through Sherrod's instruction and the supportive faces in the audiences, participants explore story and language as powerful resources, that like picketing and marching, can change their identities and their town. In standing up and telling their experiences, young people learn to see testifying as another mode of direct action. For the young woman speaking about her mother's treatment at work, this truth-telling is just as important as what is happening in the streets. In the meeting, she gains practice in speaking up, connecting her speech to direct action and the broader systemic issues they are working to address. This speech, in this way, functions akin to direct action and protest. As Kidada Williams argues: "Black people's proclaiming their traumatic experiences to family members, friends, neighbors, civil authorities, civil rights organizations, and state and federal officials represents an unappreciated form of their direct action protests against racial violence" (*They Left Great Marks on Me,* 6). For many of the young people, their testimony in the mass meeting may be the first time they stand in front of an audience and craft a narrative that effectively challenges white supremacy. Activist Georgia Gilmore acknowledges this as an important aspect of the mass meeting: "Well, I attended just about all of them [mass meetings]. I was really very interested in it because you could go and you could learn about so many things that you didn't know exist, and so many people would tell you how they was being mistreated and they were glad that they were able to come out and not have to take the same treatments that they once had taken and was afraid to admit" (Gilmore, Interview, 7). Testimony provided a key way for people to share experiences of mistreatment, and in so doing, bring deeper awareness to the group as they also cultivated their rhetorical capacities for speaking up about what they have endured and their will to change it.

Weaving Testimonies Together

Like the young people who speak the truth about Hattiesburg, the older Black community are also invited to stand up and speak. Sherrod organizes this transition and sets the stage for another group of testimonies. In this instruction, he applauds the young people for coming up to share their stories, emphasizing the difficulty in testifying. Then he works to help everyone come together across age difference to recognize the power of this collective. He begins:

> Now what has been said . . . what the young people been saying is that they are ready to move. But they need the help of everybody. We all got to get into this. You see how the young people stepped up here. I didn't pull them up here, I said anybody who want to come, come on. Ain't nobody pull them up here. Plenty more people out there wanted to talk too. Plenty of them would talk. Now, what the young people, and what the old people need, now the old people are getting what they need, they need the young people to stand up and say they're ready. And you know the young people need some of us older persons live in Hattiesburg to come up and do the same thing that they been doing. To come up and say that we ready. Now we can't let our young people down. Now can we? (Hattiesburg Mass Meeting Recordings, Tape N74)

To frame and extend the time for testimony, Sherrod begins with summative statements about the stories shared so far. These stories, as Big Boy and the young woman exemplify, varied widely, from simple stories of the day to reflections on past experiences with racism. Yet Sherrod brings them together here in his framing, saying that what the testimonies collectively reveal is a desire for change and the courage to make it so. This concluding statement serves as a rhetorical pivot to call on the older people in Hattiesburg to tell their truth as well. Sherrod argues that to realize the young's people desire for change, the entire community will have to participate, irrespective of age, and one of these kinds of participation is testifying. As he tells it, the young and old people need one another; their group identity depends on Black people, young and old, coming together to protest and to testify before one another about what they have seen, during the day's campaign, and especially for the older group, throughout their lives.

Before inviting the older people up to the platform, Sherrod expands his discussion and definition of testimony. He shifts into explicit minister language and explains that standing up to testify is like a conversion experience, where to come up from their seat in the audience to the front and tell their story demonstrates faith in God and their will to make Hattiesburg different:

> Now I know some of you people, I heard someone over there say, that's right. Gave it a Amen. I heard a whole lot of more Amens all over. So I know you're getting ready. But get outta that seat. It's like a *conversion.* You know when the preacher stands up here and says, Whoever will let him come. And take over. Take up his burden and follow the way of the cross. This is the way of the cross. (That's right) This is the way of the cross. And nobody can come over there and pull you out of your seat and make you walk this long mile. It's a long mile from there to here and many of you have never stood up here and talked. You think these children have ever stood up here and talked before? They could hardly stand over there in that school, in that thing they call school over there and say what they feel. Can't even stand up in Sunday school and say what they feel.
>
> But in the mass meetings is the place where we can stand up and say what we feel. And this is the time to do it. Can't wait until tomorrow. That's too late tomorrow. We got to do it tonight. Tonight your soul will be required in paradise. Tonight, you know the story, I don't have to tell you the story, you been here longer than I have. Taught me the story. The only difference is some others of us are trying to believe those stories that you taught us. (Hattiesburg Mass Meeting Recordings, Tape N74)

To catalyze the older group's testimony, Sherrod appeals to their faith, defining coming up to testify as an expression of spiritual commitment to the movement. He explains walking up from their seat as following in the example of Jesus. Calling on language from the gospels in the Bible—"This is the way of the cross"—Sherrod frames testimony as speech that catalyzes and reveals new identity. As this theory goes, people of faith participate in the Black freedom movement: it is to follow Jesus. People who are Christians and part of the movement have to tell stories that demonstrate that they have indeed been converted. The language of conversion thus describes the path from one's seat in the meeting to the platform to testify, offering everyone a sense of the magnitude of speaking in the meeting and of how it serves as an identity shift moment. The second biblical reference, "Tonight your soul will be required in paradise" comes from the gospel of Luke. Sherrod refers here to a verse that appears in a parable about a young rich ruler. This man has power and possessions, and when faced with a call to follow Jesus, cannot give them up. As the parable is told, God speaks to the rich man and says, "Fool, this night your soul is required of you, and the things you have prepared, whose will they be?" (English Standard Version of the Bible, Luke 12:20). Sherrod weaves this reference in to reinforce and extend the conversion theme. Following Jesus requires sacrifice, a willingness to sacrifice all power and possessions and to walk into an unknown future, in search of a new, mysterious identity. From these theological inflections as a rationale for their testimony, Sherrod closes by reminding the older people of the wisdom and knowledge they hold. It is the older Black people in Hattiesburg who most intimately know and understand their place, and the group needs to hear this wisdom. Sherrod thus works to empower them to see their experiential knowledge and its significance and to share it from a position of faith.

From Story to Exhortation

People in the audience respond to Sherrod's invitation and stand up and tell their stories. The longest testimony from this portion of the evening, and from the entire night, is delivered by an African American woman. She begins like everyone else by describing her experiences with demonstrating, focusing on her own attempt to register to vote. Then she shifts into narrating her philosophy of the movement and how she understands change to happen:

> Most of all I prayed to God last night and this morning asking him to open our hearts and help us to see ourselves and see God's word that God died for all men to be free and the only way that we will be able to see God's face, that we must fellowship here one with another. It's no divided place. It's no two heavens, and two hells . . . (Hattiesburg Mass Meeting Recordings, Tape N74)

Following Sherrod in using spiritual language, this speaker "verbally acknowledge[es] and affirm[s] the power of a greater being" (Lathan, "Testimony as a Sponsor of Literacy," 41). She also uses this discussion to provoke her audience to consider the universal aspects of the Christian faith presumably shared among many in the crowd. By explaining that heaven and hell will not be segregated, this speaker creates a powerful exhortation for her audience. If heaven and hell are not divided, it follows that divine authority and scripture authorize the freedom they are demonstrating for; they are working to make the changes they believe are mandated by the faith they hold to. Her testimony dials up the spiritual features of testimony, drawing from both Christian practices and commonplaces, and then in closing, the Bible.

This speaker also takes rhetorical advantage of testimony's malleable boundaries to shift from story-telling and experience-sharing to preaching and exhortation:

> The Scripture says we must love those that despise and misuse us, no matter how hard and how tough it is, we must still love and treat them right. But what we are trying to get is rightfully ours. We are not trying to take anything that doesn't belong to us. Because God died so that we might all have freedom. (Hattiesburg Mass Meeting Recordings, Tape N74)

The shift this speaker makes at the end of her testimony, from telling her story to exhorting her audience, is important. In the nineteenth century, some abolitionist leaders such as William Lloyd Garrison policed the boundaries of Black testimony. Garrison, for instance, encouraged Douglass to stick to his story and to avoid shifting from testimony to argument. Douglass felt that Garrison's advice limited his ability to deliver more effective and persuasive performances, and they eventually split over this issue (Logan, *Liberating Language* 73). As the passages about Sherrod's instruction and the testimony indicate, SNCC leaders taught testimony as a free and open genre, offering audience members the opportunity to tap its fuzziness and say anything they wanted to. The leaders emphasized that they share an experience as a starting point, in this case participating in a demonstration, but they also left open and indeed encouraged the possibility that an audience member might shift from testimony into exhortation, as the woman mentioned above does. This openness empowered speakers to truly feel their way into activism, to craft activist selves who told stories, explored problems, and encouraged and exhorted the group to action or developed theological frames for understanding movement work.

Testifying Across Race

Testimony operates cross-racially in the meeting, as the white ministers stand up and speak as well. Guyot takes the lead to facilitate this transition from local African Americans to the final group of the evening, the visiting white clergy. In his instruction, he picks up on a thread introduced by one of the teenagers. In this young woman's testimony, she referenced that she saw "many priests" marching but not as many African Americans. Guyot clarifies her point, noting that by priests, she likely meant white men and was referring to the large group of white ministers visiting from out of state:

I think everybody should talk. I would like to say I heard the remark of one of the young ladies that she was very hurt when she saw the priests, or I think what she wanted to say but didn't know quite how to handle it, was the white man fighting for the freedom of the Negro. And I'd just like to say that people fight in this human struggle for human rights. I think what we should do is listen to some of these people. I'd like for any of the ministers to at this time have anything that you would like to say. Perhaps you can select three from your group to do so. (Hattiesburg Mass Meeting Recordings, Tape N74)

Thus, like a good teacher, Guyot uses a comment of one of the student activists to highlight the importance of the white ministers' presence. This presence, he argues, shows them something important about the movement, that it is a "human struggle." Behind Guyot's remarks lies a controversy in SNCC. The question of how much white outsiders should participate in the Hattiesburg movement was a much-debated question and one that would eventually lead to splintering within the organization (Hogan, *Many Minds, One Heart*). But for the moment, Guyot threads the young lady's comment with his own argument that it is important to have support from white ministers and that this group should be the next and final group to testify.

Five white ministers come to the front and offer moving anecdotes of traveling very far to participate in the demonstrations.[7] They all tell the story of how they came to be involved with the movement, and most of them describe what a privilege it is to work with Hattiesburg African Americans, calling it an experience they will always remember. Many of them too testify about their fears in coming down to Mississippi. For instance, one white minister uses fear as a mode of structuring his testimony, building on other accounts from the evening:

One thing that really struck me in the remarks that were already said were when the people were telling how afraid they were to go down there. Well I want to tell you how afraid I was. I was coming in to Hattiesburg in a car. There were four of us in the car. The closer we got to Hattiesburg, the more excuses we found to stop for a little while. In fact we decided that they were going to be waiting for us. We knew that for sure. To outsmart them we would go on the highway past Hattiesburg and come in from the South. Well we got clear of the SNCC office before we saw anyone. I think they were so busy with that inauguration that they didn't know that time that we were coming or how many of us were coming.

But we weren't the only ones who were afraid, the four of us in the car and me. But all of the others of us who are here, coming in from other states were also afraid. Even though a lot of us have been picketing and demonstrating where we are. We had heard just how bad it was here. In terms of never any demonstration lasting longer than 15 minutes, usually about 3 minutes. And we came with the same feeling that we were going to have our heads used for targets for clubs. We were trying to figure out what is the nonviolent position you assume when a dog is coming. So we were afraid . . .

But then I heard people say that they're not afraid now. They've been there today, and for the first time ever in Mississippi a demonstration has gone on and has continued throughout the whole day. And it was at least that much was completed. And, therefore, I heard people say they are not afraid: there is a new person who is afraid, and it is the white citizen of Hattiesburg. (Hattiesburg Mass Meetings Recording, Tape N74)

This minister thus uses his emotional response to demonstrating, fear, as a means of drawing together the stories of African Americans, other white ministers, and lay Christian people in the North. He shifts the emotional response they all share—being afraid—to the white citizen of Hattiesburg. Like the Black woman from the community, this minister leverages his testimony to inspire his listeners. He does not exhort as she did; rather, he uses his experience as a mode of drawing together the testimonies of the evening and then juxtaposing them with the imagined response of the white citizen. In this way, his testimony explicitly does the work that Sherrod and Guyot have been calling for and demonstrates a collective understanding of the movement, a shared experience that is powerful, to create change in Hattiesburg.

Taken as a whole, this Hattiesburg event highlights the rich variety of testimony as theorized and practiced in the mass meeting. For young people, testimony enabled a next step into the movement, one where they gained facility with speaking truth about their experiences. They also generated deeper understanding of how racism functions in their town and their will to change their circumstances. By delivering and listening to testimonies, many Hattiesburg activists were transforming their sense of themselves and who they could be. As ordinary young people stand and speak, they participate in creating this identity for themselves and for their group. For the older group, testimony offers opportunity to exhort and encourage, as well as to craft the collective's narrative and identity. Testimony also helps to forge cross-racial alliances, as the white ministers participate in story-making. This

flexibility and variety was necessary for the diverse group, empowering anyone to stand up and speak without fear of saying the wrong thing or mis-
understanding the conventions of the genre. Fuzziness, thus, provided the
Hattiesburg movement with a genre that worked well for catalyzing and
creating individual and group identity and for developing an understanding
of the movement and the problems they were working together to solve.

Danville, Virginia, December 1963:
Testimony and the Burden of Audience

As the Hattiesburg meeting demonstrates, testimony played a key role in
crafting activist identity, empowering the group, and bringing them together
across age and class. Participants narrated their experiences and emotions
and at times used them as resources to create exhortations for their listeners.
In this way, the genre afforded activists a mode to speak truth and love at
once, crafting together their group and their collective account of the movement. The Hattiesburg meeting provides a view of diverse groups of activists
testifying together, and they did so in the presence of a recorder. Unafraid of
who might hear, participants stood up and told their stories.

This fearlessness about being recorded was not always the case at mass
meetings, however. In Danville, Virginia, a mass meeting held in December 1963 illustrates that at times, people needed a break from the recorder
to testify. From the audio recording of this meeting, we learn the usual
facts about the evening, except that when the meeting shifts to a time for
testimony, activists request that the recorder be turned off (Danville Mass
Meeting Recordings, Tape N38). The short debate as well as the rest of the
meeting reinforce the variety and flexibility of testimony. This meeting illuminates two additional dimensions to an understanding of testimony: (a) it
took tremendous courage for activists to deliver testimonies on the record,
as they did in the Hattiesburg meeting and so many other locations; and
(b) at times, the mass meeting had to shift toward enclosure and secrecy to
provide the security necessary for activists to offer testimonies as lament or
critique.

Among some activists, Danville was viewed as equivalent to a Jackson
or Selma in terms of racism and police corruption. As Southern Christian
Leadership Conference (SCLC) staffer Wyatt T. Walker put it, it was "one
of the worst cities I've ever visited across the South. The police brutality
here is worse than Mississippi or Alabama" (quoted in Simon Hall, "Civil
Rights Activism in 1960s Virginia," 254). Danville was one of many small
towns across the South where African Americans responded to national attention on civil rights campaigns. In historian Simon Hall's view, much of
this response was generated by media portrayals of Birmingham: "In the

spring of 1963, as a shocked nation watched Bull Connor unleash police dogs and high pressure hoses on Black school children in Birmingham, African Americans took to the streets across the South. The year 1963 saw more than 20,000 people arrested in more than 900 demonstrations: At least 115 cities were affected, including Danville, a tobacco and textile city situated in southern Pittsylvania County" (253). While Danville had been a site for civil rights organizing before the spring of 1963, the events in Birmingham heightened Danville African Americans' perceptions of the need for direct action campaigns (253).

May 1963 marked the moment when Danville civil rights organizers moved forward with direct action protests. These protests centered on marches arguing for an end to segregation and better jobs for African Americans. Leaders of the marches included two ministers, Reverend Lawrence Campbell and A. I. Dunlap, members of the newly formed Danville Christian Progressive Association (DCPA). An affiliate of the SCLC, the DCPA launched the campaign in late May, and by June 10 it came to an end with "Bloody Monday" when policeman used fire hoses against marchers and made thirty-seven arrests. A group of sixty-six activists decided to go to the jail and protest these arrests. When the group arrived at the jail, they sang hymns as they marched outside. Police Chief E. G. McCain came out and commanded them to stop singing. Protestors resisted his orders and continued singing. As activist James Forman recounts: "Chief McCain bellowed, 'Let 'em have it' and firemen turned hoses on the people, many of them women and teenagers. Nightstick wielding police and deputized garbage collectors smashed into the group, clubbing Negroes who were bunched for safety against parked cars. Some were washed under the cars; others were clubbed after the water knocked them down. Bodies lay on the street, drenched and bloody" (Forman, *The Making of Black Revolutionaries*, 328–29). Between June and December 1963, African American support for the movement in Danville waned. While there was a successful voter-registration drive in the summer months, by the end of the year support from student activists had diminished considerably for reasons that remain unclear. It is true that Martin Luther King Jr. offered little encouragement for the Danville movement, and organizational tensions in the town ran high that year (Simon Hall, "Civil Rights Activism in 1960s Virginia," 259). However, these two factors did not always result in decreased activism in other areas.

The December mass meeting was intended to explore and overcome this decreased activist participation. Toward this goal, the meeting program included the standard features, singing and a pep talk, with a time of dedicated testimony at the end. The pep talk by the local minister, Reverend Campbell, made clear that the purpose of the meeting was to generate more support for the movement. For instance, he closed his address with these words: "We are first class citizens of the United States. We are still children of God. For that reason, we will not rest, nowhere in America, until Black boys and girls will be able to walk with dignity through every street in every city" (Danville Mass Meeting Recordings, Tape N38). These few sentences adequately capture the tone of the meeting, emphasizing the importance of continued direct action for first class citizenship.

To lead the time of testimony, Campbell turned the meeting over to Bruce Baines. Baines offers an important model of testimony for his audience. He shows them how important it is to testify about one's troubles as a mode of resistance and to narrate them toward a purpose. Baines begins with some facts about himself. While he had been absent from Danville for some time, it is his home. His absence has been due to his activism in another Southern city, Shreveport. He describes these events in his opening:

> Freedom Fighters, core members of Danville, I am glad to be back in the city of Danville. I have called Danville my home now since the time I had left. . . . I am glad to be here after being down in Shreveport, Louisiana, where I have been shot at about 4 times. I have been beaten down there by the policeman, and I felt very sad when Larry called me and said nothing was going on in Danville. (Danville Mass Meeting Recordings, Tape N38)

Baines opens with these facts to show his audience how testimony works: he explains his experiences with their city and with civil rights organizing. Moreover, he leverages his testimony toward testifying to the violence he experienced as a civil rights protestor working in another area. He goes on to elaborate this point, comparing his experiences to the ones he has had working for change in Danville:

> Now we are having a hard time down in Shreveport, but the Negroes there are together and they are trying to move. Now down there you can't picket, they have all types of laws, but here we have a chance to carry on things. Now we have jobs, about 36 Negroes working down in the downtown area of Danville. Look like now the young people want to give up. And we cannot give up now. We have to keep moving. Now I am looking forward to seeing everybody tomorrow night at the mass meeting. Why? Larry is going to speak. Larry Wilson will be speaking tomorrow night. I hope you will come out and hear the young man speak. I feel bad. I feel just like crying. No more people at the church this afternoon. I feel hurt. Of all the time that we have, the friends that I have been to jail with this summer. The time that we

have pulled, the days we stayed in the jail down in the Danville. The trouble we have gave Chief McCain and Mayor Stinson and other white people here in Danville. (Danville Mass Meeting Recordings, Tape N38)

Baines uses his comparisons between Danville and Shreveport as a means of motivating his listeners toward continued activist participation. He endured police brutality in Shreveport much worse than they had experienced in Danville, he says, but the important thing is that the people are together and attempting to create change. There is no reason, it follows, that African Americans in Danville should not also be together and working toward more changes. He also recalls the difficult circumstances he endured while he was working in Danville, illustrating that he as well as many others have provided solid ground for continued work.

After modeling how to testify to activist experiences, Baines shifts toward explaining the time of testimony. Like Sherrod and Guyot, he prompts his audience to come up and speak about their experiences with demonstrations in Danville. His instructions, however, are more pointed:

And yet you have stopped. I want to know. I just want to know. What's wrong? I want to ask the question, what's wrong? Are we afraid? Are we turned chicken? I want to know. That's what I want to know now. (Danville Mass Meeting Recordings, Tape N38)

Baines frames the purpose of activists' speech differently from Guyot and Sherod. He employs testimony here as a heuristic for understanding movement problems. He poses questions to prompt a specific mode of activist testifying, accounts that will help to explain the lack of support. Baines' prior speech illuminates a model of testimony that narrates struggles and describes will and purpose toward overcoming them. He then prompts activists toward narrating struggles so that together, as a collective, they might discern how to overcome them. In this way, testimony functions as a heuristic for discerning issues and inventing solutions.

While Baines's work prompting and scaffolding testimony reveals this planned purpose for testimony, it is not possible to know how activists responded to him or if they learned from his model. The recorder is turned off so that audience members might come forward and speak. However, the conversation that precedes this moment is in itself illuminating, for it shows the affective burdens associated with testifying at meetings while they are being recorded, as well as insight into how recording was understood by movement activists. Here is the dialogue between Baines, an unidentified speaker, and Moses Moon (birth name Alan Ribback), the recorder:

> *Unidentified speaker:* I'd like to say Reverend, since our friend is recording, I think maybe our complaints should be when he's not recording.
>
> *Baines:* No I think they should be. See a lot of this stuff is going to be used for a book.
>
> *Unidentified speaker:* I think before we can put Danville in the spot like this we should get permission from the executive board of the community.
>
> *Baines:* See it's going to be about 5 to 10 years before it comes out.
>
> *Unidentified Speaker:* I still think we are really probing deep into the community here. I don't think we are in the position to speak for this entire community.
>
> *Alan Ribback* (Moses Moon): I'll cut it off. (Danville Mass Meeting Recordings, Tape N38)

This conversation illustrates that some activists saw the recorder as a hindrance to testimony as heuristic, the type of testifying that might shift into complaint, critique, or lament. For the local Danville activists, many of them students, the affective burden of providing testimony like this that might circulate was too great; they likely felt it would inhibit their ability to speak freely and productively, especially as their accounts would presumably *not* testify toward solutions they could recognize or movement progress. In this way, to speak freely before the mass-meeting group, they desired the seclusion of a space where their stories might not circulate beyond the group. Given the pressure to circulate narratives of "successful" "peaceful" civil rights activists, this desire is understandable and suggests that as a tool for exploring movement problems, testimony benefits from disconnection from audiences external to the movement and the burden of a recorder. Stories of progress, of movement victories, of overcoming—these are the testimonies that activists delivered out in the open and for wide circulation, because they are the ones that generated greater support for the movement.[8]

The Danville meeting then illustrates another important function of testimony at the mass meeting, as a heuristic for exploring movement problems. At the same time, it complicates the view of the space of the meeting, reminding that at times the meeting did attempt to go off the record and out of public view. These moments, as this meeting illuminates, are strategic; in this case, Ribback intervenes in the debate about the purpose of recording and who can speak for the community to simply say: "I'll turn it off" (Danville, Virginia Mass Meetings Recordings, Tape N38). This debate and intervention then reiterate Williams's assertion that testimony is a form of direct action, one that is arduous in any moment but perhaps especially in moments of social unrest or movement volatility. In this way, the flexibility of testimony is its most important resource. While it can be a public genre with legal inflections, and while it can operate as a kind of protest, testimony also functions completely behind-the-scenes and out of view of wider audiences and does not depend on any institution or audience. As a social action, testimony can serve as clear resistance or protest; it can also lament or critique or complain. While I cannot speculate about the features, functions, or actions of the testimonies absent from the historical record, the act of shutting the recorder off conveys an exigence for space away from speech and symbolic action designed to circulate for those outside the movement. Off the record and out of public view, the young people of Danville told their stories.

Conclusion: Testimony as Faithful Genre

Writing about Hamer speaking in the Delta, Brooks explains: "[This activist] identity sought to empower local people in a manner that would transform their self-conceptions from victims of an oppressive system to agents of change within a more just nation" (*A Voice That Could Stir an Army*, 47). Brooks focuses on how Hamer encouraged this transformation in her audiences, the ways that her incisive rhetorical abilities enabled her to push people to see themselves anew. Hamer was extraordinarily important as a speaker in telling her story and exhorting audiences to join her in the movement for Black freedom. As this chapter maintains, however, there were many, many people like Hamer who did this rhetorical work, who made the long walk from a seat in the audience to the platform to tell their stories and to encourage one another to do the same. The point is not that many people had the same rhetorical prowess as Hamer; Hamer is certainly exceptional. The point is that speaking up for oneself is an important step forward in catalyzing political agency, and this collective story-making helped everyone to recognize the systems of oppressive that marked their lives and experiences and then to participate in changing them.

In the mass meeting, testimony provided this opportunity, an opening and invitation for ordinary people, young and old, Black and white, to stand up and speak the truth about their experiences. This speech cannot be reduced to a handful of features, and it is difficult to connect to one specific, recurring social action. Yet as the figures studied in this chapter convey, testimony was a powerful next step into movement participation. Like song and prayer, it created political agency and identity; it transformed people's sense of self and possibility. By standing up and speaking before large audiences, men and women, girls and boys, delivered testimony as direct action and spoke about their experiences. At times, these testimonies spoke more softly and to smaller audiences, as meeting organizers revised the mass meeting's purpose to enable a safer, more exclusive space for testimonies that could serve as heuristics. Testimony enabled wide, collective participation, and it functioned to foster activists' truth-telling about many different types of experiences—from difficult experiences of abuse to more light-hearted stories of participation in protest.

As a faithful genre, testimony is unique. Unlike freedom songs and prayer, it is easily disentangled from its religious dimensions. It persists through the contextual shifts that occur during the Black Power phase of civil rights efforts. Not only does testimony continue to be important, where freedom songs and prayer diminish in usefulness, but as far as I have been able to tell, testimony does not receive the same type of criticism and interrogation from activists that prayer and song do. While some activists deeply question the reliance on freedom songs and prayers, they turn again and again to testimony throughout the tumultuous 1960s.[9] Given its flexibility, this endurance makes rhetorical sense: as Sherrod, Guyot, and Baines teach the genre, testimony can be defined by its user. Speakers may choose to discuss deeply difficult topics, or they may tell humorous stories about their experiences. They may speak from a position of faith, or they may mute the sacred dimensions of the genre and adapt a different frame. The purpose of testimony might be legal, or it might be for laughter or joy. Speakers may use their testimonies to shift into argument or exhortation, or they may, given some protections, shift into inquiry, lament, or critique. Given this immense variety and openness, testimony stands out among the key genres of the mass meeting for its fluid movement from the church to new contexts and its capacity to be severed from its religious dimensions.

FIVE

Reckoning with
White Violence and Resistance

A poster publicizing a 1961 NAACP mass meeting in Savannah, Georgia, reads: "Come One, Come All: Everybody Welcome!" In addition to the time, date, and location, the poster indicates the purpose of the event as "Freedom Now," stating that "Supporters of the 'Freedom Now' Movement Will Overflow the NAACP Mass Meeting." Historical evidence reveals that white people, including community members, Northerners, reporters, police detectives, fire department officials, and segregationists, responded to invitations like this one and attended meetings as friends and foes. In the Hattiesburg meeting studied in chapter 4, for instance, the audio recording demonstrates that members of the Klan and the Citizens' Council were present at the event. In other cities, such as Selma and Birmingham, Alabama, much of the evidence of mass meetings comes from police surveillance tapes. In southwest Georgia, accounts in the *New York Times* as well as activists' testimonies demonstrate yet again the presence of local police at meetings.

Activists took full advantage of the opportunity to engage these interlocutors and spoke with police, segregationists, and reporters. To offer one well-known example, in 1965 King and Abernathy encouraged activists in Selma, Alabama, to continue working toward voting rights, doing so in the presence of a surveillance device planted by police detectives. On one occasion, Abernathy delivered his "doo-hickey speech," speaking to those eavesdropping while also motivating activists to persevere. Abernathy's speech is no exception. In each of the instances cited above, leaders including Charles Sherrod and James Bevel responded to the presence of outsiders as they continued to use the meeting toward their own ends—sustaining the group affectively, planning next steps, and interpreting how the movement was being received by media. The performances of Abernathy, Sherrod, and Bevel point to the ways that activists maintained ownership of their space while speaking to Southern whites, police, and the press.

While scholars have noted outsiders' presence at events, the external engagement dimension of the mass meeting has not received much attention or analysis. Moving into the complex question of meeting audiences, this chapter investigates activists' fluid movements among internally focused rhetorics, countermovement response, and media savvy. Studying activists' rhetorical movements calls attention to the burden of the mass meeting as a watched, visible space and the strategic ways that activists responded to these watchful eyes. I claim that leaders exploited countermovement groups' presence in meetings to circulate and teach radical pacificist engagements.[1] "Radical pacifism" and "Christian nonviolence" refer to activists' fusion of Gandhian protest strategies, biblical teaching, and racial justice.

To build this argument, I approach the mass meeting holistically and read liturgies in their entirety, as I do in chapter 1. Chapter 1 revealed how as a holistic event, the mass meeting functioned as a pedagogical arena, empowering collectives toward participatory readiness or civic speech and action. This chapter expands the view of the meeting's holistic functions to show how collectives learned and practiced Christian nonviolent rhetorics. These responses also demonstrate how activists gained media advantage and circulated narratives of dignified, joyful Black protestors welcoming hostile outsiders into their space. Inspecting meeting scenes in Hattiesburg, Mississippi; Albany, Georgia; and Selma, Alabama, I examine how in each of these locales, meeting leaders and participants cultivated strategic responses to white hatred, interruption, and surveillance.[2]

One note on this chapter and its attention to white people's role in mass meetings. In the preceding chapters I deliberately ignored the presence of certain groups—local police, the Citizens Council, the Klan, and even reporters—to privilege Black people and the African American rhetorics at the heart of mass meetings. I make a different move here and attend to the persistent white violence and resistance that activists dealt with because it is a real and recurring aspect of the mass meeting. Activists' responses reveal the range of sophisticated rhetorical modes they developed as they maintained ownership over their space and its purposes. Even in the sort-of behind-the-scenes space of the meeting, activists recharged and found renewal as the world looked on, at times in appreciation of their liturgy, but all too often with intent to harm or thwart their work.

Inventing and Speaking Radical Pacificism:
Christian Nonviolence in the Mass Meeting

In his 1935 book *The Power of Nonviolence*, Richard Gregg defines "radical pacificism" as "moral jiu-jitsu" and as "a way of throwing the oppressor off balance" (43). Reflecting on this theory, Keith Miller observes: "Whereas martial arts are physical arts, moral jiu-jitsu involves both verbal and physical performance. Protestors used language—to orate, write, conduct press conferences, pray, and sing—and their bodies to sit in, march, and picket" ("Afterword," 337). As Miller maintains, Christian nonviolence is a rhetorical phenomenon carried out through language and symbolic action. Civil rights activists inventively embodied nonviolence through a range of direct action strategies, from sit-ins to swim-ins to marches. Likewise, as discursive response, the Christian nonviolence of the movement is richly varied, and the mass meeting provided a key arena for developing these strategies. The liturgy scaffolded this process of adapting nonviolence as a theory and contextualizing it for the movement. Individuals and collectives inhabited freedom songs, prayer, and testimony as sites of peaceful identity and action, and these same genres were useful for speaking with and responding to countermovement groups. The invitation to white outsiders to join the meeting catalyzed the invention and rehearsal of nonviolent performances. Before examining this process and the specific discursive strategies activists devised, this section overviews how radical pacificism emerged as a dominant rhetorical approach to Black freedom.

Activists including James Farmer, Bayard Rustin, and Pauli Murray saw radical pacificism as a possible tactic of Black freedom early in the twentieth century. Two organizations, the Fellowship of Reconciliation (FOR) and the Congress of Racial Equality (CORE), explored these possibilities through experiments centered on Gandhi's teachings on nonviolence in the context of the United States and Black life (Wolcott, "Radical Nonviolence, Interracial Utopias," 33). The FOR formed during World War I to oppose organized violence of all kinds and provided an intellectual haven for thinkers like Richard Gregg and A. J. Muste to develop and refine pacificism as theology and political theory. Through their work in FOR, Gregg and Muste began to see nonviolence as "a calculated performance attuned to the sympathies of audiences, especially those created by new forms of mass media" and "a moral crusade that was simultaneously a stunning display of creative political strategy" (Kosek, *Acts of Conscience,* 10). The CORE, founded by Farmer and Rustin who were also members of FOR, situated these insights directly in response to segregation and racial injustice. These activists read Krishnalal Shridharani's *War without Violence*, looking to Gandhian nonviolence for cues on how to peacefully create racial justice. Inspired by Shridharani, Farmer and Rustin called for the development of communal living experiments, interracial sites where radical pacifism might be refined through ordinary life together (Wolcott, "Radical Nonviolence, Interracial Utopias," 34).

In addition to communal living experiments, CORE activists explored nonviolent direct action through public protests—displays that helped craft a blueprint for the sit-ins, marches, and Freedom Rides of the 1960s. Rhetorical scholar David Miguel Molina makes this point through study of Murray's projects in Washington, DC. In the 1940s, Murray explored *satyagraha*, which she defines as "nonviolent resistance coupled with goodwill," in her work with young activists at Howard University (*Song in a Weary Throat*, 178). Murray, a Howard law student, was tasked with advising the Civil Rights Committee of the DC chapter of the National Association for the Advancement of Colored People (NAACP). Murray and the student activists, many of them young women, experimented with nonviolent direct action in a series of protests. In April 1943, three young women entered establishments in Washington, DC, and requested service. The establishment, Little Palace Café, refused them, in accordance with a "white trade only" policy. In response, the young women found open tables, set empty cafeteria trays down, and began to read. Over the course of the day, several groups came in and followed the same pattern, requesting service and then sitting at tables with empty trays and reading materials. The following year the group carried out a similar campaign at Thompson's Café (Molina, "'Our boys, our bonds, our brothers,'" 35–37). Reflecting on her work with these activists, Murray writes: "We had proved that intelligent, imaginative action could bring positive results and, fortunately, we had won our first victory without an embarrassing incident" (*Song in a Weary Throat*, 269). Analyzing this work, Molina identifies these campaigns as precursors to the 1960s sit-ins, and more generally, they reveal how Christian nonviolent approaches to civil rights emerged in the United States. Experiments with radical pacificism in the 1940s afforded figures like Murray, Farmer, Rustin, and others opportunities to develop their understanding of how Gandhian nonviolence could support racial justice in the United States. For Murray, these protests revealed how civil disobedience might "draw upon the situatedness of black Americans' everyday life" (Molina, "'Our boys, our bonds, our brothers,'" 47).

In the 1950s, civil rights leaders, most famously Martin Luther King Jr., built on this work, exploring how radical pacifism might structure collective campaigns across the South. Historian Victoria Wolcott writes: "Radical pacificism shaped the tactics of the SCLC, SNCC, and CORE and offered an alternative to the NAACP's legalism and racial liberals' gradualism" ("Radical Nonviolence, Interracial Utopias," 49). The example of the 1955 Montgomery bus boycott is instructive in showing how civil rights activists came to see radical pacifism as a viable movement strategy and applied it to mass-meeting design. While the boycott was peaceful from the start, in terms of self-defense, Montgomerians were comfortable with armed resistance, and King himself purportedly had guns in his home early in the movement. At a critical moment in February 1956, leaders from FOR, first Rustin and later Glenn Smiley, arrived in Montgomery to persuade the Montgomery Improvement Association (MIA) to explore pacifist ideals and embed them into the broader movement strategy. For example, Smiley gave King a copy of Gregg's *The Power of Non-violence*, and then distributed it to libraries at historically Black colleges and universities (HBCUs) across the South. King cited the book as one of his key influences during and for many years after the boycott, and as of 1960, it was a top title on the Student Nonviolent Coordinating Committee's (SNCC) recommended reading list (Kosek, *Acts of Conscience*, 224, 229).

Radical pacifism took hold in the civil rights movement in no small part because it resonated with Black church traditions and genres. Activist James Lawson explained nonviolence as "creative Christian love that comes from the inside of a person, that—that in a sense heals a person inwardly and enables him then to really be a free man" (Lawson, Interview). Discussing teaching nonviolence during the movement, Lawson describes how Christianity informed his work: "Some of the most exciting experiences I've had in, in teaching and in training have been in the Delta of Mississippi where I primarily spoke in biblical terms, and used biblical illustrations, and biblical stories, and myths to . . . illustrate and document the whole idea of Christian nonviolence, and found people . . . exceedingly responsive and aware of this fact. I've had people say to me . . . 'Reverend Lawson, I have always felt . . . that the only way to change this situation or to change what we have to put up with is through Christian love and through what Christ talked about'" (Lawson, Interview). As Lawson explains, in the movement for Black freedom, nonviolence had to be taught, and religious rhetoric was crucial to this teaching. For many, Christianity implicitly supported nonviolent direct action through the teachings of Jesus.

The nonviolent workshops Lawson describes were a key training tool in the movement. The mass meetings provided another opportunity for translating, adapting, and teaching Christian nonviolence.[3] The mass meeting, as holistic event, worked as a pedagogical forum of nonviolent action, where through engagement with white groups who sought to intimidate, threaten,

Figure 5.1. King Speaking at Maggie Street Baptist Church, Montgomery, Alabama, February 1968. Photographed by Jim Peppler, Alabama Department of Archives and History.

or surveil activists' work, leaders offered instruction and practice in radical pacifist response (see fig. 5.1 for an example of press coverage of meetings). The liturgy of the meeting thus provided opportunity for situating these responses in already accepted Christian genres, experimenting with their possibilities as faithful and overtly peaceful actions.

Narrative Contrast in Hattiesburg, Mississippi, 1964

As chapter 4 demonstrated, the key purpose of the 1964 Hattiesburg mass meeting was to empower the group to speak truth in love, to feel their way to civil rights activism through narrating experiences and creating collective testimony. Yet in one small moment in this event, the moderator reveals the presence of members of the Ku Klux Klan (KKK) and the White Citizen's Council. This small moment is easy to miss. From the strong and fearless speech of the young people, on first listen the event seems an intimate space attended only by insiders to the movement for Black freedom. However, a close listen to the whole meeting indicates these countermovement groups were in attendance. The moderator uses their presence as an opening for teaching Christian nonviolence as creative response. One of the principles of nonviolent direct action is that it is not passive and that instead it responds creatively to the oppressor and exposes his injustice (Hoover, "The Nashville Sit-Ins," 96). The moderator shows activists gathered how to put this principle to work, in this case, through a strategy of narrative contrast. To model the practices of nonviolence, the moderator speaks directly to countermovement groups in the beginning of the meeting. This brief speech contrasts their hatred with movement love and brotherhood, appeals to them to repent, and then moves on to speak as though they are not there. The moderator throws the violent groups off moral balance through story and appeal and then returns to the meeting liturgy's internal design. Through his example, he teaches the audience how to speak with countermovement groups.

In modeling this strategy and enacting Christian nonviolence, the moderator names the countermovement groups and positions them in the faithful vision of social change that inflects the work of the meeting. This narrative locates the members of the Klan and the Citizen's Council as outsiders to civil rights activity and by extension to divine acceptance and justice. Speaking to this group, the moderator explains:

> Even the White Citizen's Council representatives that are here: You need it. (Amen) God wants your hearts to be changed. God wants you to be converted. I have been to many of these meetings for the past few years, and I know some of you, but God knows you best. (That's right) Amen. (Amen)
>
> And to the Ku Klux Klan representatives: we are all brothers, whether you accept it or not. And until you realize, my brother, that I am your brother, and that God is the Father of us all, you are living a false life. It's time for all of us to repent. Somewhere in this blessed book, God to spoke to some of His children: Stop being slaveholders. Stop hating Negroes and Jews. Stop all of your . . . hateful ways. . . .
>
> For our Scripture lesson, may I read the 46th Psalm. God is our refuge and strength. (Hattiesburg Mass Meeting Recordings, N76)

In this brief speech, the moderator makes clear to everyone gathered that the presence of the Citizen's Council and the Klan is not unnoticed, and he embodies and models a radical pacificist response. To the countermovement group, the moderator prompts repentance and recognition of their "false life." Here, he creates a narrative contrast, asserting God is displeased with their hatred and insistence on racial divisions. He extends the point and calls them to see that if they are Christians, then they are unified with their Black brothers (and sisters) as part of the family of God. In the narrative crafted here, this group is on the wrong side of justice. As brothers and sisters of the activists gathered, they are part of a multiracial family of God, whether they accept it or not. Through this appeal, the moderator invites the countermovement groups to become what Danielle Allen calls political friends and to start again in renewed relationship. As Allen writes: "Friendship teaches citizens how to start over again with symbolically significant acts that regenerate trust where it has disintegrated" (*Talking to Strangers*, 136). Repentance entails casting racial hatred aside and changing their ways. As a strategy of Christian nonviolence, this move does not deeply consider white groups' needs or spend time reflecting on it. The moderator contrasts countermovement groups and their hatred with the loving, truthful activists gathered and moving closer toward a just world, securing the moral upper hand, and then moves on.

The moderator enacts nonviolent direct action through his speech, and at the same time, he models this practice for the activists gathered. As a teaching moment, the moderator reveals rhetorical moves of Christian nonviolence: narrative contrast, a call to repentance, and a return to planned movement purposes. Through his speech, the moderator prepares activists for engaging with violent groups. He shows them how to throw oppressors off "moral balance" through resources the meeting liturgy provides, in this case biblical ideals of brotherhood and repentance. Beyond this specific moment in the Hattiesburg event, more generally the design of the meeting space also catalyzed these types of responses. As discussed in the introduction to the chapter, meeting publicity materials often emphasize the space as "welcoming" and "open." If members of the Klan or the Citizens' Council showed up and wanted to attend, they were not denied entry. All were welcome at the civil rights mass meeting. This welcoming, hospitable approach to meeting design had many rhetorical advantages. The Hattiesburg meeting reveals modelled behavior as one key element, as activists in the meeting see Christian nonviolence in action and learn how to use the meeting liturgy to invent a peaceful response.

Collective Testimony in Southwest Georgia, 1962

Albany, Georgia, is not usually remembered as an example of civil rights activists' greatest use of nonviolent direct action. This strand of the movement instead often serves as a counterpoint, a moment when radical pacifism failed to achieve public sympathy for activists and create political gains on the national level. As this story goes, when Albany police chief Laurie Pritchett learned of civil rights activity in his area in the early 1960s, he studied Martin Luther King Jr.'s work to date. He read *Stride Toward Freedom: The Montgomery Story*; he learned about Gandhi; he schooled himself in how nonviolence worked. Then he anticipated the SCLC's next moves. In advance of demonstrations, he filled all the jails in his county, so there could be no arrests. To prevent law enforcement from being cast as unjust by the media, he trained his officers to minimize the use of force. Pritchett describes his strategy as follows: "I lectured to the men that the news media could either be our ally or our enemy and we wanted them as an ally. We would not have any force. . . . We're going to out non-violent [them]" (Pritchett, Interview, 3). When King himself was jailed in Albany, Pritchett arranged for him to be released on bail, confounding King and causing him to leave unexpectedly. Historian Wesley Hogan sums up the events: "Movement people struggled, and failed, to find a way to focus the community's rage on a nonviolent action that would invite the national attention and the moral authority of the Montgomery bus boycotts or the student sit-ins" (Hogan, *Many Minds, One Heart*, 71).

Yet Hogan also notes that while the Albany movement failed to achieve immediate gains, SNCC activists' long-term work in southwest Georgia is nonetheless remarkable. The leadership and teaching of Charles Sherrod created lasting change in the African American community in southwest Georgia and unsettled many whites' views of social harmony, thus exposing racial injustice and prompting change (Hogan, *Many Minds, One Heart*, 71; Sokol, *There Goes My Everything*). Hogan offers this description: "[Sherrod] demonstrated that blacks did not have to remain within the powerful but hopelessly outmoded behavioral code called 'segregation.' The price of this education was, for an extended time, the survival of continued terror" (75). In 1961, Sherrod traveled to Terrell County, Georgia, to test an injunction laid down by a federal judge. Initially focused on voter registration, SNCC's goals expanded to include total desegregation of this southwest corner of the state. Sherrod, with the rest of SNCC staff, successfully encouraged local Albany State students and residents to create an organization to join these efforts. What SNCC worked with local activists to achieve was nothing short of political consciousness, and as Hogan labels it, a kind of democratic education.

This analysis focuses on a July 1962 mass meeting held in Terrell County, a rural area near Albany, Georgia. In this region, African Americans comprised almost two-thirds the population and less than 1 percent of registered voters. Recognizing that federal help was a long way off, Sherrod and other SNCC leaders used mass meetings as sites for instilling courage, developing new political imaginaries, and teaching groups how to respond to counter-movement groups.

At this event, southwest Georgia law officer Sherriff Matthews and a group of segregationists interrupted the meeting. Sherrod and local activists gathered toward the objectives laid out above, for voter registration, but more broadly, to participate in and model democracy as a racially inclusive, just project. The meeting account, published in *The New York Times,* reveals how Sherrod, like the Hattiesburg moderator, modelled Christian nonviolence in action. Next, the event moved into an additional type of teaching, where Sherrod scaffolds activists' invention and performance of radical pacificist responses. Here, he steps back to catalyze activists' collective testimony before the countermovement group. Activists first listen as Sherrod enacts Christian nonviolence through the faithful genres of the meeting, and then they speak directly as truth-tellers to the countermovement group.

The liturgy for the meeting went as follows: "Pass Me Not, O Gentle Savior," the Lord's Prayer, a Scripture reading, and the hymn "Climbing Jacob's Ladder." Sherrod led the group through each, offering encouragement and exhortation throughout, making clear that by following the liturgy, they could find collective strength no matter the interruption. The group was able to begin the event as planned, singing the opening hymn and praying the Lord's Prayer without outsiders present. Then, when he got to the reading of the Scripture passage, Romans 8, Sherrod indicated to the group that the segregationists and police were about to enter the meeting. He paused and said: "I'm going to read it again for they're standing on the outside." Rereading the passage, Sherrod continued: 'If God be for us, who can be against us. We are counted as sheep for the slaughter'" (quoted in Sitton, "Sherriff Harasses Negroes at Voting Rally in Georgia"). Sherrod had been tipped off before the event that the group of police and segregationists might show up, so he was likely unsurprised by the sounds of whites gathering in the parking lot outside (Hogan, *Many Minds, One Heart*). Reading Scripture and remaining committed to the meeting liturgy enabled the group to persevere, continuing the event as planned.

After Sherrod finished reading, the white group entered the church and attempted to disrupt the meeting. Sherrod modelled how to use the liturgy as nonviolent response in his prayer: "Give us the wisdom to try to understand this world. Oh, Lord God, we've been abused so long; we've been down so long; oh, Lord, all we want is for our white brothers to understand that in Thy sight we are all equal. We're praying for the courage to withstand the brutality of our brethren" (quoted in Sitton, "Sherriff Harasses Negroes at Voting Rally in Georgia"). Through the prayer, Sherrod revealed the radical pacificist resources available through meeting genres. In line with the Hattiesburg moderator's speech, Sherrod admonished the white segregationists to acknowledge and repent of the brutal abuse Blacks have suffered. For activists, he modeled how to use prayer to speak and act peacefully while feeling intimidation, fear, or anger. For everyone, he asserts a central tenant of their work, acknowledgment of the equality that all Americans share before God.

Unlike the silent group of Klan and Citizens' Council members in the Hattiesburg meeting, Matthews took the floor at this event and attempted to reroute the meeting purpose. Through this rowdy behavior, Matthews and the rest of his group step into the role of unjust opponent, amplifying the meeting's capacity to reveal committed Black people working for justice. In his speech, Matthews asked all African Americans from Terrell County to stand and then proceeded to question them, perhaps expecting them to affirm his view of Sherrod and other SNCC members as "outside agitators."[4] Matthews's speech suggests he may have believed, as many white southerners did at the time, that the explanation for the demonstrations and campaigns was influence from leaders visiting the area (Sokol, *There Goes My Everything*, 56–57). The African Americans from that county took Matthew's interruption as an opportunity to perform Christian nonviolence. Here, the group speaks back directly to Matthews and all those gathered in the meeting.

> *Matthews:* Are any of you disturbed?
> *Terrell residents:* Yes.
> *Matthews:* Can you vote if you are qualified?
> *Terrell residents:* No.
> *Matthews:* Do you need people to come down and tell you what to do?
> *Terrell residents:* Yes.
> *Matthews:* Haven't you been getting along well for a hundred years?
> *Terrell residents:* No. (Sitton, "Sherriff Harasses Negroes at Voting Rally in Georgia")

Intending to upset the meeting's direction and prove SNCC's presence unnecessary, Matthews's speech instead becomes an opportunity for local Black people to testify to their experiences of oppression and their resolution to partner with civil rights workers to create peaceful change. They throw Matthews off moral balance through their collective voice, unsettling the view of Terrell County as a peaceful, just place. Through their collective testimony, they assert their actions as significant to democracy, exposing Matthews and segregationists as unwise obstacles to justice and equality. Like Sherrod and the moderator in Hattiesburg, they appeal to countermovement groups to see them as political friends and equals.

Accounts of this meeting emphasize the enormous affective burden the white interruption presented for Terrell County African Americans. Reporter Claude Sitton writes that even before the meeting was interrupted, "The sound of voices around the automobiles parked beside the church could be heard as license numbers were called out. And the faces of the audience stiffened with fear" (Sitton, "Sherriff Harasses Negroes at Voting Rally in Georgia"). He goes on: "Now and then one of the audience [members] would look up from the pine floor to steal a fearful glance at the door." The entrance of the police and segregationists surely brought with it intimidation, fear, and anger associated with the possibility of violence. Sherrod modelled how to turn the affective burden to rhetorical advantage. He shows the group to recognize the surveillance and interruption to their space as opportunity for enacting Christian nonviolence. Then through collective voice, the group performed radical pacificism to the countermovement group. Through their response, Black activists frankly spoke the truth of the situation in Terrell. Outsiders were not the reason for the campaigns and demonstrations; racial injustice and white supremacy were at the heart of their participation.

In speaking these collective truths, they encountered one of the most difficult elements of Christian nonviolence. This type of rhetorical confrontation is incredibly risky, putting bodies, homes, jobs, families, and churches on the line. To expose the oppressor's violence is often to experience loss. Indeed, just six weeks later, the church where this meeting was held burned to the ground; after the vandalism of their church, activists continued their meetings in a tent (Hogan, *Many Minds, One Heart,* 74).[5]

This Terrell County event then continues to show the mass meeting as a pedagogical forum, where leaders modelled radical pacifism. In this case, the event adds a new layer of learning, as activists themselves performed these strategies when given the opportunity. Here, it reveals another dimension of the meeting as pedagogical forum. In welcoming countermovement groups into the space, activists gained the opportunity for collective participation in direct action, to continue waging nonviolent war on white supremacy through their liturgy. In this event, they learn through practice, stepping up when Matthews created an opening for their nonviolent performance. Yet they practice in a space where the stakes could not be higher. As a key arena for teaching, the mass meeting uniquely straddles pedagogical forum and direct enactment of movement principles.

Black Joy in Selma, Alabama, 1965

This final section turns to Selma, Alabama, 1965, a civil rights scene well known for its violent and hostile police chief, Sheriff Jim Clark. Indeed, this chief attracted the SCLC to Selma in the first place, as the organization was focused on repeating the strategy that achieved the Civil Rights Bill in 1964. Hogan explains the plan: to "go to a town with a traditional southern style of law enforcement, augmented at the top by an especially authoritarian police chief. Attract the media, demonstrate, suffer through the resulting violence, agitate for a new broader Civil Rights Bill" (*Many Minds, One Heart,* 220). Wise to watch out for figures like Pritchett, the SCLC did their homework and believed that Clark would play into their media strategy. Much scholarly attention is paid to events of the summer—the marches across Pettis Bridge, Bloody Sunday, and the resulting 1965 Voting Rights Act—but here I focus on a mass meeting held earlier in the year. King, Abernathy, and the rest of the SCLC centered their efforts in Selma beginning in winter 1965. While the height of the drama reveals how activists' public demonstrations made use of this strategy, the marches and the violence of Bloody Sunday actually represent what occurred at the end of the Selma movement.

In fact, civil rights activists enacted peaceful protests over the course of the winter and spring of 1965, and they included months of organizing, campaigning, and movement renewal. The first mass meeting held during the campaign offers insight into such renewal, for it was held after a particularly challenging day of demonstrating. On January 25, as many as 250 Selma activists participated in direct action around voting rights registration by gathering at the courthouse in downtown Selma. As historian Taylor Branch observes, on this day "prevailing local sentiment shifted in favor of Sheriff Clark [the especially authoritarian police chief] against outside interference" (*Pillar of Fire*, 566). Activists were working to follow rules for peaceful assembly laid out in a court order by District Judge Daniel Thomas. According to the order, demonstrators were to gather in an alleyway by the courthouse with assigned numbers. Apparently, Sheriff Clark interpreted this rule to mean that no one could stand on sidewalks, and thus, briskly moved among activists waiting on the sidewalk, pushing them back. When Clark pushed activist Annie Lee Cooper, she had had enough: she told him not to twist her arm and then punched him. Cooper had after all already been fired from her job at Dunn Rest Hall for participation in an earlier voter-registration campaign. The conflict resulted in Cooper pinned down on the ground, clubbed by Clark and two deputies, and then arrested (Branch, *Pillar of Fire*, 563–64).

By many accounts, leaders sympathized with Cooper's retaliation. As King put it, "she had been provoked" (Dallas County, AL, Sheriff's Department Surveillance Tapes). Nonetheless, this single interaction became the media narrative of the day, distracting from what leaders hoped would be stories of Selma activists nonviolently attempting to register to vote and being unjustly prohibited by local law enforcement (Branch, *Pillar of Fire*, 563). When the group gathered at the mass meeting later that evening, King, Abernathy, and other activists "ardently fought the day's gloom" (563). In light of these sentiments, the purpose of the meeting and its liturgy was twofold: first, to recharge and to renew enthusiasm after the day's challenges and second, to analyze and interpret media and countermovement narratives of events that vilified Cooper.

Toward the first internal purpose, to rejuvenate activists, the liturgy of-fered people opportunities to recharge through singing hymns like "I Feel Like Going On" and listening to leaders urge them to remember the pro-found, even eternal significance of their work. In his address, King encour-aged activists to continue attempting to vote despite violence against them. Reflecting on his own feelings that day, King spoke candidly: "I must con-fess, sometimes I feel discouraged in Alabama. Sometimes I feel my work's in vain. Then, the Holy Spirit revives my soul again. There is balm in Gilead to make the wounded whole" (Dallas County, Alabama, Sheriff's Department Surveillance Tapes).[6] To bolster activists' spirits, King assures them that he too feels downcast at times. Yet this anguish serves as a turn to faith and a reminder that they are on the side of justice: the balm in Gilead, a reference to the book of Jeremiah, is available only to those wounded righteously. Building on King's affective claims, meeting moderator Reverend Anderson also heightened meeting *pathos*. After King's speech and a time of singing, he stood before the crowd and exclaimed: "This is a glorious time. I know we must feel about like Peter did on the Mount of Transfiguration. Let's build three tabernacles! This is a great time here" (Dallas County, Alabama, Sher-iff's Department Surveillance Tapes). Like King, Anderson sought to create feelings of belonging and purpose among activists by turning to the book of Matthew in the Bible. While the direct-action portion of the day had been difficult and discouraging, at the meeting activists confessed and reframed discouragement, remembering their goals and the religious imaginaries that supported their work.

In addition to rejuvenating the group's spirits, this meeting was the site for interpreting and analyzing the day's events, particularly media and coun-termovement accounts. King takes this purpose on as well, analyzing the interactions between Cooper and Sheriff Clark and the media's account of it. King first offers a legal interpretation of the injunction issued by the Dis-trict Judge. He maintains that the SCLC lawyers are still working to under-stand exactly what it means for their demonstrations, but he asserts that what is clear is that "Sheriff Clark has already violated [the] injunction" (Dallas County, Alabama, Sheriff's Department Surveillance Tapes). He goes on to apply this interpretation to Cooper's response to Clark. Here, he asserts that the real story has not yet been told and offers his analysis: "The truth of the situation is that Mrs. Cooper, if she did anything, was provoked by Sheriff Clark. At that moment he was engaging in some very ugly, usual business of action. We are going to get more of that." King seeks to engage the group in a new understanding of the events that reveal the unwillingness of Clark and other Selma law enforcement officials to adhere to the law; this reveals them as brutal oppressors. This interpretation of the day's events overturns narratives about the civil rights demonstrations turning violent, and in this way, King's message overall worked with the rest of the meeting's program to renew activists and prepare them for more demonstrating.

The affective renewal of activists and the interpretation of the day's events are key purposes that explain much about the meeting's internal functions as a site for separating temporarily to recharge and to reflect on movement reception. Recognizing these internal purposes of the meeting and its liturgy, however, does not tell the whole story of this meeting, an event recorded by the placement of a surveillance device on the podium in the front of the church (Dallas County, Alabama, Sheriff's Department Surveillance Tapes; Fager, *Selma 1965*, 46). Indeed, the Dallas County Police Department planted the device at some point in advance of the meeting, and it was not lost on activists that their speech was being recorded. Rather, they exploited the opportunity to continue with the meeting as planned and purposed—to encourage the group gathered and to interpret the negative messages circulating through the press about Cooper. Then, Abernathy, Bevel, and other leaders took further rhetorical advantage by calling out the device as a "doohickey." Here, they repurposed what was intended for surveillance as a site for laughter.

Through these references to the "doohickey," figures invite activists to tap the power of Black joy as nonviolent response. Philosopher Lindsey Stewart writes: "Black joy . . . rejects the implicit requirement of Black abjection for political recognition . . . and foregrounds a flourishing relation of the self to the self . . . [or] how Black folks relate to each other" and "serves as a refusal to entertain the white gaze" (*The Politics of Black Joy*, 7, 9). To perform Christian nonviolence, collectives were often taught to enact middle-class respectability, juxtaposing Black dignity and manners with white oppressors' behavior. Judith Hoover call attentions to this tactic in Nashville, where activists were instructed not to "laugh out" or "slouch" and to "dress nicely" (quoted in Hoover, "The Nashville Sit-Ins," 101, 100). Marilyn Delaure observes how striking this image appeared in television news coverage: "The lunch counter demonstrations were the epitome of orderly decorum: in their dress and comportment, the student protestors exemplified middle-class respectability" ("Televisuality and the Performance of Citizenship," 247). The second example in this chapter might be read as an extension of this strategy. However, in this Selma meeting, Abernathy and Bevel reveal another dimension of Christian nonviolence performed in the civil rights movement, one where Black people refuse the oppressor's gaze (or in this case, ear). In response to the surveillance device, Abernathy invites the group to laugh with one another, and their peaceful response is the joy they share.

Abernathy employs the first half of the "doohickey" speech to extend King's reinterpretation of the day's events and bolster activists' spirits, and these strategies precede his instruction in responding to white surveillance through joy. When Abernathy takes the podium, he opens by joking with the crowd for not standing up to greet him. Saying he does not believe "in half-doing anything," he tells the crowd: "If you're gone stand up, stand up. So, everybody stand up" (Dallas County, Alabama, Sheriff's Department Surveillance Tapes). He goes on to encourage respect for all the leaders, including Reverend Reese and John Lewis, in the Selma movement. Next, he claims he needs "to put one or two things on the record tonight." Repeating this phrase, he builds on King's interpretation of the day's events, highlighting Sheriff Clark as the violent agitator in provoking Clark. Moreover, he defines Clark's violence as emblematic of the white supremacy in Selma they are working against, using it to reveal the importance of continued demonstrating. Here, his speech extends the purposes set out from the beginning of the meeting, to renew activists and to reframe media narratives.

The audio recording of this meeting indicates that with the phrase, "put it in the record," Abernathy invited audience's attention to the surveillance device on the podium. As soon as he spoke the phrase, the audience begins roaring with laughter. Using this phrase as an entrée, he created new meaning for the device likely visible to the audience. What the local police intended to invoke fear and to reroute the meeting's purpose, Abernathy reclaims as cause for laughter. He repeats the phrase "Now you get it in the record" twice in the first half of his speech, preparing activists for his more overt reference to the device as "doohickey" that serves as his conclusion. Here, he shifts into call-and-response engagement with the group gathered inviting them to "talk to the doohickey" with him. He continues: "Talk to the doohickey. We are not going to take it. There are some things that destroy our manhood. How can I go home at night and look my children in the eyes, when I . . . have not been free to walk downtown any way that I choose to walk downtown?" By referring to the surveillance device as doohickey, he develops a strategy for responding to the varied perspectives present in the space. For the audience of police detectives, this naming and mocking acknowledges their surveillance and demonstrates resolution to proceed with movement plans. Calling their microphone a "doohickey" exchanges what they intended to surveil and intimidate for comedic relief and pedagogical opportunity, thus refusing the surveillor's attempt to own the tone and purposes of the meeting.

For activists, Abernathy reveals joy as Christian nonviolent response. They laugh together at the oppressor and his attempt to intervene in a key movement space. Charles Fager recalls: "The people laughed with delight. Abernathy had a droll, earthy humor in his speeches which had quickly become so popular . . . The whole audience convulsed with laughter at his performance. People held their sides and wiped their eyes; they had never seen anything to match it" (*Selma 1965*, 46). Rather than ignoring the device as others (including King) had done, Abernathy took rhetorical and pedagogical advantage of its presence, calling out police detectives and inviting the group to relish their relationships to one another.

In this way, Abernathy's appeal to joy enacts and teaches radical pacificism. Like the Hattiesburg moderator and Sherrod, Abernathy models how to engage with countermovement groups and their attempts to intervene in the meeting space. And like Sherrod, he creates an opening for the collective to participate and practice cultivating radical pacifist response. After calling out the device as doohickey, he invites the crowd to speak as a group. Here, Selma activists collectively speak together to police detectives:

> *Abernathy:* Are you going to take it?
> *Crowd:* No!"
> *Abernathy:* Talk to the doohickey. Are you going to take it? Then what
>   do you want?
> *Crowd:* Freedom!
> *Abernathy:* I don't believe the doohickey heard. What do you want?
> *Crowd:* Freedom!
> *Abernathy:* What do you want?
> *Crowd:* Freedom!
> *Abernathy:* What do you want?
> *Crowd:* Freedom!
> *Abernathy:* When do you want it?
> *Crowd:* Now!
> *Abernathy:* When do you want it?
> *Crowd:* Now!
> *Abernathy:* Aw, shucks now. (Dallas County, Alabama, Sheriff's
>   Department Surveillance Tapes)

Responding to Abernathy's cues, the audience speaks back, shifting from joy and laughter to explicit collective statement of their commitment to Black freedom. Here, they remind themselves and the audience of police that the Selma movement will not back down. This performance reveals Abernathy's skill as pedagogue within meetings, a role he also takes on in Birmingham (Holmes, "'Hear Me Tonight'" 157). This scene further demonstrates the ways in which Abernathy teaches the crowd to recognize and exploit white surveillance and turn it to a rhetorical advantage. Rather than enact a quiet dignity, however, this performance of Christian nonviolence centers collective joy and laughter.

Abernathy's doohickey address in Selma was not the first or last time that leaders used this trope to laugh about surveillance. In this meeting, after Abernathy finished speaking, James Bevel took the platform to discuss how to proceed with demonstrating the next day. As he explains plans for the campaign, he says: "Not only that, the doohickey's still here" (Dallas County). This statement seems to be a clue to the audience that they should expect continued harassment on the part of the police, and perhaps a directive to police that Bevel's instructions are veiled in ways they will not be able to fully understand. At the Selma mass meeting, Abernathy invites laughter at the device and Bevel follows his lead, reminding audiences of its presence.

These speeches in Selma were also not the first time activists laughed about police detectives' devices. Writing about a Birmingham 1963 mass meeting, historian Andrew Manis notes that minister Ed Gardner also described a transmitter as a doohickey (*A Fire You Can't Put Out,* 356). Abernathy picked the trope up later in the evening: "You hear that, little doohickey? . . . And biting dogs and ain't nothing else going to stop me. . . . We ain't afraid of white folks anymore" (quoted in Manis, *A Fire You Can't Put Out,* 356). Like in Selma, leaders used the doohickey trope to recenter this Birmingham mass meeting on activist goals, laughing with one another and enjoying the power of the collective. Taken together, these instances of calling out and laughing at the doohickey reveal the importance of Black joy as creative response to oppression. This strand of Christian nonviolence contrasts oft-cited images of civil rights activists' quiet dignity and expands the view of radical pacifism in action.

Conclusion: Crafting Peaceful Resistance through Liturgy

Lawyer Hodding Carter III observes: "The civil rights movement both tapped the American conscience, and it piqued the American conscience. It appealed to it and it developed it. It came out of a consensus that you couldn't allow what was going on in the South to continue, but it also focused that consensus" (Carter, Interview, 15). The primary purpose of the meeting was cultivating group identity and positioning participants for civic engagement, and these rhetorical purposes were animated by the event's liturgy. Yet another purpose, as this chapter reveals, was to "ta[p] the American conscience" and teach radical pacifism. The meeting served as a catalyst space for Christian nonviolence as direct action, where activists performed the liturgy of the mass meetings before a range of audiences, including segregationists and local law enforcement. These audiences at times sought to interrupt and intimidate, and they often intended to thwart activists plans and unsettle meetings as sites for fervor and renewal. Yet for over a decade, civil rights leaders remained committed to welcoming outsiders into meetings.

Studying these countermovement responses shows the varied, creative ways activists spoke with the outsiders who entered meetings. In Hattiesburg, activists largely ignored the presence of the KKK and White Citizen's Council. In Terrell Country, the collective relied on the liturgy for strength and quiet dignity, and they also spoke back directly as truth-tellers. In Selma, leaders encouraged the group to laugh together and find strength in their shared joy. These scenes offer insight into the rich variety of Christian nonviolent rhetorics performed and taught in the mass meeting.

Conclusion

Faith, Racial Justice, and Rhetorical Activism
in the Twenty-First Century

Historian Wesley Hogan remarks: "Almost no historians have been able to clearly explain how civil rights or Black Power activists accomplished their feats, except through highly generalized abstractions about people transforming the social and political landscape of the nation. The specifics have remained beyond reach" (*Many Minds, One Heart,* 230). Considering this comment, Meagan Parker Brooks reflects on what rhetoricians bring to the study of the civil rights movement. Brooks offers a deep examination of Fannie Lou Hamer's discourse and then moves past the impasse marked out by Hogan and reveals specificity, nuance, and texture in the story of who Hamer was and how she participated in transforming the nation through her rhetorical career. The lesson for future studies, according to Brooks, is that "taking movement discourse seriously is one way to learn more about how particular activists and the broader movement accomplished what it did" (*A Voice That Could Stir an Army,* 246). One of the key objectives of this book was to get at these specifics for one key space in the civil rights movement, the mass meeting. Rather than focus on an individual activist or a particular locale, my interest was in recovering one movement tool and how through its recurrence, individuals and collectives incited change in themselves and their places. Studying the particular space of the mass meeting, then, revealed the nuances and textures of a rhetorical process that activists used across the civil rights movement for a variety of social change ends. In this conclusion, my goals are to reflect on the story of transformation the book conveys and the ways that the project resonates with racial justice activism in the twenty-first century.

As the first book-length reconstruction of mass-meeting scenes across the movement, *Liturgy of Change* locates the transformative power of the mass meeting in the religious and rhetorical patterns of these events. As a liturgy made up of faithful genres, the meeting invited individuals and groups to take first steps into the movement for Black freedom and then provided continuing rhetorical and democratic education. This process of identity making turned on the event's careful and strategic generic structure and the range of rhetorical participation the liturgy afforded meeting attendees. Sacred songs had protest uses before they were sung in mass meetings, but at these events people like Mrs. J. N. Rucker made them freedom songs and invented a musical genre specific to the movement. These leaders along with local collectives forged the genre and their civic identity together. The mass meeting offered a forum for participants to mine prayer's gestural and quiet resources for holding together reverence and resistance and embodying a paradox of uncivil civility. Testimony, the most flexible of the genres examined, afforded individuals a free and open space to experiment with language and narrative, speaking as prophets, storytellers, and democratic agents. Participating in these genres at the mass meeting provided an experience of a changed world, one where Black people's dignity was recognized before God, the law, and the nation. Activists participated in these genres to constitute new modes of thinking and acting in the world. They inhabited these new modes first in the meeting and then as they performed direct action in more public sites.

Beyond the rhetorical transformations facilitated through the liturgy and its genres, the mass meeting was transformative through its spatial orientation. As a space that coordinated rhetorical movement, these events provided preparation and scaffolding for stepping out of the meeting into more public arenas of civil rights activity. Through regular freedom singing, meeting participants practiced finding solace and energy in music; this affective resolve then provided strength and guidance when activists sang during marches or other public protests. Prayer, likewise, prepared activists to endure and persevere and then more literally provided scaffolding for collectives' movement out of meeting spaces and into the streets. Testimony's particular resources for movement emerge from its flexibility. As a malleable genre, activists could dial down the religious dimensions of the genre as they sought to tell their stories in more secular settings beyond the meeting. Mass meetings were able to provide teaching toward this kind of rhetorical dexterity because of their unique and innovative positioning to audience(s). Through the liturgy's pedagogy of peaceful resistance, participants had opportunities to develop internal rhetorics just for themselves while also gaining practice in performing before the press or countermovement groups.

As the book demonstrates, the mass meeting's capacity to encourage multidimensional rhetorical performances, education, and experience emerged from its rhetorical pattern and its spatial particularities. To see these many rhetorical functions entails looking closely at the mass meeting as a space unique to the movement for Black freedom. Scholars of social movement theory emphasize the importance of spaces where individuals can experience—however temporarily—the changes they seek to create (Brown and Pickerill, "Space for Emotion in the Spaces of Activism," 29). The mass meeting provided this kind of haven and prefigurative experience while also maintaining a nuanced relationship to external audiences, and this in-between positioning served key pedagogical functions.

This study also brings to light the public, social significance of everyday religious rhetorics. As chapter 1 emphasizes, the mass meeting's reliance on liturgy enabled it to feel like a familiar church service and worship experience. For the mass meeting, this familiarity was key to practical, rhetorical functions—inviting people in, encouraging participation, and trying out the genres. Yet beyond this familiarity, this aspect of the mass meeting has to be viewed as another dimension of its capacity to move people rhetorically—to draw them into the movement, to sustain them during difficult moments, and to propel them toward the next steps before them. In studying how movement spaces sustain participants affectively, the spiritual rhetorical components cannot be ignored, and in the case of the mass meeting, these spiritual elements point to the importance of examining everyday religious rhetorics as they shape action, identity, and feeling. Civil rights mass meetings aligned the routine experience of the meeting with a faithful vision of social change; this alignment prefigured the world activists were working to create.

Through the focus on the civil rights mass meeting as a prefigurative rhetorical and religious experience, the book helps to draw out a point that is well known: religion was at the heart of the civil rights movement. Davis Houck and David Dixon (*Rhetoric, Religion, and the Civil Rights Movement, 1954–1965, Volumes I and II*), Gary Selby (*Martin Luther King and the Rhetoric of Freedom*), Keith Miller (*Voice of Deliverance*), David Holmes (*Where the Sacred and the Secular Harmonize*), Kirt Wilson ("Interpreting the Discursive Field of the Montgomery Bus Boycott"), and Maegan Parker Brooks (*A Voice that Could Stir an Army*), in rhetorical studies, and Tobin Shearer ("Invoking Crisis"), Ansley Quiros (*God with Us*), Charles Marsh (*The Beloved Community* and *God's Long Summer*), and David Chappell (*A Stone of Hope*), in history, among others, are scholars whose work argues this point admirably. Rhetorical scholars have amassed significant insight into the religious language, strategies, and appeals that animated key speeches and made the movement move. *Liturgy of Change* adds to the story of religion's role in the movement through attention to faith at the conceptual and collective rhetorical level. Recognizing the mass meeting as a liturgy provides greater insight into the ways it operated "as church," to return to activist

John Lewis's phrase. The liturgy that animated the mass meeting reveals faith as a collective force, a felt experience, a rhetorical structure for self and group transformation, and a genre set poised to speak internally and externally. Seeing the mass meeting function in this way, as a rhetorical liturgy, shows faithful experience and participation as key modes of activist-making. By examining the liturgy's specific dimensions as it shaped the participatory genres of song, prayer, and testimony, we can extend recovery and analysis of religious speech to think about emotion and experience and to uncover the collective performances that faithful genres made possible.

The Limits of Liturgy and Twenty-First-Century Racial Justice Movements

The twenty-first century has been marked by an upsurge in collective organizing around antiblackness. On the national stage, Black Lives Matter (BLM) activists respond to the persistent force of white supremacy, particularly as it emerges in police brutality and the unjust loss of Black lives as a result. BLM is arguably the most prominent form of racial justice activism in the early decades of the new millennium in the United States. Scholars contend that BLM reveals a deliberate turn away from the Black church and its rhetorical resources and a turn toward Black feminism (Ransby, *Making All Black Lives Matter;* Jackson, "Ask a Feminist"). While BLM does seek to demonstrate respect for activism of the past, as a movement it is distinct from the faithful genres of civil rights mass meetings, distinctions I reflect on below through attention to a series of meeting paradoxes. Examining BLM's strategic departures from Black church ideologies deepens appreciation of the intellectual and sociopolitical vision of BLM, while also pointing toward the limits of liturgy as an animating concept in the movement for Black freedom. For all its transformative power and significance, the liturgy of the mass meeting circumscribed the participation of women along with queer and young activists and at times forwarded a myopic, gendered vision of freedom and citizenship.

Paradox #1: The liturgy of the mass meeting was designed to invite the collective participation of ordinary people; it was not, however, designed to promote an egalitarian leadership structure. One of the goals of this book was to reveal how the mass meeting provided a key space for ordinary people to show up and develop resolve and rhetorical prowess. Like historian Jeanne Theoharis, from the outset of the project I believed that "the modern Black freedom struggle remains one of the most important examples of the power of ordinary people to change the course of the nation. But the popular stories we get impoverish our ability to see how change happens" (*A More Beautiful and Terrible History,* xvii). The mass meeting was a key space for local people's first steps into making change, and these steps were strategically invited and taught through the faithful genres the book recovers. Popular stories of the movement for Black freedom tend to focus on talented leaders, most often men, and obscure the daily work of transformation and the many people who accomplished it. Through examination of collective rhetorical work at the mass meeting across places and moments, this book contributes to creating a fuller, more expansive picture of how the movement drew ordinary people in and cultivated a desire to work toward Black freedom, no matter the costs. In each chapter of the book, we learn how the mass meeting provided a forum for the rhetorical performance of relatively unknown players in the movement, such as Elizabeth Burgess in Nashville and Irene Johnson in Hattiesburg. We learn too how these performances built upon the earlier work of unsung figures such as Pauli Murray.

As much as the liturgy opened up possibilities for anyone in the group to participate through singing, praying, and testifying, it was not a perfect forum where rhetorical participation was wholly egalitarian. As I discuss in chapter 1, the mass meeting was a gendered space, one that did not overcome the sexist hierarchies of Black church leadership structures in place throughout the South at the time. Activist Ella Baker puts the point strongly: "The role of women in the southern church . . . was that of doing the things that the minister said he wanted to have done. It was not one in which they were credited with having creativity and initiative and capacity to carry out things" (quoted in Ransby, *Ella Baker and the Black Freedom Movement*, 184). While historian Barbara Ransby provides some caveats for this comment, Baker points to a shortcoming of the movement's reliance on the institution and resources of the Black church. Women's rhetorical leadership was limited by the space and authority structure—and I would add genres—of the same tradition that helped transform the South and the nation. Besides women, queer people were also denied leadership positions because of reliance on church-based structures. Bayard Rustin, for example, played crucial roles behind the scenes in 1950s campaigns like the Montgomery Bus Boycott and the Prayer Pilgrimage for Freedom, but because he was a gay man, he was passed over for public leadership positions (Ransby, *Ella Baker and the Black Freedom Movement*, 179). The exclusions of queer people and women from leadership reflect the broader sociopolitical context. These issues were not particular to the civil rights movement, or its liturgical genres, but the movement's key organizations did little to question leaderships models.

In examining the dynamics of the Southern Christian Leadership Conference (SCLC), scholars bring attention to the difficult reality that this group was very skilled at recognizing unjust hierarchies in the nation but far less equipped to turn the same critical eye toward their organization and churches (see for example, Ransby, *Ella Baker and the Black Freedom Movement*, 175–76). This book adds to the evidence documenting these complexities. The faithful genres of the meeting both opened up and closed off avenues of participation and leadership: in the case of the freedom songs, women were clearly authorities on the genre and frequently in charge of this aspect of the liturgy. Prayer and countermovement engagements, however, appear less available as rhetorical opportunities to women or anyone not credentialed or known to be a minister. In these chapters, I do not center women's voices because archival holdings do not provide evidence of these performances. While there is always the possibility the archive will fill out and offer new insights, for meeting genres like prayer and the sermon it is generally true that pastoral authority did position some individuals as "experts" and "authorities" and others without power. Martin Luther King Jr. explained this view of authority: "Leadership never ascends from the pew to the pulpit, but . . . descends from the pulpit to the pew" (quoted in Ransby, *Ella Baker and the Black Freedom Movement*, 168). Thus, like the movement generally, the mass meeting tapped key transformative resources the Black church provided, but it also replicated its patriarchal approach to leadership. This limitation likely constrained meeting liturgies' potential not just for participation and leadership but also for how the genres catalyzed invention, action, and identity.

BLM's leadership structure demonstrates a deliberate attempt to overcome this limitation of the civil rights movement. Most obviously, the movement emerged from the digital organizing of three queer Black women. Alicia Garza, Patrisse Cullors, and Opal Tometi founded BLM after the acquittal of George Zimmerman, the man who shot and killed 17-year-old Trayvon Martin; their first collective action was creating Tumblr and Twitter accounts where people could give accounts in response to the hashtag #blacklivesmatter (Jamilah King, "How Three Friends Turned a Spontaneous Facebook Post into a Global Phenomenon"). In the intervening years, as the movement has grown and evolved, women have persisted as the most visible and public leaders of the movement, and they have sought to root their leadership in grassroots and group-centered approaches (Ransby, *Making All Black Lives Matter*, 3). The vision and leadership of these women, however, is not always credited to them, revealing that the issues women faced in the 1950s and 1960s are still present. For example, in some of Melissa Harris-Perry's initial coverage of BLM on MSNBC, she failed to discuss the origin story of the hashtag and did not include any interviews with these founders. Responding to the trend to overlook the significance of her work with Cullors and Tometi, Alicia Garza comments: "To feel like something gets taken from you, used, and you're completely erased from the conversation is infuriating" (quoted in Jamilah King, "How Three Friends Turned a Spontaneous Facebook Post into a Global Phenomenon"). Garza's reflection reminds that while Black women have taken the lead in BLM, racism, sexism, and queerphobia persist and render their work as well as egalitarian leadership structures difficult for the public to accept and celebrate.

Paradox #2: The mass meeting invited groups to engage with a vast, faithful vision of freedom and social change; leaders of the movement often behaved in ways that appeared hypocritical or unprincipled when juxtaposed with this vision. As I discuss throughout the book, the vision of the civil rights movement was grand, encompassing every aspect of life and being. At the mass meeting held at the end of the Montgomery bus boycott, King, for instance, charged the group with recognizing it as "a victory for justice and a victory for goodwill and a victory for the forces of light" ("Nov. 14, 1956, Address to MIA Mass Meeting," 428). He went on to explain the implications for their behavior: "So let us not limit this decision to a victory for Negroes. Let us go back to the buses in all humility and with gratitude to the Almighty God (Yes) for making this decision possible. (Yes)" (428). Freedom, in the view of King and other ministers including Sherrod, Lawson, and Abernathy, depended on Christian morality and ethics, deeply held commitments to making change through peaceful protests lovingly performed. In this example, King calls Montgomerians to respond with peace and love even after the cameras are gone and desegregation has been legislated. After all, he is a minister and an activist and in these roles fuses sociopolitical strategy and pastoral encouragement.

This vision was incredibly important to the successes of the movement, particularly regarding nonviolence and media narratives. It was also, however, difficult to live up to in private. If the vision of change activists were working toward meant behaving with kindness toward a violent white neighbor, then it reasonably followed that it meant treating one another within the movement with the same depth of respect and humility. Yet as historians have probed the internal dynamics of the movement, they concur that activists, particularly men, often fell short of this bar (Ransby, *Ella Baker and the Black Freedom Movement*; Payne, "'Sexism is a helluva thing'"). As outlined above, most civil rights organizations replicated the structural hierarchies that existed outside the movement. As individuals, many leaders struggled to live up to the sexual ethics of Christianity, and these failures disproportionately affected the women of the movement, who endured sexual violence and the pressure to keep quiet about it. As Ransby writes: "During my research on Ella Baker, I remember vividly the stories women in the civil rights movement told me about sexual harassment and assault in movement circles in the 1960s. At that time, few women dared to report instances except to close girlfriends. And some still whispered about it decades later. They feared that their revelations might be used against movement organizations and leaders by those who wanted to discredit the work" (*Making All Black Lives Matter,* 115). Women in the movement bore the burdens of diminished leadership opportunities and sexual harassment and abuse, while recognizing that calling attention to either might thwart movement progress. Victims and witnesses to such internal sexual violence grappled with hypocrisy in leaders' proclamations of peaceful nonviolent action as a way of life.

BLM is not above criticism, but it is a movement that recognizes misalignments between vision, private behavior, and internal movement dynamics as problems to be faced head on and addressed by leadership. In striving to respond to these now well-known issues in civil rights organizing, many BLM activists embrace restorative justice to respond to internal failures and especially sexual violence within the movement. Restorative justice, as explained by activist Jamala Rogers, refers to "a healing process that takes into full account both accountability and personal salvation" (quoted in Ransby, *Making All Black Lives Matter,* 113). This approach does not wholly absolve BLM of tensions, problematic dynamics, or the possibility of violence. As Ransby writes: "Political work is not done by angels or robots but by people—complicated and beautifully imperfect human beings, all of whom have been socialized in a hetero-patriarchal capitalist society" (113). However, the restorative justice approach does help discourage silence around these issues and creates a mechanism for healing and accountability.

Paradox #3: Through the genres of the meeting, collectives explored and defined a vision of change and democratic citizenship for themselves; on the national stage, this vision belonged to the men of the movement and missed key aspects of the injustice Black people in the United States faced. One of the points that I have emphasized throughout the book is that the collective genres of song, prayer, and testimony opened rhetorical opportunities for groups to collectively craft the movement vision and goals. In the chapter on testimony, for example, we see how a young woman uses her story-telling moment in the meeting to discuss her specific experiences; we see too how many do not testify in faith-specific frames or language. These individuals found space in testimony to explore and feel out their own understanding of freedom and citizenship, defining these terms for themselves. This aspect of the liturgy is important: individuals developed their agency and their understanding of the movement in a range of ways that we miss when we focus only on leaders' performances at meetings.

However, it is also true that at the national level, with a few notable exceptions like Fannie Lou Hamer, genres circulated in ways that aligned largely with internal power structures of the movement. This alignment meant that the vision of freedom and change that took hold nationally omitted the collective theorizing that could happen in the meeting. The ministers and their sermonic addresses were authoritative, and this authority meant that these were the figures who were most often sought out to craft and explain the movement vision beyond the meeting space. Within the mass meeting, faithful genres created opportunities for people to engage, question, and reconceive of movement ideals; beyond the meeting, faithful genres could not be severed from public perceptions that the ministers were the experts, and women and laypeople's contributions were subservient to these leaders. As historian Laurie Green observes, this aspect of the movement obfuscates a truly just vision of change and point to ways "ideals of freedom itself may have been gendered" ("Challenging the Civil Rights Narrative," 61). In Greene's analysis, for instance, freedom at the national level often was defined through Black men's experiences of political exclusions and ideals of male dignity, failing to account for the public hypersexualization and domestic abuses that marked many Black women's lives (61–63).

BLM's vision of justice expands considerably on the demands of civil rights activists. BLM works to account for all Black people's experiences, recognizing that this means confronting a wide range of structures and ideologies including capitalism, heteronormativity, and the prison system. Ransby explains BLM's vision: "politically and ideologically grounded in the US-based Black feminist tradition, a tradition that embraces an intersectional analysis while insisting on the interlocking and interconnected nature of different systems of oppression; advocates the importance of women's group-centered leadership; supports LGBTQIA issues; and seeks to center the most marginalized and vulnerable members of the Black community in terms of the language and priorities of the movement" (*Making All Black Lives Matter*, ix). BLM is by no means monolithic; activists understand and define freedom in complementary and varied ways. However, the movement is generally held together by a Black feminist tradition that seeks inclusivity and broad, structural transformations. Many BLM activists trace this tradition back to civil rights figures such as Baker, Hamer, and Murray. For example, explaining her involvement in BLM, activist Aislinn Pulley observes: "No one is free until we are all free [to paraphrase Fannie Lou Hamer], and that includes those who are employed, unemployed, those who are incarcerated or in gangs, or who are sex workers. What we are fighting for is a world where our full humanity is honored and protected and valued, and that includes all of who we are" (quoted in Ransby, *Making All Black Lives Matter*, 157). Pulley, like many activists in BLM, finds inspiration in civil rights activists like Hamer, who were both active in the movement for Black freedom and outspoken critics of its injustices.

Reflecting on this series of meeting paradoxes provides a glimpse into some of the shortcomings of liturgy as a support for social change and complicates a view of the mass meeting as beautifully and perfectly transformative. The civil rights mass meeting was beautifully and *imperfectly* transformative. In recognizing and interrogating these imperfections, BLM seeks to craft its vision, leadership structure, and approach to internal movement problems such that they might move racial justice forward in more radically inclusive ways, while still showing respect for civil rights activism and honoring some of the women most important to the movement.

Liturgies and Faithful Genres of Racial Justice in the Twenty-First Century

BLM reveals ways that twenty-first century racial justice activism departs from church-based approaches. Given the clear distinctions BLM sets out, it might seem that just as the civil rights movement ended and gave way to the new, more secular activism of Black Power, the decline in faith-based religious activism that marked the transition from the 1960s to the 1970s persisted in a downward trend. It is generally true that church structures no longer undergird a collective, nationally recognized approach to racial justice activism as they did during the civil rights movement. However, throughout the Black Power movement and in the context of BLM organizing, individuals do seek racial justice through sacred rhetoric.[1] In the twenty-first century, activists, scholars, and lawyers such as Barack Obama, Bryan Stevenson, Jemar Tisby, Bree Newsome, Ekemini Uwon, and Michael Eric Dyson turn to liturgy and the genres of hymn, prayer, and testimony to carry on the enduring, still-too-needed work of racial justice.[2] In this final section, I highlight examples of the ways Dyson, Obama, and a group of religious leaders in Boston creatively adapt and circulate faithful genres in response to white supremacist violence and police brutality. A comprehensive look at the ways in which faith intersects with racial justice activism in the early decades of the twenty-first century would take another book. My goal here is simply to point to examples as a way of complicating the decline narrative and promoting diversity of activists' rhetorical approaches.[3]

The first example is a *liturgy of change*. In 2017, pastor, scholar, and activist Michael Eric Dyson published *Tears We Cannot Stop: A Sermon to White America*. This book, a response to the election of Donald Trump to the Oval Office and ongoing police violence against Black people, invites white readers to worship with Dyson and turn toward specific actions in support of racial justice. As he explains: "America is in trouble, and a lot of that trouble—perhaps most of it—has to do with race. . . . Black despair piles up with each body that gets snuffed up on video and streamed on social media. We have, in the span of a few years, elected the nation's first Black president and placed in the Oval Office the scariest racial demagogue in a generation" (3). This opening charge makes up the "Call to Worship," the first liturgical genre of the book. The table of contents reveals the pattern of faithful genres that comprises the rest of the text:

I. Call to Worship
II. Hymns of Praise
III. Invocation
IV. Scripture Reading
V. Sermon
   Repenting of Whiteness
   1. Inventing Whiteness
   2. The Five Stages of White Grief
   3. The Plague of White Innocence
   Being Black in America
   4. Nigger
   5. Our Own Worst Enemy?
   6. Coptopia
VI. Benediction
VII. Offering Plate
VIII. Prelude to Service
IX. Closing Prayer

The book is certainly religious in its structure, but Dyson notes at the beginning that he does not just intend it for Christian readers; rather, this is a liturgy for all. As he explains: "All of us . . . share a language of moral repair. That language is our common meeting ground, our tool of analysis, and yes, our inspiration for repentance, our hope for redemption" (*Tears We Cannot Stop*, 4). The book, then, is religiously inclusive, and this thread is carried through in the choice of language and sources, which are often secular. Thus, the structure of the book, the liturgy, is its most emphatic religious component. As the outline conveys, Dyson moves readers through each genre of a worship service, leading up to the sermon that calls the audience to repentance and to deeper understanding of the Black experience in the United States. The Sermon, the longest section of the book, is deeply explanatory, a kind of illumination of the chasm between white and Black experience. It is followed by the Benediction, which is a call to action. Here, Dyson lays out a path forward for readers, offering practical suggestions for responding to racism and repenting of whiteness.

This benediction reveals a rhetoric of faithful activism enabled by the liturgical structure of the text. In this section, Dyson outlines a number of actions—reparation, education, participation, interracial friendship, speaking up, crossing racial lines, and empathy. Each of these actions is unpacked with practical suggestions. For example, in calling white readers to cross racial lines, Dyson explains that this can mean visiting Black people in schools, jails, and churches. He writes about his own experience visiting his brother in prison and how he makes time to go to other jails and prisons as well to talk with people and learn about what their lives are like. This call to cross racial lines, like each of the other actions, is also explained with pithy social analyses that reveal the systemic racism that underpins the need for action. For instance, in explaining the need to visit and understand jails and prisons, Dyson writes: "There is a pipeline, my friends, one that runs from the playground to the prison. When you visit the incarcerated you'll see how utterly decent most of these men and women are, how they got a bad deal because they were poor with no one to advocate for them" (*Tears We Cannot Stop*, 210). This quick and clear analysis identifies the reason for the action, structural whiteness, and it does so as a call to repair, to action, and to greater justice. As a rhetoric of faithful activism, Dyson's call is expansive, a call to individual and collective action that aims to address social as well as systemic issues. However, it is not an explicit call to legal or political action, though the critiques that undergird the actions encourage readers to develop an awareness of these dimensions of the problem. Ultimately, the book encourages readers to respond and act with greater awareness and understanding of racial problems in America, and the liturgy of the book is central to this call. Written in a secular context and for secular and faithful readers of all religions, *Tears We Cannot Stop* works to make liturgy inclusive, an experience of worship that can be shared through a commitment to racial justice. As a minister, Dyson understands the power of liturgy to shape identity and to encourage reflection on moral repair. Taking this power outside of the context of the church and penning it in book form, he works to create an identity of racial awareness for White Americans and then to lay out the next steps for this identity.[4]

Tears We Cannot Stop indicates the enduring rhetorical possibilities of liturgies of change. The individual faithful genres of the book continue to circulate as well, though also through adaptations and new modes of circulation. To move to the next example of sacred song, when asked to respond to the tragic shooting at Emanuel Baptist Church in South Carolina, then-President Barack Obama found sacred song to be an appropriate mode of lament and call to action. Generally, sacred songs do not have the kind of collective, activist power that they did in the civil rights movement. Sound studies scholars, for the most part, agree that this shift has been emphatic, affecting music's social and activist significance broadly (Sterne, "A Groove We Can Move To," 69). Still, individuals publicly turn to faithful music to respond to racial injustice, and in 2015, Obama provided a prominent example of a public enactment of hymn when he spoke at the Emanuel Baptist Church. Obama was called upon to speak to congregants after they lost nine members to the gun violence of white supremacist Dylan Roof. In his eulogy, Obama turned to the genre of hymn. In closing, he sang, "Amazing grace, how sweet the sound, that saved a wretch like me; I once was lost, but now I'm found; was blind but now I see" (The White House). He then went on to use the hymn as the linchpin of his conclusion:

> Clementa Pinckney found that grace.
> Cynthia Hurd found that grace.
> Susie Jackson found that grace.
> Ethel Lance found that grace.
> DePayne Middleton-Doctor found that grace.
> Tywanza Sanders found that grace.
> Daniel L. Simmons, Sr. found that grace.
> Sharonda Coleman-Singleton found that grace.
> Myra Thompson found that grace.
> Through the example of their lives, they've now passed it on to us.
> May we find ourselves worthy of that precious and extraordinary gift,
> as long as our lives endure. May grace now lead them home. May God
> continue to shed His grace on the United States of America. (The
> White House)

Obama turned to a faithful genre to support the work of his eulogy, the hymn. His hybrid speech responded to the heinous crime of Roof and the racial injustice carried out against Pinckney, Hurd, Jackson, Lance, Middleton-Doctor, Sanders, Simmons, Coleman-Singleton, and Thompson. This 2015 moment in Charleston points to the enduring rhetorical power of the genre of hymn as a mode for addressing white supremacists' violence. Fittingly, Obama turned to the language and resources of the church to respond to a tragedy carried out inside it. Like Matthew Jones in Jackson, Mississippi, Obama thinks of song as a mode for grieving murders at the hands of racial hate.

To turn to the final example, prayer too circulates today and provides a way of responding to racial injustice. In the summer of 2020, when footage of George Floyd's brutal death at the hands of police circulated, protests erupted across the United States. One strand of these protests was the prayer march. For example, a group of Black clergy in Boston, Massachusetts, led hundreds of marchers from Roxbury's Nubian Square to the Boston Police Department. Upon reaching the plaza, the group paused in silence for eight minutes and forty-nine seconds, the length of time Floyd suffered with a police officer kneeling on his neck. This event, according to organizers, was a gathering to pray for justice in response to police violence against Black people. For this group, prayer provided a way to center and organize the march and a generic reason for silence; silence is a feature of prayer. Similar to the marchers in St. Augustine, Florida, the coalition mined the resources of prayer for protest, finding rhetorical power in the interplay of reverence and resistance. Summer 2020 also saw prayer circulate in this moment as a structure for gatherings, or vigils. The day before the prayer march, Bostonians gathered at a prayer vigil held outside City Hall. An interfaith group of religious leaders spoke and prayed. Bishop John Borders III prayed: "O God, our land is in need of healing. . . . The lack of resolve for the endless mutilation of black bodies, the disparity between the haves and the have-nots, is worsening and causing more unrest" (quoted in Jenkins, "At protests, some clergy pray, others put their bodies and souls on the line"). While prayer marches center on embodied action, prayer vigils afford more time for spoken prayers, particularly lament, cries for justice, and calls for divine action. These two examples are reminders that prayer remains a viable response to racial injustice for many.

Taken together, these figures and their rhetorical work reveal that liturgies of change and faithful genres continue to offer academics, politicians, and activists ways of responding to police brutality and white supremacy in the twenty-first century. While there are many differences and unique aspects of this twenty-first century rhetorical activism, the circulation of these genres makes clear that religion has not declined as a force marking rhetorics about race. These examples bring to life the point Martin Camper makes in his article "The Future of the History of Rhetoric Is Religious": he reminds scholars and activist alike that faith remains a viable mode of engaging publics in issues of racial justice. In this way, the work and performances of Michael Eric Dyson, Barack Obama, and the clergy in Boston should be viewed as glimpses of new possibilities for liturgy and faithful genres. Far from anomalies, faithful individuals continue to participate, adapt, revise, and even lead in activist efforts. The mass meetings studied in this book then are not historical blips reminding of a time when religion *could* be a resource for productive civic engagement. Instead, they should be viewed as roadmaps with rhetorical lessons that resonate today, showing moral vision, creativity, perseverance, and urgency that is still much needed. While these events cannot be replicated or fully described, as faithful enactments of a changed world, the rhetorical work of mass meetings might help point the way to a more just future.

NOTES

Introduction

1. For a critique of this movement periodization, see Keith Miller, "Afterword: Chiseling at a Fossilized Memory—Connections, Questions, and Implications" and Jacquelyn Dowd Hall, "The Long Civil Rights Movement and the Political Uses of the Past."

2. Historians have made clear that the movement for Black freedom relied on the resources of the Black church tradition, and rhetorical scholars have investigated the role that religious language and appeals played in individual's speeches at civil rights mass meetings and the movement. For historical treatments, see, for example, David Chappell, *Stone of Hope,* and Charles Marsh, *God's Long Summer.* In rhetorical studies, see Brooks, *A Voice That Could Stir an Army*; Holmes, *Where the Sacred and the Secular Harmonize*; Houck and Dixon, *Rhetoric, Religion, and the Civil Rights Movement*; Andrew King, "The Rhetorical Legacy of the Black Church"; Rhea Estelle Lathan, *Freedom Writing: African American Civil Rights Literacy Activism, 1955-1967;* Keith Miller, *Voice of Deliverance: The Language of Martin Luther King, Jr., and Its Sources*; and Wilson, "Interpreting the Discursive Field of the Montgomery Bus Boycott."

3. For examinations in this vein, see Wilson, "Interpreting the Discursive Field of the Montgomery Bus Boycott"; Selby, *Martin Luther King and the Rhetoric of Freedom*; Holmes, *Where the Sacred and the Secular Harmonize* and "'Hear Me Tonight'"; and Brooks, *A Voice That Could Stir an Army.*

4. For studies of the civil rights march, see Davi Johnson Thornton, "The Rhetoric of Civil Rights Photographs: James Meredith's March Against Fear" and Susan Santoli, Paige Vitulli, and Rebecca Giles, "Picturing Equality: Exploring Civil Rights' Marches Through Photographs." Vanessa Beasely offers an important critique of the ableism underlying the march and the tactic's role in social movement; see her "The Trouble With Marching: Abelism, Visibility, and Exclusion of People with Disabilities."

5. In naming a "keyword" for movement studies, I have in mind Christina Foust's call for a "commons" and critique of studies of social change rhetorics that can be characterized as "nomadic" ("'Social Movement Rhetoric',," 51). Foust suggests that critics work toward a "commons," "an undifferentiated reality, openly available and accessible to humans . . . rendered more bountiful with each creative act that springs forth from it—acts of artistry that are only possible through the commons' shared wealth" (63).

6. For earlier work on genre and social movement, see Richard Fulkerson, "The Public Letter as a Rhetorical Form"; Herbert Simons, "Requirements, Problems, and Strategies: A Theory of Persuasion for Social Movements"; Kathleen Jamieson, "Antecedent Genre as Rhetorical Constraint"; Karlyn Kohrs Campbell and

Kathleen Jamieson, "Form and Genre in Rhetorical Criticism: An Introduction"; and John C. Hammerback and Richard J. Jenson, "Ethnic Heritage as Rhetorical Legacy: The Plan of Delano." For overviews of genre theory, see Anis Bawarshi and Mary Jo Reiff, *Genre: An Introduction to History, Theory, Research, and Pedagogy*, and Amy Devitt, *Writing Genres*.

7. See, for example, Gerard Hauser's *Vernacular Voices: The Rhetoric of Publics and Public Spheres*.

8. For discussion of the significance of this type of study for civil rights history, see Sharon Monteith, " 'I second that emotion': A Case for Using Imaginative Sources in Writing Civil Rights History." Specific to civil rights rhetoric, see for example Stephen Schneider, *You Can't Padlock an Idea*, and Elizabeth Ellis Miller, "Reframing Rhetorical Failure: Confession and Conversion in Sarah Patton Boyle's *Desegregated Heart*."

9. For other scholarship related to genre and identity-making, see Victoria Gallagher, "Displaying Race: Cultural Projection and Commemoration" and Kelly Jakes, "La France en Chantant: The Rhetorical Construction of French Identity in Songs of the Resistance Movement."

10. For earlier theorizing and case studies in this vein, see Richard B. Gregg, "The Ego-Function of the Rhetoric of Protest"; Erin J. Rand, "A Disunited Nation and Legacy of Contradiction: Queer Nation's Construction of Identity"; and Tasha Dubriwny, "Consciousness-Raising as Collective Rhetoric: The Articulation of Experience in the Redstocking's Abortion Speak-Out of 1969." For overviews specific to collective identity in social movement rhetoric, see Charles Stewart, Craig Smith, and Robert Denton, *Persuasion and Social Movements*, 6th ed., and John W. Bowers, Donovan, J. Ochs, Richard J. Jensen, and David P. Shulz, *The Rhetoric of Agitation and Control*, 3rd ed.

11. I gesture here toward debates about over constitutive vs. instrumental rhetorics. For a critique of a constitutive view of rhetoric in the study of social movement, see Dana Cloud, "The Null Persona: Race and the Rhetoric of Silence in the Uprising of '34." For an overview of the broader discussion, see Amy Pason, Christina R. Foust, and Kate Zittlow Rogness, "Introduction: Rhetoric and the Study of Social Change."

12. Joshua Gunn (*Maranatha*) and Linda Williams ("Film Bodies: Gender, Genre, and Excess") call for attention to "body genres"; Mary Jo Reiff ("Geographies of Public Genres") and Risa Applegarth ("Genre, Location, and Mary Austin's Ethos") emphasize the need for attention to material and spatial dimensions to genres; and Carolyn Miller, Amy Devitt, and Victoria Gallagher ("Genre: Permanence and Change") mark out these areas as significant for future inquiry.

13. For scholarship on the role of the body in rhetorical studies, see Karma Chávez, "The Body: An Abstract and Actual Rhetorical Concept"; Debra Hawhee, *Moving Bodies*; Melanie Yergeau, *Authoring Autism: On Rhetoric and Neurological Queerness*; Jacqueline Rhodes, "Slutwalk Is Not Enough: Notes Toward a Critical Feminist Rhetoric"; and Jack Selzer, "Habeas Corpus: An Introduction."

14. For an overview of the distinction between emotion and affect and its significance to rhetorical studies, see Jenny Rice, "The New 'New': Making a Case for Critical Affect Studies." For cultural theorists who contend with affect and emotion, see for example Sara Ahmed, *The Cultural Politics of Emotion*; Lauren Berlant, *The Female Complaint: The Unfinished Business of Sentimentality in American Culture*; and Brian Massumi, *Parables for the Virtual*.

15. Enoch extends a larger conversation among feminist scholars about rhetoric, gender, and space; see her *Domestic Occupations: Spatial Rhetorics and Women's Work.* See also Lindal Buchanan, *Regendering Delivery;* Nan Johnson, *Gender and Rhetorical Space in American Life, 1866–1910;* and Linda W. Kerber, "Separate Spheres, Female Worlds, Woman's Place: The Rhetoric of Women's History."

16. In addition to studying the intersections of belief and rhetorical action, the lived theology approach might also examine elements of rhetorical history and theory. Scholars consider, for example, how sacred understandings inform rhetorical concepts including ethos and kairos. For more on this topic, see Kenneth Zagacki, "The Ethos of Rhetoric and Thomas Merton's 'Letters to a White Liberal'" and Richard Benjamin Crosby, "Cathedral of Kairos: Rhetoric and Revelation in the House of Prayer."

CHAPTER 1
Becoming Hopeful

1. For discussion of translation as rhetorical practice, see Claudia Carlos, "Translation as Rhetoric: Edward Jerningham's 'Impenitence'."

2. "Genre set" and "genre repertoire" are Devitt's terms for explaining relationships among genres (*Writing Genres*). An ecological view of genres refers to Rivers and Weber's study of the Montgomery bus boycott, where they observe social movement as "[a] complex concatenation of texts and rhetorical acts, both mundane and monumental, propelled the movement—logistical and organizational texts to keep the boycott going, informational and motivational texts to inspire the boycotters, and advocacy, public relations, ally building, fundraising, and legal texts to represent the movement to various other publics" ("Ecological, Pedagogical, Public Rhetoric," 200).

3. The topic of religious rhetoric has emerged as an important subfield in rhetoric studies. As starting points specific to Christianity, see Michael-John DePalma and Jeffrey Ringer, *Mapping Christian Rhetorics: Connecting Conversations, Charting New Territories*, and Elizabeth Vander Lei, Thomas Amorose, Beth Daniell, and Anne Ruggles Gere, *Renovating Rhetoric in the Christian Tradition*. Other important studies include Michael Bernard-Donals and Janice W. Fernheimer, *Jewish Rhetorics: History, Theory, Practice*; Carol Mattingly, *Secret Habits: Catholic Literacy Education for Women in the Early Nineteenth Century*; Rasha Diab, *Shades of Sulh: The Rhetorics of Arab-Islamic Reconciliation*; and Davida Charney, *Persuading God: Rhetorical Studies of First-Person Psalms*.

4. For a secular discussion of this idea, see Chris Earle's essay, " 'More Resilient than Concrete and Steel': Consciousness-Raising, Self-Discipline, and Bodily Resistance in Solitary Confinement." Earle calls attention to the techniques of the self in the work of Michel Foucault. According to Earle, the techniques of the self describe how "subjects are constructed and positioned by power but possess and can cultivate the capacities to critically reflect their self-understandings and work to transform themselves, to become different from what we are or have been told we must be" (133).

5. As a rhetorical approach to religious language and experience, liturgy need not be limited to Christian traditions. For discussion of liturgy as a broad, multi-faith concept, see Moyaert and Geldhof, eds., *Ritual Participation and Interreligious Dialogue: Boundaries, Transgressions, and Innovation*.

6. For critiques of Christianity and its relationship to politics of race, see Robert P. Jones, *White Too Long: The Legacy of White Supremacy in American Christianity*, and Jemar Tisby, *The Color of Compromise: The Truth About the American Church's Complicity in Racism*.

7. Another way to think about this question is through the lens of a social gospel. Historian and theologian Gary Dorrien writes about this topic particular to the civil rights movement in *Breaking White Supremacy: Martin Luther King Jr. and the Black Social Gospel*. For rhetorical scholars who study the social gospel, see Lisa Zimmerelli, "'The Stereoscopic View of Truth': Frances Willard's Woman in the Pulpit as a Feminist Rhetoric of Theology" and William Duffy, "Transforming Decorum: The Sophistic Appeal of Walter Rauschenbusch and the Social Gospel."

8. For overviews of African American rhetoric, see Keith Gilyard and Adam J. Banks, *On African American Rhetoric*, and Vershawn Young and Michelle Robinson, *The Routledge Reader of African American Rhetoric: The Longue Duree of Black Voices*.

9. For discussions of the sermon and the Black church, see Andrew King, "The Rhetorical Legacy of the Black Church"; Beverly Moss, *A Community Text Arises*; and Roxanne Mountford, *The Gendered Pulpit*; for scholars who examine it as a site for rhetorical education, see Shirley Logan, *Liberating Language: Sites of Rhetorical Education in Nineteenth-Century Black America*, and Maegan Parker Brooks, *A Voice That Could Stir an Army*; for analysis of its role as a space for hush harbor rhetorics, see Vorris Nunley, *Keepin' It Hushed: The Barbershop and African American Hush Harbor Rhetoric*.

10. Activist Fannie Lou Hamer called out the "chicken eatin' preachers," or according to Brooks, "those religious leaders who were content to stay out of the risky movement for social change" (33). Hamer put the point plainly, "Every church door in the state of Mississippi should be open for these meetings, but preachers have preached for years what he didn't believe himself. And if he's willing to trust God . . . he won't mind opening the church door" ("We're on Our Way," 49).

11. For discussion of Nashville civil rights rhetoric and the sit-ins, see Judith D. Hoover, "The Nashville Sit-Ins: Successful Nonviolent Direct-action through Rhetorical Invention and Advocacy."

12. In *Education and Equality*, Allen names these three rhetorical modes as important for the broad civic and political agency that she is describing.

13. Commenting on a turn away from inquiry into emotion in the twentieth century, Robert Hariman and John Lucaites claimed emotion was "rhetoric's major liability" ("Dissent and Emotional Management in a Liberal-Democratic Society," 6). Hariman and Lucaites define emotions as "group properties, triggered by events or performances, established through communication, involving complex social forms, and producing social cohesion and persuasion" ("Dissent and Emotional Management in a Liberal-Democratic Society," 16). Since Hariman and Lucaites's article was published, much work has been done and this renewed conversation about emotion and rhetoric is too vast to summarize here. For starting points, see Lisa Blankenship, *Changing the Subject: A Theory of Rhetorical Empathy*; Lisa Corrigan, *Black Feelings: Race and Affect in the Long Sixties*, Laura Micciche, *Doing Emotion: Rhetoric, Writing, Teaching*, and Shari Stenburg, "Teaching and (Re)learning the Rhetoric of Emotion."

14. Historian John Dittmer, for instance, observes the pattern of meetings in the Mississippi Delta to include a "combination of spontaneous testimony, old-fashioned preaching, wickedly hilarious observations about the character of the

white opposition, and inspiring oratory from the young organizers" (*Local People*, 131). He goes on to emphasize the significance of music in the events: "Local people were especially moved to action by the freedom songs" (131). In contrast with an urban location like Nashville, Tennessee, the pattern Dittmer notes is more fluid and free form than the carefully ordered program put forth by the NCLC.

15. For more on the topic of dress in the civil rights movement, see Marisa Chappell, Jenny Hutchinson, and Brian Ward, "'Dress modestly, neatly . . . as if you were going to church": Respectability, Class and Gender in the Montgomery Bus Boycott and the Early Civil Rights Movement."

16. In making a distinction between place and space, I follow scholars such as Jessica Enoch who see place as particular and space as general (*Domestic Occupations*).

17. Lisa Shaver follows up on this point in her study *Beyond the Pulpit: Women's Rhetorical Roles in the Antebellum Religious Press.*

18. Maegan Parker Brooks's work on Fannie Lou Hamer's speeches at mass meetings is a notable exception. David Holmes discusses this as a research issue in the conclusion to *Where the Sacred and Secular Harmonize.* See also Houck and Dixon, "Introduction: Recovering Women's Voices from the Civil Rights Movement."

19. Media coverage of civil rights events also contributed to and reinforced gendering of the movement narrative. See Keith Miller, "Afterword: Chiseling at a Fossilized Memory—Connections, Questions, and Implications."

CHAPTER 2
Sounding Civic Identity

1. For an overview of the rhetoric of music in the civil rights movement, see Kerran Sanger, *"When the Spirit Says Sing!": The Role of Freedom Songs in the Civil Rights Movement.* Sanger writes: "Whenever activists met, they engaged in the behavior of singing, perhaps the most powerful rhetorical behavior of all in the Civil Rights movement" (15). For other scholars writing about rhetoric and freedom songs, see Stephen A. King, "People Get Ready: The Civil Rights Movement, Protest Music, and the Rhetoric of Resistance"; Keith Miller, "City Called Freedom: Biblical Metaphor in Spirituals, Gospel Lyrics, and the Civil Rights Movement"; and Stephen Schneider, *You Can't Padlock an Idea.*

2. Historian Robert Darden observes: "Most historians have overlooked the impact of the singing itself during . . . those [mass] meetings" (*Nothing but Love in God's Water*, 134).

3. Some feminist theorists emphasize genre as both inflected by power and a site for agency and thus raise questions about the conceptual utility of evolutionary metaphors. Applegarth writes: "Instead of viewing genres as ecosystems that evolve, with or without human intervention and in response to limitations and pressures that are inherent, we can retain our awareness that social artifacts like genres are the product of power-inflected historical choices, and that the limitations and pressures that shape them are human constructions" ("Rhetorical Scarcity," 457).

4. See Lawrence Levine ("African American Music as Resistance") for an extensive discussion of music's role in enslavement.

5. During Reconstruction and the early twentieth century, Levine notes that the overt protest functions of religious music diminished ("African American Music as Resistance," 593). In this period, African Americans in churches began to sing gospel music in the traditions of Charles Tindley, the rural blues and the

Holiness-Pentecostal style (Burnim, "Spirituals," 67). While this music was not overtly politicized, it nonetheless operated as a subtle form of resistance in its stark departure from the musical styles animating white churches. Singing remained a collective experience valuable for many African Americans simply because of their experiences in churches. Civil rights leaders built upon this familiarity with singing as they developed the freedom song genre.

6. For more discussion of rhetoric, race, and citizenship, see Robert Terrill, *Double Consciousness and the Rhetoric of Barack Obama: The Price and Promise of Citizenship* and Candace Epps-Robertson, *Resisting Brown: Race, Literacy, and Citizenship in the Heart of Virginia.*

7. King and Abernathy both use the terms "first" and "second-class citizenship." As far as I know, these terms have not received much analysis. For historical discussion, see, for example, David Garrow, *Bearing the Cross: Martin Luther King, Jr., and the Southern Christian Leadership Conference,* and Taylor Branch, *Parting the Waters: America in the King Years 1954–1963.*

8. Of the singing of "Leaning on the Everlasting Arms," Wilson observes: "The overarching message of this hymn is that peace and tranquility are possible, but only when one depends or 'leans' on God. Whereas 'Onward Christian Soldiers' provided the audience with an active agency, an identity that grappled with evil, 'Leaning on the Everlasting Arms' reassured the audience that God was omnipotent and would protect them if only they submitted to his agency" ("Interpreting the Discursive Field of the Montgomery Bus Boycott," 318).

9. Roy writes: "In the early period of the Civil Rights movement, before freedom songs were widely known and sung, it was religious music that bound the participants together in solidarity. From its birth, the movement was bathed in the music of the church" (*Reds, Whites, and Blues,* 184).

10. Hale writes about the recordings as creating modes of "participatory democracy" ("Participatory Democracy"). The varied documentary genres that accompanied civil rights work deserve more attention as key rhetorical texts.

11. For genealogies of particular freedom songs, see Darden, *Nothing but Love in God's Water;* Roy, *Reds, Whites, and Blues;* and Sanger, *"When the Spirit Says Sing!": The Role of Freedom Songs in the Civil Rights Movement.*

12. As King's Holt Street Address indicates, unity was always important and vulnerable for civil rights collectives. Here I mean that as college students entered, their particular views about music created new and unique challenges to keeping the group unified around how to understand the role of song in the movement.

13. Rhetorical scholar Jonathan Stone writes about the role of Alan and John Lomax in sound history; see "Listening to the Sonic Archive: Rhetoric, Representation, and Race in the Lomax Prison Recordings."

14. For more discussion of Guy and Candie Carawan's participation in shaping the freedom song genre, see Elizabeth Ellis Miller, "Remembering Freedom Songs: Repurposing an Activist Genre" and Kristen Turner, "Guy and Candie Carawan: Meditating the Music of the Civil Rights Movement."

15. Turner provides the most in-depth treatment of Guy's leadership in terms of musical sources for these selections; see "Guy and Candie Carawan: Meditating the Music of the Civil Rights Movement."

16. For more on activists' debates about the freedom song genre, see the collection of essays and quotes included in *Freedom Is a Constant Struggle: Songs of the Freedom Movement,* edited by Guy and Candie Carawan. Scholar Tammy Kernodle also offers discussion and context related to these complexities in the genre in "'I Wish

I Knew How It Would Feel to Be Free': Nina Simone and the Redefining of the Freedom Song of the 1960s."

17. For historical treatment of the freedom songs after civil rights, see Stephen Sacks, "Headed for the Brink: Freedom-singing in U. S. Culture After 1968."

CHAPTER 3
Embodying Peace

1. For extensive discussion of the rhetoric of the sit-ins, see Sean Patrick O'Rourke and Lesli K. Pace, eds., *Like Wildfire: The Rhetoric of the Civil Rights Sit-Ins*. Focused specifically on the Greensboro sit-ins, Laura Michael Brown reveals (in "Remembering Silence: Bennett College Women and the 1960s Greensboro Student Sit-Ins") the complicated and gendered rhetorical history of commemoration of these events and the women who organized and envisioned the protest. While beyond the scope of my argument here, erasure and forgetting seem to apply to this prayerful aspect of the protest as well.

2. Historians have paid more attention to civil rights prayers than rhetorical scholars. See, for example, historian Tobin Miller Shearer, "Invoking Crisis: Performative Christian Prayer and the Civil Rights Movement"; Carolyn Dupont, *Mississippi Praying: Connecting Conversations, Charting New Territories;* Ansley Quiros, *God with Us;* and Stephen Haynes, *The Last Desegregated Hour.*

3. To describe the power of prayer in mass meetings, activist Bernice Reagon explains: "This [mass meeting] was . . . the first time I heard the text in some of the old prayers, and it felt as if they were saying exactly what we were going through. 'Lord, you know me, you know my conditions, and I'm asking you to come by here and see about me' was prayed every second Sunday in Mt. Olive Baptist Church, No. 2, by the mother of the church. But when she did it in a mass meeting just before a march, those words named our situation. It was like an amazing light of understanding opening up within me. That prayer, which had sounded old, was new and immediate; it was about us, pressed down by racism and wanting the power in the universe to be with us as we marched" ("Since I Laid My Burden Down," 150).

4. Chapter 1 explores the two-sides of religion as support for racial justice movements and source of oppression and scaffold for colonialist projects.

5. Literary scholar Katherine Bassard (*Transforming Scriptures*) writes about Stewart's relationship to prayer.

6. Given the observations of Johnson (*God's Trombone*) and Reagon ("Since I Laid My Burden Down"), prayer, like the freedom songs, would seem to be a genre open to women. However, I have not been able to find recorded examples of these performances.

7. For extensive discussion of this protest, see William Lawson, *No Small Thing.*

8. The relationship between nonviolence and the night march is complicated, given that provoking retaliation was part of the SCLC's strategy. Historians debate how to make sense of this aspect of Christian nonviolence in the civil rights movement. See Fairclough, *To Redeem the Soul of America*, 226–29, and Joseph Kosek, *Acts of Conscience.*

9. Lisa Corrigan writes about political shame as a resource in the civil rights movement: "White guilt was an emotional vector that, for King, had tremendous potential to motivate white political change through a new politics of responsibility. This is, in part, because shame is a communal feeling. And because it is so closely

associated with failure and relies on being *seen* in order to emerge, shame is a lingering (political) feeling" (*Black Feelings*, 32, emphasis in original).

10. Another way to read this silence is through Kenneth Burke's theory of mortification. See Burke, *The Rhetoric of Religion*. For critical discussion of religious rhetoric and mortification, see for example Christopher Oldenburg, "Redemptive Resistance through Hybrid Victimage: Catholic Guilt, Mortification, and Transvaluation in the Case of the Milwaukee Fourteen."

11. There are many examples of civil rights activists describing praying in response to public violence. In an interview, activist Cleveland Sellers remembers praying after James Chaney, Andrew Goodman, and Michael Schwerner were murdered (Sellers, Interview).

CHAPTER 4

Speaking Truth in Love

1. See Maegan Parker Brooks, *A Voice That Could Stir an Army: Fannie Lou Hamer and the Rhetoric of the Black Freedom Movement.*

2. In the most narrow religious sense of the genre, testimony is the sharing of a spiritual experience, such as testifying to what God has done. Testimony also has a narrow legal definition, where to testify is literally to give account of events in a court of law or before a judicial committee.

3. For more insight into Sherrod's leadership, see Ansley Quiros, *God with Us: Lived Theology and the Freedom Struggle in Americus, Georgia, 1942–1976* and David P. Cline, *From Reconciliation to Revolution: The Student Interracial Ministry, Liberal Christianity, and the Civil Rights Movement.*

4. For further explanation, see the collection, "United States of America vs. Theron C. Lynd, Registrar of Voters for Forrest County, Mississippi- Legal case, held at the University of Southern Mississippi." For a general overview, consult the online finding aid.

5. This recording can be found in the Moses Moon Collection at the National Museum of American History. See Jackson and Hattiesburg Mass Meetings Recordings, Tapes N68–N72, January 1964. Transcript in author's possession.

6. For other work on consciousness-raising rhetoric, see Sara Hayden, "Toward a Collective Rhetoric Rooted in Choice: Consciousness Raising in the Boston Women's Health Book Collective's *Ourselves and Our Children.*"

7. See also historian James Findlay, *Church People in the Struggle: The National Council of Churches and the Black Freedom Movement, 1950–1970.*

8. For more on the recording aspect of the civil rights movement, see Grace Hale, "Participatory Democracy: Recording the Sound of Equality in the Southern Civil Rights Movement."

9. For discussion of autobiography as a persistent genre, see Kathryn Nasstrom, "Between Memory and History: Autobiographies of the Civil Rights Movement and the Writing of Civil Rights History."

CHAPTER 5

Reckoning with White Violence and Resistance

1. In this chapter, I use the terms "radical pacifism" and "Christian nonviolence" interchangeably to refer to what activists are teaching and performing through mass

meetings. Here, I follow historians Victoria Wolcott ("Radical Nonviolence, Interracial Utopias") and Joseph Kosek (*Acts of Conscience*) who write about these theories as they animated civil rights protests and strategies.

2. For discussion of mass-meetings audiences in relationship to public sphere theory, see Elizabeth Ellis Miller, "Between Enclave and Counterpublic." For broader discussion of public sphere theory, see Nancy Fraser, "Rethinking the Public Sphere"; Jurgen Habermas, *The Structural Transformation;* and Catherine Squires, "Rethinking the Black Public Sphere."

3. For more on the mass meeting as a site of nonviolent teaching, see Kosek, *Acts of Conscience.*

4. Historians use the phrase "outside agitator" to name a common view among white Southerners at the time. This view wrongly believed that civil rights protests emerged from leaders coming to the South from other parts of the United States. King responds to this view in "Letter from Birmingham Jail." For analysis of the "Letter," see Michael Leff and Ebony Utley, "Instrumental and Constitutive Rhetoric in Martin Luther King Jr.'s 'Letter from Birmingham Jail.'" For more discussion of the "outside agitator" mindset among white Southerners, see also Jason Sokol, *There Goes My Everything.*

5. Ruth Osorio writes about truth-telling, material risks, and the body; see her "Embodying Truth: Sylvia Rivera's Delivery of *Parrhesia* at the 1973 Christopher Street Liberation Day Rally." For earlier work on *parrhesia,* see Arthur E. Walzer, "*Parrhesia,* Foucault, and the Classical Rhetorical Tradition."

6. I'm referring to the speeches of King and Abernathy as "addresses" because they do not fall clearly into the sermon category. Still, it should be noted these men are preachers, and sermonics are key to their rhetorics. Their rhetorics fill this role in the liturgy, even as the addresses deviate from preaching at times. King refers to this portion of the meeting as a "pep talk" (*Stride Toward Freedom*). It is beyond the scope of this chapter to unpack this genre's role in the meeting liturgy.

Conclusion

1. For work on religion in Black Power, see Kerry Kimblott, *Faith in Black Power: Religion, Race, and Resistance in Cairos, Illinois.*

2. Tisby also works to describe, analyze, and historicize faithful activism for twenty-first century audiences. See *How to Fight Racism,* and his podcast, *Pass the Mic.* For a starting point on the podcast, see episode, "MLK50: Bree Newsome (Interview)."

3. For a comprehensive overview of religion in relationship to contemporary activism and politics, see Jack Jenkins, *American Prophets: The Religious Roots of Progressive Politics and the Ongoing Fight for the Soul of the Country.*

4. The other important example of rhetorical liturgy around racial justice operating in the twenty-first century is William Barber II and the Poor People's Campaign. Mass meetings have been a feature of this organization for years and reveal another example of the endurance of liturgy as a social change tool.

BIBLIOGRAPHY

Abernathy, Ralph. Interview. By Blacksides, Inc., for *Eyes on the Prize: America's Civil Rights Years (1954–1965)*, November 5, 1985, transcript, Henry Hampton Collection, Washington University Libraries, Film and Media Archive. https://library.wustl.edu/.

Ahmed, Sara. *The Cultural Politics of Emotion*. New York: Routledge, 2014.

Alexander, Jonathan, and Susan Jarratt. "Introduction." In *Unruly Rhetorics: Protest, Persuasion, and Publics*, edited by Jonathan Alexander, Susan Jarratt, and Nancy Welch, 3–23. Pittsburgh: University of Pittsburgh Press, 2018.

Alexander, Jonathan, Susan Jarratt, and Nancy Welch, eds. *Unruly Rhetorics: Protest, Persuasion, and Publics*. Pittsburgh: University of Pittsburgh Press, 2018.

Allen, Danielle. *Education and Equality*. Chicago: University of Chicago Press, 2016.

———. *Talking to Strangers: Anxieties of Citizenship since Brown v. Board of Education*. Chicago: University of Chicago Press, 2006.

Americus Mass Meetings Recordings, August 1963. Tapes A.M 1.2-1.3. Moses Moon Collection, National Museum of American History, Archives Center, Washington, DC.

Anderson, Dana. *Identity's Strategy: Rhetorical Selves in Conversion*. Columbia: University of South Carolina Press, 2007.

Applegarth, Risa. "Genre, Location, and Mary Austin's Ethos." *Rhetoric Society Quarterly* 41, no. 1 (2011): 41–63

———. "Rhetorical Scarcity: Spatial and Economic Inflections on Genre Change." *College Composition and Communication* 63, no. 3 (February 2012): 453–83.

———. *Rhetoric in American Anthropology: Gender, Genre, and Science*. Pittsburgh: University of Pittsburgh Press, 2014.

Auken, Sune. "Contemporary Genre Studies: An Interdisciplinary Conversation with Johannine Scholarship." In *The Gospel of John as Genre Mosaic*, edited by Kasper Bro Larsen, 47–66. Göttingen, Germany: Vandenhoekc & Ruprecht, 2015.

Banfield, William. "The Music Kept Us From Being Paralyzed: A Talk with Bernice Johnson Reagon." In *Black Notes: Essays of a Musician Writing in a Post-Album Age*, 193–197. Lanham, MD: Scarecrow Press, 2004.

Bassard, Katherine. *Transforming Scriptures: African American Women Writers and the Bible*. Athens: University of Georgia Press, 2010.

Bawarshi, Anis. "The Genre Function." *College English* 62, no. 3 (January 2000): 327–52.

Bawarshi, Anis, and Mary Jo Reiff, eds. *Genre: An Introduction to History, Theory, Research, and Pedagogy*. Anderson: Parlor Press, 2010.

———. "Introduction." In *Genre and the Performance of Publics*, 3–22. Boulder: University of Colorado Press, 2016.

Beasley, Vanessa. "The Trouble with Marching: Ableism, Visibility, and Exclusion of People with Disabilities." *Rhetoric Society Quarterly* 50, no. 3 (2020): 164–74.

Belser, Frances. Interview. By Blacksides, Inc., for *Eyes on the Prize: America's Civil Rights Years (1954–1965)*, November 6, 1985, transcript, Henry Hampton Collection,

Washington University Libraries, Film and Media Archive. https://library.wustl.edu/.

Berlant, Lauren. *The Female Complaint: The Unfinished Business of Sentimentality in American Culture*. Durham, NC: Duke University Press, 2008.

Bernard-Donals, Michael, and Janice W. Fernheimer, eds. *Jewish Rhetorics: History, Theory, Practice*. Waltham, MA: Brandeis University Press, 2014.

Blankenship, Lisa. *Changing the Subject: A Theory of Rhetorical Empathy*. Boulder: University of Colorado Press, 2019.

Bowers, John W., Donovan J. Ochs, Richard J. Jensen, and David P. Shulz. *The Rhetoric of Agitation and Control*, 3rd ed. Long Grove, IL: Waveland Press, 2009.

Branch, Taylor. *Parting the Waters: America in the King Years 1954–1963*. New York: Simon & Schuster, 1989.

———. *Pillar of Fire: American in the King Years 1963–65*. New York: Simon & Schuster, 1998.

Brooks, Maegan Parker. *A Voice That Could Stir an Army: Fannie Lou Hamer and the Rhetoric of the Black Freedom Movement*. Jackson: University of Mississippi Press, 2014.

Brooks, Maegan Parker, and Davis Houck. "Introduction: Showing Love and Telling It Like It Is." In *The Speeches of Fannie Lou Hamer: To Tell It Like It Is*, edited by Maegan Parker Brooks and David Houck, xi–xxxii. Jackson: University of Mississippi Press, 2009.

Brown, Gavin, and Jenny Pickerill. "Space for Emotion in the Spaces of Activism." *Emotion, Space and Society* 2, no. 1 (2009): 24–35.

Brown, Laura Michael. "Remembering Silence: Bennett College Women and the 1960s Greensboro Student Sit-Ins." *Rhetoric Society Quarterly* 48, no. 1 (2018): 49–70.

Buchanan, Lindal. *Regendering Delivery: The Fifth Canon and Antebellum Women Rhetors*. Carbondale: Southern Illinois University Press, 2005.

Burke, Kenneth. *The Rhetoric of Religion*. Berkeley: University of California Press, 1961.

Burnim, Mellonee. "Spirituals." In *African American Music: An Introduction*, edited by Mellonee Burnim and Portia K. Maultsby, 50–72. New York: Routledge, 2006.

Campbell, Karlyn Khors. "The Rhetoric of Women's Liberation: An Oxymoron." *Quarterly Journal of Speech* 59, no. 1 (1973): 74–86.

Campbell, Karlyn Khors, and Kathleen Jamieson. "Form and Genre in Rhetorical Criticism: An Introduction." In *Form and Genre: Shaping Rhetorical Action*, 9–32. Falls Church, VA: Speech Communication Association, 1978.

Camper, Martin. "The Future of the History of Rhetoric Is Religious." *Journal for the History of Rhetoric* 23, no. 1 (2020): 104–5.

Campt, Tina. *Listening to Images*. Durham, NC: Duke University Press, 2017.

Carawan, Guy and Candie. *Freedom Is a Constant Struggle: Songs of the Freedom Movement*. New York: Oak Press, 1968.

———. *Sing for Freedom: The Story of the Civil Rights Movement Through Its Songs*. Montgomery: NewSouth Books, 2007.

———. *We Shall Overcome*. New York: Oak Press, 1963.

Carlos, Claudia. "Translation as Rhetoric: Edward Jerningham's 'Impenitence' (1800)." *Rhetoric Review* 28, vol. 4 (2009): 335–51.

Carter, Hodding III. Interview. By Blackside, Inc., for *Eyes on the Prize: America's Civil Rights Years (1954–1965)*, October 30, 1985, transcript, Henry Hampton Collection, Washington University Libraries, Film and Media Archive. https://library.wustl.edu/.

Ceraso, Steph. *Sounding Composition: Multimodal Pedagogies for Embodied Listening.* Pittsburgh: University of Pittsburgh Press, 2018.

Chafe, William. *Civilities and Civil Rights: Greensboro, North Carolina, and the Struggle for Black Freedom.* New York: Oxford University Press, 1980.

Chappell, David. *A Stone of Hope: Prophetic Religion and the Death of Jim Crow.* Chapel Hill: University of North Carolina Press, 2005.

Chappell, Marisa, Jenny Hutchinson, and Brian Ward. "Dress modestly, neatly . . . as if you were going to church": Respectability, Class and Gender in the Montgomery Bus Boycott and the Early Civil Rights Movement." In *Gender in the Civil Rights Movement,* edited by Peter J. Ling and Sharon Monteith, 69–100. Shrewsbury: Garland Press, 1999.

Charland, Maurice. "Constitutive Rhetoric: The Case of the *Peuple Quebecois.*" *The Quarterly Journal of Speech* 73, no. 2 (1987): 133–50.

Charney, Davida. *Persuading God: Rhetorical Studies of First-Person Psalms.* Sheffield: Sheffield Phoenix Press, 2015.

Chávez, Karma. "Counter-Public Enclaves and Understanding the Function of Rhetoric in Social Movement Coalition-Building." *Communication Quarterly* 59, no.1 (2011): 1–18.

———. "The Body: An Abstract and Actual Rhetorical Concept." *Rhetoric Society Quarterly* 48, no. 3 (2018): 242–50.

Clark, Gregory. "Rhetorical Experience and the National Museum in Harlem." In *Places of Public Memory: The Rhetoric of Museums and Memorials,* edited by Greg Dickinson, Carole Blair, and Brian Ott, 113–38. Tuscaloosa: University of Alabama Press, 2010.

Cline, David. *From Reconciliation to Revolution: The Student Interracial Ministry, Liberal Christianity, and the Civil Rights Movement.* Chapel Hill: University of North Carolina Press, 2016.

Cloud, Dana. "The Null Persona: Race and the Rhetoric of Silence in the Uprising of '34." *Rhetoric & Public Affairs* 2, no. 2 (Summer 1999): 177–209.

Colburn, David. *Racial Change and Community Crisis: St. Augustine, Florida, 1877–1980.* New York: Columbia University Press, 1985.

Colsten, Melva. "Music in the Liturgy of African American Congregations." *Journal of the Interdenominational Theological Center* 31, no. 2 (Spring 2003): 113–50.

Corrigan, John. "Introduction: How Do We Study Religion and Emotion?" In *Feeling Religion,* edited by John Corrigan, 1–22. Durham, NC: Duke University Press, 2017.

Corrigan, Lisa. *Black Feelings: Race and Affect in the Long Sixties.* Jackson: University Press of Mississippi, 2020.

Crosby, Richard Benjamin. "Cathedral of Kairos: Rhetoric and Revelation in the House of Prayer." *Philosophy and Rhetoric* 46, no. 2 (2013): 132–55.

Dallas County, Alabama, Sheriff's Department Surveillance Tapes, 1965. Tapes 1–6. Birmingham Public Library Archives, Birmingham, Alabama.

Danville, Virginia Mass Meetings Recordings, December 1963. Tapes N36–N39. Moses Moon Collection, National Museum of American History, Archives Center, Washington, DC.

Darden, Robert. *Nothing but Love in God's Water: Volume 1: Black Sacred Music from the Civil War to the Civil Rights Movement.* University Park: Pennsylvania State University Press, 2014.

Davis, Elizabeth. "Making Movement Sounds: The Cultural Organizing Behind the

Freedom Songs of the Civil Rights Movement." PhD diss., Harvard University, 2017. ProQuest no. 39987965.

DeLaure, Marilyn. "Televisuality and the Performance of Citizenship on NBC's 'Sit-In.'" In *Like Wildfire: The Rhetoric of the Civil Rights Sit-In*, edited by Sean Patrick O'Rourke and Lesli K. Pace, 243–60. Columbia: University of South Carolina Press, 2020.

DePalma, Michael John. "Austin Phelps and the Spirit (of) Composing: An Exploration of Nineteenth-Century Sacred Rhetoric at Andover Theological Seminary." *Rhetoric Review* 27, no. 4 (September 2008): 379–96.

DePalma, Michael-John, and Jeffrey Ringer. "Charting Prospects and Possibilities for Scholarship on Religious Rhetorics." In *Mapping Christian Rhetorics: Connecting Conversations, Charting New Territories*, edited by DePalma and Ringer, 262–88. New York: Routledge, 2014.

DePalma, Michael-John, and Jeffrey Ringer, eds. *Mapping Christian Rhetorics: Connecting Conversations, Charting New Territories*. New York: Routledge, 2014.

Devitt, Amy. *Writing Genres*. Carbondale: Southern Illinois University Press, 2004.

Diab, Rasha. *Shades of Sulh: The Rhetorics of Arab-Islamic Reconciliation*. Pittsburgh: University of Pittsburgh Press, 2018.

Dittmer, John. *Local People: The Struggle for Civil Rights in Mississippi*. Champaign: University of Illinois Press, 1994.

Dorrien, Gary. *Breaking White Supremacy: Martin Luther King Jr. and the Black Social Gospel*. New Haven: Yale University Press, 2018.

Douglass, Frederick. *Narrative of the Life of Frederick Douglass, an American Slave, Written by Himself*. New York: Random House, 2000.

Dreyer, Dylan. "From the Editors." *Composition Forum* 31 (2015).

Du Bois, W. E. B. "Give Us Grace." In *Conversations with God: Two Centuries of Prayers by African Americans*, edited by James Melvin Washington, 105. New York: HarperCollins, 1994.

———. *The Souls of Black Folk: Essays and Sketches*. New York: Bantam, 1989.

Dubriwny, Tasha. "Consciousness-Raising as Collective Rhetoric: The Articulation of Experience in the Redstockings' Abortion Speak-Out of 1969." *Quarterly Journal of Speech* 91, no. 4 (2005): 395–422.

Duffy, William. "Transforming Decorum: The Sophistic Appeal of Walter Rauschenbusch and the Social Gospel." In *Mapping Christian Rhetorics: Connecting Conversations, Charting New Territories*, edited by Michael-John DePalma and Jeffrey M. Ringer, 222–39. New York: Routledge, 2014.

Dupont, Carolyn. *Mississippi Praying: Southern White Evangelicals and the Civil Rights Movement, 1945–1975*. New York: New York University Press, 2015.

Dyson, Michael Eric. *Tears We Cannot Stop: A Sermon to White America*. New York: St. Martin's Press, 2017.

Earle, Chris. "'More Resilient than Concrete and Steel': Consciousness-Raising, Self-Discipline, and Bodily Resistance." *Rhetoric Society Quarterly* 50, no. 2 (February 2020): 124–38.

Enck-Wanzer, Darrel. "Trashing the System: Social Movement, Intersectional Rhetoric, and Collective Agency in the Young Lords Organization's Garbage Offensive." *Quarterly Journal of Speech* 92, no. 2 (May 2006): 174–201.

The English Standard Version of the Bible. New York: Oxford University Press, 2009.

Enoch, Jessica. *Domestic Occupations: Spatial Rhetorics and Women's Work*. Carbondale: Southern Illinois University Press, 2019.

Epps-Robertson, Candace. *Resisting Brown: Race, Literacy, and Citizenship in the Heart of Virginia*. Pittsburgh: University of Pittsburgh Press, 2018.

Fager, Charles. *Selma 1965: The March That Changed the South*. Boston: Beacon Press, 1974.

Fairclough, Adam. *To Redeem the Soul of America: The Southern Christian Leadership Conference and Martin Luther King, Jr.* Athens: University of Georgia Press, 2001.

Field, Uriah J. "Minutes of Montgomery Association Founding Meeting." In *The Papers of Martin Luther King, Jr. Volume III: Birth of a New Age, December 1955–December 1956*, edited by Clayborne Carson, Stewart Burns, Susan Carson, Dana Powell, and Peter Halloran, 70. Oakland: University of California Press, 1997.

Findlay, James. *Church People in the Struggle: The National Council of Churches and the Black Freedom Movement, 1950–1970*. New York: Oxford University Press, 1997.

FitzGerald, William. *Spiritual Modalities: Prayer as Rhetoric and Performance*. University Park: Pennsylvania State University Press, 2012.

Forman, James. *The Making of Black Revolutionaries*. Seattle: University of Washington Press, 1972.

Foust, Christina. "'Social Movement Rhetoric': A Critical Genealogy, Post–1980." In *What Democracy Looks Like: The Rhetoric of Social Movements and Counterpublics*, edited by Christina R. Foust, Amy Pason, and Kate Zittlow Rogness, 46–74. Tuscaloosa: University of Alabama Press, 2017.

Fraser, Nancy. "Rethinking the Public Sphere." *Social Text* 25, no. 26 (1990): 56–80.

Friere, Paulo. *Pedagogy of the Oppressed*. New York: Bloomsbury Academic, 2000.

Fulkerson, Richard. "The Public Letter as a Rhetorical Form: Structure, Logic, and Style in King's 'Letter from Birmingham Jail.'" *Quarterly Journal of Speech* 65, no. 2 (1979): 121–36.

Gallagher, Victoria. "Displaying Race: Cultural Projection and Commemoration." In *Rhetorics of Display*, edited by Lawrence Prelli, 177–96. Columbia: University of South Carolina Press, 2006.

Garrow, David. *Bearing the Cross: Martin Luther King, Jr., and the Southern Christian Leadership Conference*. New York: HarperCollins, 2004.

Gearhart, Sally. "Womanpower: Energy Re-Sourcement." In *The Politics of Women's Spirituality: Essays on the Rise of Spiritual Power Within the Feminist Movement*, edited by Charlene Spretnek, 386–93. Norwell: Anchor Press, 1982.

Gere, Anne Ruggles. "Revealing Silence: Rethinking Personal Writing." *College Composition and Communication* 53, no. 2 (Dec. 2011): 203–23.

Gibson, Lydialyle. "Sentimental Education." *The University of Chicago Magazine* 100, no. 6 (2008).

Gilmore, Georgia. Interview. By Blackside, Inc., for *Eyes on the Prize: America's Civil Rights Years (1954–1965)*, February 17, 1986, transcript, Henry Hampton Collection, Washington University Libraries, Film and Media Archive. https://library.wustl.edu/.

Gilyard, Keith, and Adam J. Banks. *On African-American Rhetoric*. New York: Routledge, 2018.

Glenn, Cheryl. *Unspoken: A Rhetoric of Silence*. Carbondale: Southern Illinois University Press, 2005.

Gray, Fred. *Bus Ride to Justice: The Life and Works of Fred Gray*. Montgomery: NewSouth, 2002.

Greene, Laurie. "Challenging the Civil Rights Narrative: Women, Gender, and the 'Politics of Protection.'" In *Civil Rights History from the Ground Up: Local Struggles,*

A National Movement, 52–80, edited by Emilye Crosby. Athens: University of Georgia Press, 2011.

Greenwood Mass Meeting Recordings, Fall/Winter 1963. Tape N60. Moses Moon Collection, National Museum of American History, Archives Center, Washington, DC. Transcript in author's possession.

Gregg, Richard B. "The Ego-Function of the Rhetoric of Protest." *Philosophy & Rhetoric* 4, no. 2 (1971): 71–91.

Gregg, Richard. *The Power of Nonviolence*. Philadelphia: Fellowship, 1959.

Gunn, Joshua. "*Maranatha.*" *Quarterly Journal of Speech* 98, no. 4 (2012): 359–85.

Gwin, Minrose. *Remembering Medgar Evers: Writing the Long Civil Rights Movement*. Athens: University of Georgia Press, 2013.

Habermas, Jurgen. *The Structural Transformation of the Public Sphere*. Translated by Thomas Burger. Boston: Massachusetts Institute of Technology Press, 2001.

Halberstam, David. "Negroes Meet Nightly Despite Tension in Delta." *New York Times,* June 29, 1964.

Hale, Grace Elizabeth. "Participatory Democracy: Recording the Sound of Equality in the Southern Civil Rights Movement." In *Remaking Reality: US Documentary Culture After 1945*, edited by Sara Blair, Joseph Entin, and Franny Nudelman, 99–119. Chapel Hill: University of North Carolina Press, 2018.

Hall, Jacquelyn Dowd. "The Long Civil Rights Movement: The Political Uses of the Past." *Journal of American History* 91, no. 4 (March 2005): 1233–63.

Hall, Prathia. "Freedom-Faith." In *Hands on the Freedom Plow: Personal Accounts by Women in SNCC*, edited by Faith S. Holsaert, Martha Prescod Norman Noonan, Judy Richardson, Betty Garman Robinson, Jean Smith Young, and Dorothy M. Zellner, 172–80. Urbana, IL: University of Illinois Press, 2012.

Hall, Simon. "Civil Rights Activism in 1960s Virginia." *Journal of Black Studies,* 38, no. 2 (2007): 251–67.

Hamer, Fannie Lou. "I Don't Mind My Light Shining." In *The Speeches of Fannie Lou Hamer: To Tell It Like It Is,* edited by Maegan Parker Brooks and Davis Houck, 3–6. Jackson: University of Mississippi Press, 2011.

———. "We're On Our Way." In *The Speeches of Fannie Lou Hamer: To Tell It Like It Is,* edited by Maegan Parker Brooks and Davis Houck, 46–56. Jackson: University of Mississippi Press, 2011.

Hammerback, John C., and Richard Jenson. "Ethnic Heritage as Rhetorical Legacy: The Plan of Delano." *Quarterly Journal of Speech* 80, no. 1 (1994): 53–70.

Hariman, Robert, and John Lucas Lucaites. "Dissent and Emotional Management in a Liberal-Democratic Society: The Kent State Iconic Photograph." *Rhetoric Society Quarterly* 31, no. 3 (2001): 5–31.

Hattiesburg Mass Meetings Recordings, January 1964. Tapes N73-74. Moses Moon Collection, National Museum of American History, Archives Center, Washington, DC. Transcript in author's possession.

Hauser, Gerard. *Vernacular Voices: The Rhetoric of Publics and Public Spheres*. Columbia: University of South Carolina Press, 2008.

Hawhee, Debra. *Moving Bodies: Kenneth Burke at the Edges of Language*. Columbia: University of South Carolina Press, 2012.

Hawhee, Debra, and Christa Olson. "Pan-Historiography: The Challenges of Writing Across Time and Space." In *Theorizing Histories of Rhetoric*, edited by Michelle Ballif, 90–105. Carbondale: Southern Illinois University Press, 2013.

Hayden, Sara. "Toward a Collective Rhetoric Rooted in Choice: Consciousness Raising in the Boston Women's Health Book Collective's *Ourselves and Our Children*. *Quarterly Journal of Speech* 104, no. 3 (2018): 235–56.

Haynes, Stephen. *The Last Desegregated Hour: The Memphis Kneel-Ins and the Campaign for Southern Church Desegregation*. New York: Oxford University Press, 2012.

Hogan, Wesley. *Many Minds, One Heart: SNCC's Dream for a New America*. Chapel Hill: University of North Carolina Press, 2007.

Holding, Cory. "The Rhetoric of the Open Fist." *Rhetoric Society Quarterly* 45, no. 5 (2015): 399–419.

Holmes, David. "'Hear Me Tonight': Ralph Abernathy and the Sermonic Pedagogy of the Birmingham Mass Meeting." *Rhetoric Review* 32, no. 2 (2013): 156–73.

———. *Where the Sacred and the Secular Harmonize: Birmingham Mass Meeting Rhetoric and the Prophetic Legacy of the Civil Rights Movement*. Eugene: Wipf and Stock, 2017.

Holsaert, Faith S., Martha Prescod Norman Noonan, Judy Richardson, Betty Garman Robinson, Jean Smith Young, and Dorothy M. Zellner, eds. *Hands on the Freedom Plow: Personal Accounts by Women in SNCC*. Urbana, IL: University of Illinois Press, 2012.

Hoover, Judith. "The Nashville Sit-Ins: Successful Nonviolent Direct Action through Rhetorical Invention and Advocacy." In *Like Wildfire: The Rhetoric of the Civil Rights Sit-Ins*, edited by Sean Patrick O'Rourke and Lesli K. Pace, 94–120. Columbia: University of South Carolina Press, 2020.

Houck, Davis W. and David E. Dixon, eds. "Introduction: Recovering Women's Voices from the Civil Rights Movement." In *Women and the Civil Rights Movement, 1954–1965*, ix–xxvii. Jackson: University of Mississippi Press, 2009.

———. *Rhetoric, Religion, and the Civil Rights Movement, 1954–1965, Volumes I and II*. Waco: Baylor University Press, 2014.

Houston, Ben. *The Nashville Way: Racial Etiquette and the Struggle for Social Justice in a Southern City*. Athens: University of Georgia Press, 2012.

Jackson Mass Meeting Recordings, Fall/Winter1963. Tape N57-58. Moses Moon Collection, National Museum of American History, Archives Center, Washington, DC. Transcript in author's possession.

Jackson, Sarah J. "Ask a Feminist: A Conversation with Cathy Cohen on Black Lives Matter, Feminism, and Contemporary Activism." *Signs* 41, no. 4 (Summer 2015): 775–92.

Jakes, Kelly. "La France en Chantant: The Rhetorical Construction of French Identity in Songs of the Resistance Movement." *Quarterly Journal of Speech* 99, no. 3 (2013): 317–40.

Jamieson, Kathleen. "Antecedent Genre as Rhetorical Constraint." *Quarterly Journal of Speech* 61, no. 4 (December 1975): 406–15.

Jenkins, Jack. *American Prophets: The Religious Roots of Progressive Politics and the Ongoing Fight for the Soul of the Country*. New York: HarperOne, 2020.

———. "At Protests, Some Clergy Pray, Others Put Their Bodies and Souls on the Line." *Religion News Service*, June 1, 2020.

Johnson, James Weldon. *God's Trombones*. New York: Penguin, 2008.

Johnson, Nan. *Gender and Rhetorical Space in American Life, 1866–1910*. Carbondale: Southern Illinois Press, 2002.

Jones, Jamila. Interview. By Joseph Mosnier, April 27, 2011, transcript, Washington, DC. Southern Oral History Program, Civil Rights History Project, Smithsonian Institution's National Museum of African American History & Culture and the

Library of Congress, Washington, DC. https://www.loc.gov/collections/civil-rights-history-project/

Jones, Robert P. *White Too Long: The Legacy of White Supremacy in American Christianity*. New York: Simon & Schuster, 2020.

Kerber, Linda W. "Separate Spheres, Female Worlds, Woman's Place: The Rhetoric of Women's History." *Journal of American History* 75, no. 1 (1989): 9–39.

Kernodle, Tammy. "'I Wish I Knew How It Would Feel to Be Free': Nina Simone and the Redefining of the Freedom Song of the 1960s." *Journal of the Society of American Music* 2 (2008): 295–317.

Kimblott, Kerry. *Faith in Black Power: Religion, Race, and Resistance in Cairos, Illinois*. Lexington: University Press of Kentucky, 2016.

King, Andrew A. "The Rhetorical Legacy of the Black Church." *Central States Speech Journal* 22, no. 3 (1971): 179–84.

King, Coretta Scott. Interview. By Blackside, Inc., for *Eyes on the Prize: America's Civil Rights Years (1954–1965)*, December 20, 1985, transcript, Henry Hampton Collection, Washington University Libraries, Film and Media Archive. https://library.wustl.edu/.

King, Jamilah. "How Three Friends Turned a Spontaneous Facebook Post into a Global Phenomenon." *The California Sunday Magazine*, March 2015.

King, Martin Luther, Jr. Dec. 5, 1955, Holt Street Address. In *The Papers of Martin Luther King, Jr. Volume III: Birth of a New Age, December 1955–December 1956*, edited by Clayborne Carson, Stewart Burns, Susan Carson, Dana Powell, and Peter Halloran. Oakland: University of California Press, 1997.

———. "Letter from Birmingham Jail." In *I Have a Dream: Speeches and Writings that Changed the World*, edited by J. M. Washington, 83-100. San Francisco: Harper, 1986.

———. "Nonviolence: The Only Road to Freedom." In *A Testament of Hope: The Essential Writings and Speeches of Martin Luther King, Jr*, edited by James M. Washington. New York: HarperOne, 203.

———. Nov. 14, 1956, Address to MIA Mass Meeting at Holt Street Baptist Church. In *The Papers of Martin Luther King, Jr. Volume III: Birth of a New Age, December 1955–December 1956*, edited by Clayborne Carson, Stewart Burns, Susan Carson, Dana Powell, and Peter Halloran. Oakland: University of California Press, 1997.

———. *Stride Toward Freedom: The Montgomery Story*. New York: Beacon, 2010.

King, Stephen A. "People Get Ready: The Civil Rights Movement, Protest Music, and the Rhetoric of Resistance." In *Social Controversy and Public Address in the 1960s and 1970s*, edited by Richard Jensen, 251–90. East Lansing: Michigan State University Press, 2017.

Kirsch, Gesa. "From Introspection to Action: Connecting Spirituality and Civic Engagement." *College Composition and Communication*: 60 (2009): W1–W15. Print.

Kosek, Joseph. *Acts of Conscience: Christian Nonviolence and Modern American Democracy*. New York: Columbia University Press, 2011.

Larson, Kate Clifford. *Bound for the Promised Land: Harriet Tubman Portrait of an American Hero*. New York: One World, 2004.

Lathan, Rhea Estelle. *Freedom Writing: African American Civil Rights Literacy Activism, 1955–1967*. Champaign: NCTE Press, 2015.

———. "Testimony as a Sponsor of Literacy: Bernice Robinson and South Carolina Sea Island Citizenship Program's Literacy Activism." In *Literacy, Economy, and Power: Writing Research Ten Years After Literacy in American Lives*, edited by John

Duffy, Julie Christoph, Eli Goldblatt, Nelson Graff, Rebecca Nowacek, and Bryan Trabold, 30–44. Carbondale: Southern Illinois University Press, 2014.

Lawson, James. Interview. By Robert Penn Warren for *Who Speaks for the Negro?* March 17, 1964, transcript, Robert Penn Warren Center for Humanities, Vanderbilt University. https://whospeaks.library.vanderbilt.edu.Lawson, William. *No Small Thing: The 1963 Freedom Vote*. Jackson: University of Mississippi Press, 2014.

Leff, Michael, and Ebony Utley. "Instrumental and Constitutive Rhetoric in Martin Luther King Jr.'s 'Letter from Birmingham Jail.'" *Rhetoric & Public Affairs* 7, no. 1 (2004): 37–52.

Lester, Julius. "Freedom Songs in the North." *Sing Out* 42 (1964): 13–14. https://sing out.org/downloads/broadside/b042.pdf.

———. "The Movement's Moving On: The New Mood." In *Freedom is a Constant Struggle: Songs of the Freedom Movement*, edited by Guy and Candie Carawan, 214–22. New York: Oak Press, 1968.

Levine, Lawrence. "African American Music as Resistance: Antebellum Period." In *African American Music: An Introduction*, edited by Melonee Burnim and Portia K. Maultsby, 587–97. New York: Routledge, 2006.

Logan, Shirley Wilson. *Liberating Language: Sites of Rhetorical Education in Nineteenth-Century Black America*. Carbondale: Southern Illinois University Press, 2008.

Lundberg, Christian. "Enjoying God's Death: The Passion of the Christ and the Practices of an Evangelical Public." *Quarterly Journal of Speech* 95, no. 4 (2009): 387–41.

Maddux, Kristy. *Practicing Citizenship: Women's Rhetoric at the 1893 Chicago World's Fair*. University Park: Pennsylvania State University Press, 2019.

Manis, Andrew. *A Fire You Can't Put Out: The Civil Rights Life of Birmingham's Reverend Fred Shuttlesworth*. Tuscaloosa: University of Alabama Press, 1999.

Marsh, Charles. *The Beloved Community: How Faith Shapes Social Justice, from the Civil Rights Movement to Today*. New York: Basic Books, 2008.

———. *God's Long Summer: Stories of Faith and Civil Rights*. Princeton, NJ: Princeton University Press, 2008.

———. "Letter From the Director." In *The Conference on Lived Theology and Civil Courage: A Collection of Essays*, edited by Charles Marsh, 1–5. Charlottesville, VA: The Project on Lived Theology, 2016.

Massumi, Brian. *Parables for the Virtual: Movement, Affect, Sensation*. Durham, NC: Duke University Press, 2002.

Mattingly, Carol. *Secret Habits: Catholic Literacy Education for Women in the Early Nineteenth Century*. Carbondale: Southern Illinois University Press, 2016.

Medway, Peter. "Fuzzy Genres and Community Identities: The Case of Architecture Students' Sketchbooks." In *The Rhetoric and Ideology of Genre: Strategies for Stability and Change*, edited by Richard Coe, Lorelei Lingard, and Tatiana Teslenko, 123–53. New York: Hampton, 2002.

Merton, Thomas. *The Seven Storey Mountain*. Boston: Mariner Books, 1999.

Micciche, Laura R. *Doing Emotion: Rhetoric, Writing, Teaching*. Portsmouth, NH: Boynton/Cook, 2007.

Miller, Carolyn. "Genre as Social Action." *Quarterly Journal of Speech* 70, no. 2 (1984): 151–67.

Miller, Carolyn, Amy Devitt, and Victoria Gallagher. "Genre: Permanence and Change." *Rhetoric Society Quarterly* 48, no. 4 (2018): 269–77.

Miller, Elizabeth Ellis. "Between Enclave and Counterpublic: Doubled Rhetorical

Space and the Civil Rights Mass Meeting." *Rhetoric & Public Affairs* 23, no. 2 (Summer 2020): 225–54.

———. "Reframing Rhetorical Failure: Confession and Conversion in Sarah Patton Boyle's *Desegregated Heart." Rhetoric Review* 35, no. 4 (Fall 2016): 294–307.

———. "Remembering Freedom Songs: Repurposing an Activist Genre." *College English* 81, no. 1 (2018): 50–72.

Miller, Keith. "Afterword: Chiseling at a Fossilized Memory—Connections, Questions, and Implications." In *Like Wildfire: The Rhetoric of the Civil Rights Sit-Ins,* edited by Sean Patrick O'Rourke and Lesli K. Pace, 332–40. Columbia: University of South Carolina Press, 2020.

———. "City Called Freedom: Biblical Metaphor in Spirituals, Gospel Lyrics, and the Civil Rights Movement." In *African Americans and the Bible,* edited by Vincent Wimbush, 546–57. New York: Continuum, 2000.

———. "On Martin Luther King, Jr. and the Landscape of Civil Rights Rhetoric." *Rhetoric and Public Affairs* 16, no. 1 (2013): 167–84.

———. *Voice of Deliverance: The Language of Martin Luther King, Jr., and Its Sources.* New York: The Free Press, 1992.

Molina, David. "'Our boys, our bonds, our brothers': Pauli Murray and the Washington, D. C., Sit-ins, 1943–1944." In *Like Wildfire: The Rhetoric of the Civil Rights Sit-Ins,* edited by Sean Patrick O'Rourke and Lesli K. Pace, 35–54. Columbia: University of South Carolina Press, 2020.

Monteith, Sharon. "'I second that emotion': A Case for Using Imaginative Sources in Writing Civil Rights History." *Patterns of Prejudice* 49, no. 5 (2015): 440–65.

"Montgomery Firm on Bus Bias Policy." *New York Times,* November 16, 1956.

More, Jane Bond. "A SNCC Blue Book." In *Hands on the Freedom Plow: Personal Accounts by Women in SNCC,* edited by Faith S. Holsaert, Martha Prescod Norman Noonan, Judy Richardson, Betty Garman Robinson, Jean Smith Young, and Dorothy M. Zellner, 326-331. Urbana: University of Illinois Press, 2012.

Morris, Aldon. *The Origins of the Civil Rights Movement.* New York: The Free Press, 1984.

Morrison, Michael. "Race, Blacksound, and the (Re)Making of Musicological Discourse." *Journal of the American Musicological Society* 72, no. 3 (2019): 781–823.Moss, Beverly. *A Community Text Arises: A Literate Text and a Literature Tradition in African American Churches.* New York: Hampton Press, 2003.

Mountford, Roxanne. *The Gendered Pulpit: Preaching in American Protestant Spaces.* Carbondale: University of Southern Illinois Press, 2003.

Moyaert, Marianne, and Joris Geldholf, eds. *Ritual Participation and Interreligious Dialogue: Boundaries, Transgressions, and Innovations.* London: Bloomsbury Press, 2016

Murray, Pauli. *Song in a Weary Throat: Memoir of an American Pilgrimage.* New York: Liveright, 2018.

Nashville Mass Meeting recordings. Guy and Candie Carawan Collection, 1955–2010, The Louis Round Wilson Library Special Collections, University of North Carolina, Chapel Hill Libraries, Chapel Hill, North Carolina. Transcript in author's possession.

Nasstrom, Kathryn. "Between Memory and History: Autobiographies of the Civil Rights Movement and the Writing of Civil Rights History." *Journal of Southern History* 74, no. 2 (2008): 325–64.

"Negroes in South in Store Sit-Down." In *Black Protest in the Sixties,* edited by August Meier, John Bracey, Jr., and Elliot Rudwick, 28. Princeton: Markus Wiener Press, 1991.

Nunley, Vorris L. *Keepin' It Hushed: The Barbershop and African American Hush Harbor Rhetoric.* Detroit: Wayne State University Press, 2011.

Oldenburg, Christopher. "Redemptive Resistance through Hybrid Victimage: Catholic Guilt, Mortification, and Transvaluation in the Case of the Milwaukee Fourteen." *KB Journal* 9, no. 1 (2013).

Olson, Christa. *Constitutive Visions: Indigeneity and Commonplaces of National Identity.* University Park: Pennsylvania State University Press, 2013.

O'Rourke, Sean Patrick, and Lesli K. Pace, eds. *Like Wildfire: The Rhetoric of the Civil Rights Sit-Ins.* Columbia: University of South Carolina Press, 2020.

Osorio, Ruth. "Embodying Truth: Sylvia Rivera's Delivery of *Parrhesia* at the 1973 Christopher Street Liberation Day Rally." *Rhetoric Review* 36, no. 2 (2017): 151–63.

Pason, Amy, Christina R. Foust, and Kate Zittlow Rogness. "Introduction: Rhetoric and the Study of Social Change." In *What Democracy Looks Like: The Rhetoric of Social Movements and Counterpublics*, edited by Christina R. Foust, Amy Pason, and Kate Zittlow Rogness, 1–28. Tuscaloosa: University of Alabama Press, 2017.

Payne, Charles. *I've Got the Light of Freedom: The Organizing Tradition and the Mississippi Freedom Struggle.* Berkeley: University of California Press, 1995.

———. "'Sexism is a helluva thing': Rethinking Our Questions and Assumptions." In *Civil Rights History From the Ground Up: Local Struggles, a National Movement*, edited by Emilye Crosby, 419–47. Athens: University of Georgia Press, 2011.

Polletta, Francesca. *Freedom Is an Endless Meeting: Democracy in American Social Movements.* Chicago: University of Chicago Press, 2004.

Popham, John. "Negroes to Keep Boycotting Buses: Montgomery Meeting Votes to Continue Protest as City Fights Integration Move." *New York Times*, April 27, 1956.

Portnoy, Alisse. *Their Right to Speak: Women's Activism in the Indian and Slave Debates.* Boston: Harvard University Press, 2005.

Pritchett, Laurie. Interview. By Blackside, Inc., for *Eyes on the Prize: America's Civil Rights Years (1954–1965)*, November 7, 1985, transcript, Henry Hampton Collection, Washington University Libraries, Film and Media Archive. https://library.wustl.edu/.

Program for MIA Mass Meeting at First Baptist Church, December 15, 1955. In *The Papers of Martin Luther King, Jr. Volume III: Birth of a New Age, December 1955–December 1956*, edited by Clayborne Carson, Stewart Burns, Susan Carson, Dana Powell, and Peter Halloran, 84. Berkeley: University of California Press, 1997.

Quiros, Ansley. *God with Us: Lived Theology and the Freedom Struggle in Americus, Georgia, 1942–1976.* Chapel Hill: University of North Carolina Press, 2018.

Raboteau, Albert J. *Canaan Land: A Religious History of African Americans.* New York: Oxford University Press, 2001.

Rand, Erin J. "A Disunited Nation and Legacy of Contradiction: Queer Nation's Construction of Identity." *Journal of Communication Inquiry* 28, no. 4 (2004): 288–306.

Ransby, Barbara. *Ella Baker and the Black Freedom Movement: A Radical Democratic Vision.* Chapel Hill: University of North Carolina Press, 2003.

———. *Making All Black Lives Matter: Reimagining Freedom in the Twenty-First Century.* Berkeley: University of California Press, 2018.

Reagon, Bernice Johnson. "Since I Laid My Burden Down." In *Hands on the Freedom Plow: Personal Accounts by Women in SNCC*, edited by Faith S. Holsaert, Martha Prescod Norman Noonan, Judy Richardson, Betty Garman Robinson, Jean Smith Young, and Dorothy M. Zellner, 146–50. Urbana: University of Illinois Press, 2012.

———. "Songs of the Civil Rights Movement 1955–1965: A Study in Culture History." PhD diss., Howard University, 1975.

———. *Voices of the Civil Rights Movement: Black American Freedom Songs, 1960–1965*. Washington, DC, Smithsonian Institution, 1997. CD.

Recording of Mass Meeting and March in St. Augustine, Florida, May 27, 1964. Paul Good Papers, 1963–1964, Stuart A. Rose Manuscript, Archives, and Rare Book Library, Emory University, Atlanta, Georgia. Transcript in author's possession.

Reiff, Mary Jo. "Geographies of Public Genres: Navigating Rhetorical and Material Relations of the Public Petition." In *Genre and the Performance of Publics*, edited by Anis Bawarshi and Mary Jo Reiff, 100–116. Louisville: University Press of Colorado, 2016.

Rhodes, Jaqueline. "Slutwalk Is Not Enough: Notes Toward a Critical Feminist Rhetoric." In *Unruly Rhetorics: Protest, Persuasion and Publics*, edited by Jonathan Alexander, Susan Jarratt, and Nancy Welch, 88–104. Pittsburgh: University of Pittsburgh Press, 2018.

Rice, Jenny Edbauer. "The New 'New': Making a Case for Critical Affect Studies." *Quarterly Journal of Speech* 94, no. 2 (2008): 200–12.

Rieder, Jonathan. *The Word of the Lord Is Upon Me: The Righteous Performance of Martin Luther King, Jr.* Boston: Harvard University Press, 2008.

Rivers, Nathaniel A., and Ryan P. Weber. "Ecological, Pedagogical, Public Rhetoric." *College Communication and Composition* 63, no. 2 (2012): 187–213.

Roberts, Gene, and Hank Klibanoff. *The Race Beat, the Press, the Civil Rights Struggle, and the Awakening of a Nation*. New York: Alfred A. Knopf, 2006.

Robinson, Jo Ann. *The Montgomery Bus Boycott and the Women Who Started It: The Memoir of Jo Ann Gibson Robinson*. Knoxville: University of Tennessee Press, 1987.

Ross, Rossetta. *Witnessing and Testifying: Black Women, Religion, and Civil Rights*. Minneapolis: Fortress Press, 2003.

Roy, William. *Reds, Whites, and Blues: Social Movements, Folk Music, and Race in the United States*. Princeton: Princeton University Press, 2010.

Royster, Jaqueline Jones. *Traces of a Stream: Literacy and Social Change Among African American Women*. Pittsburgh: University of Pittsburgh Press, 2000.

Russell, Clare. "Upheaval in Savannah: The Protest Cycle of a 'Short' Civil Rights Movement." *Journal of Contemporary History* 47, no. 4 (2012): 773–92.

Russell, Lindsay Rose. "Defining Moments: Genre Beginnings, Genre Invention, and the Case of the English-Language Dictionary." In *Genre and the Performance of Publics*, edited by Mary Jo Reiff and Anis Bawarshi, 83–99. Logan: Utah State University Press, 2016.

Sacks, Stephen. "Headed for the Brink: Freedom-singing in U. S. Culture After 1968." PhD diss., University of North Carolina, Chapel Hill, 2019.

Sanger, Kerran. *"When the Spirit Says Sing!": The Role of Freedom Songs in the Civil Rights Movement*. New York: Routledge, 1995.

Santoli, Susan, Paige Vitulli, and Rebecca Giles. "Picturing Equality: Exploring Civil Rights Marches through Photographs." *The Social Studies* 106, no. 2: (2014): 72–76.

Schneider, Stephen. *You Can't Padlock an Idea: Rhetorical Education at the Highlander Folk School, 1932–1961*. Columbia: University of South Carolina Press, 2014.

Selby, Gary. *Martin Luther King and the Rhetoric of Freedom*. Waco, TX: Baylor University Press, 2008.

Sellers, Cleveland. Interview. By Blackside, Inc., for *Eyes on the Prize II: America at the Racial Crossroads (1965 to 1985)*, October 21, 1988, transcript, Henry Hampton Collection, Washington University Libraries, Film, and Media Archive. https://library.wustl.edu/.

Selzer, Jack. "Habeas Corpus: An Introduction." In *Rhetorical Bodies,* edited by Jack Selzer and Sharon Crowley, 3–15. Madison: University of Wisconsin Press, 1999.

Shaver, Lisa. *Beyond the Pulpit: Women's Rhetorical Roles in the Antebellum Religious Press.* Pittsburgh: University of Pittsburgh Press, 2012.

Shearer, Tobin. "Invoking Crisis: Performative Christian Prayer and the Civil Rights Movement." *Journal of the American Academy of Religion* 83, no. 2 (2015): 490–512.

Sherrod, Charles. Interview. By Joseph Mosnier, June 4, 2011, transcript, Washington D.C. Southern Oral History Program, Civil Rights History Project, Smithsonian Institution's National Museum of African American History & Culture and the Library of Congress, Washington D.C. https://www.loc.gov/.

Shridharani, Krishnalal. *War Without Violence: The Sociology of Gandhi's Satyagraha.* New York: Harcourt Brace, 1939.

Simons, Herbert. "Requirements, Problems, and Strategies: A Theory of Persuasion for Social Movements." *Quarterly Journal of Speech* 56, no. 1 (1970): 1–11.

Sitton, Claude. "Sherriff Harasses Negroes at Voting Rally in Georgia." *New York Times,* July 27, 1962.

"A Slave Woman's Prayer." In *Conversations with God: Two Centuries of Prayers by African Americans*, edited by James Melvin Washington, 19. Transcribed by Stephen Hays. New York: HarperCollins, 1994.

Smitherman, Geneva. *Word from the Mother: Language and African Americans.* New York: Routledge, 2006.

Sokol, Jason. *There Goes My Everything: White Southerners in the Age of Civil Rights, 1945–1975.* New York: Vintage, 2007.

Spencer, Jon. *Protest and Praise: Sacred Music of Black Religion.* Minneapolis: Augsburg Fortress Press, 1990.

Squires, Catherine. "Rethinking the Black Public Sphere: An Alternative Vocabulary for Black Public Spheres." *Communication Theory* 12, no. 4 (2002): 446–68.

Stenberg, Shari. "Teaching and (Re) learning the Rhetoric of Emotion." *Pedagogy* 11, no. 2 (2011): 349–69.

Sterne, Jonathan. "A Groove We Can Move To: The Sound & Sense of Quebec's *Manifs Casseroles*, Spring 2012." In *Unruly Rhetorics: Protest, Persuasion and Publics*, edited by Jonathan Alexander, Susan Jarratt, and Nancy Welch, 60–71. Pittsburgh: University of Pittsburgh Press, 2018.

Stewart, Charles, Craig Smith, and Robert Denton. *Persuasion and Social Movements,* 6th ed. Long Grove, IL: Waveland Press, 2012.

Stewart, Lindsey. *The Politics of Black Joy: Zora Neale Hurston and Neo-Abolitionism.* Evanston, IL: Northwestern University Press, 2021.

Stewart, Maria. "Productions of Mrs. Maria Stewart." In *Spiritual Narratives,* edited by Sue Houchins. New York: Oxford University Press, 1988.

Stoever, Jennifer. "Black Radio Listeners in America's 'Golden Age.'" *Journal of Radio & Audio Media* 26, no. 1 (2019): 119–33.

———. *The Sonic Color Line: Race and the Cultural Politics of Listening.* New York: New York University Press, 2016.

Stone, Jonathan. "Listening to the Sonic Archive: Rhetoric, Representation, and Race in the Lomax Prison Recordings." *enculturation: a journal of rhetoric, writing, and culture* (2015). http://enculturation.net/.

Terrill, Robert. *Double-Consciousness and the Rhetoric of Barack Obama: The Price and Promise of Citizenship.* Columbia: University of South Carolina Press, 2015.

Theoharis, Jeanne. *A More Beautiful and Terrible History: The Uses and Misuses of Civil Rights History*. New York: Beacon Press, 2018.

Thorton, Davi Johnson. "The Rhetoric of Civil Rights Photographs: James Meredith's March Against Fear." *Rhetoric & Public Affairs* 16, no. 3 (2013): 457–87.

Tisby, Jemar. "Black Christians Don't Negotiate Your Dignity. With Tyler Burns. *Pass the Mic*. Podastery. July 27, 2020. https://thewitnessbcc.com/.

———. *The Color of Compromise: The Truth About the American Church's Complicity in Racism*. Grand Rapids, MI: Zondervan, 2020.

———. *How to Fight Racism: Courageous Christianity and the Journey Toward Racial Justice*. Grand Rapids, MI: Zondervan, 2021.

Tuck, Stephen. *Beyond Atlanta: The Struggle for Racial Equality in Georgia, 1940–1980*. Athens: University of Georgia Press, 2003.

Turner, Kristen. "Guy and Candie Carawan: Meditating the Music of the Civil Rights Movement." MA thesis, University of North Carolina Chapel Hill, 2011.

United States of America vs. Theron C. Lynd, Registrar of Voters for Forrest County, Mississippi- Legal case. Collection Number M 27, 1961-1967. Hattiesburg, MS: The University of Southern Mississippi McCain Library and Archives. https://lib.usm.edu/spcol/collections/.

Vander Lei, Elizabeth, Thomas Amorose, Beth Daniell, and Anne Ruggles Gere. *Renovating Rhetoric in the Christian Tradition*. Pittsburgh: University of Pittsburgh Press, 2014.

Van Rijn, Guido. *Kennedy's Blues: African American Blues and Gospel Songs on JFK*. Jackson: University of Mississippi Press, 2010.

Vondey, Wolfgang. "The Making of a Black Liturgy: Pentecostal Worship and Spirituality from African Slave Narratives to American Cityscapes." *Black Theology* 10, no. 2 (2012): 147–68.

Walzer, Arthur E. "*Parrhesia,* Foucault, and the Classical Rhetorical Tradition." *Rhetoric Society Quarterly* 43, no. 1 (2013): 1–21.

Wan, Amy. "In the Name of Citizenship: The Writing Classroom and the Promise of Citizenship." *College English* 74, no. 1 (2011): 28–49.

Warner, Michael. *Publics and Counterpublics*. New York: Zone Books, 2002.

Warnock, Raphael. *The Divided Mind of the Black Church: Theology, Piety, and Public Witness*. New York: New York University Press, 2013.

Washington, James Melvin. *Conversations with God: Two Centuries of Prayers by African Americans*. New York: HarperCollins, 1994.

Watters, Pat. *Down to Now: Reflections on the Southern Civil Rights Movement*. Athens: University of Georgia Press, 2012.

The White House. "Remarks by the President in Eulogy for the Honorable Reverend Clementa Pinckney." June 26, 2015. https://obamawhitehouse.archives.gov/.

Williams, Kidada. *They Left Great Marks on Me: African American Testimonies of Racial Violence from Emancipation to World War I*. New York: New York University Press, 2012.

Williams, Linda. "Film Bodies: Gender, Genre, and Excess." *Film Quarterly* 44, no. 4 (1999): 2–13.

Wilson, A. W. Interview. By Blackside, Inc., for *Eyes on the Prize: America's Civil Rights Years (1954–1965)*, 1979. Washington University Libraries, Film and Media Archive, Henry Hampton. https://library.wustl.edu/.

Wilson, Kirt. "Interpreting the Discursive Field of the Montgomery Bus Boycott:

Martin Luther King, Jr.'s Holt Street Address." *Rhetoric and Public Affairs* 8, no. 2 (2005): 299–26.

Wolcott, Victoria. "Radical Nonviolence, Interracial Utopias, and the Congress of Racial Equality in the Early Civil Rights Movement." *Journal of Civil and Human Rights* 4, no. 2 (2018): 31–61.

Yergeau, Melanie. *Authoring Autism: On Rhetoric and Neurological Queerness.* Durham, NC: Duke University Press, 2019.

Young, Vershawn, and Michelle Bachelor Robinson, eds. *The Routledge Reader of African American Rhetoric: The Longue Duree of Black Voices.* New York: Routledge, 2018.

Zagacki, Kenneth. "The Ethos of Rhetoric: Thomas Merton's 'Letters to a White Liberal.'" *Journal of Communication and Religion* 44, no. 3 (2021): 5–23.

Zimmerelli, Lisa. "'The Stereoscopic View of Truth: The Feminist Theological Rhetoric of Frances Willard's *Woman in the Pulpit.*" *Rhetoric Society Quarterly* 42, no. 4 (2012): 353–74.

INDEX